EDWARD AUGUSTUS BRACKETT

EDWARD AUGUSTUS BRACKETT

The Life, Art and Tumultuous Times of an American Original

Eleanor Heartney

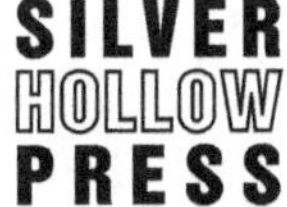

Dedication

*To all those whose forgotten efforts
have made our world possible.*

TABLE OF CONTENTS

INTRODUCTION

This is a book about a singular American artist. It is also a book about the political turmoil, spiritual aspirations and sectarian conflicts that roiled America in the 19th century. The life of Edward Augustus Brackett provides a portal to the tumultuous century which set the stage for our own fractious times.

Edward Augustus Brackett was born in 1818 and lived until 1908, a few months short of his 90th birthday. During that time, he gained recognition as an artist, abolitionist, spiritualist, poet, amateur architect and conservationist. He made valuable contributions in each of these fields, while also rubbing shoulders with such important historical figures as William Cullen Bryant, Washington Allston, William Lloyd Garrison, William James, John Brown, Wendell Phillips, Charles Sumner, Horace Greeley and Edmonia Lewis. Brackett's life was intimately tied up with such important aspects of 19th century American history as the westward expansion, the promotion of a uniquely American art and culture, the abolitionist movement, the postwar spiritualist frenzy, the dawning of environmental consciousness and the changes unleashed by mind spinning new developments in science and technology.

Brackett is little known today. However, his name pops up frequently in 19th century American art reviews, popular publications, patent applications, government reports and memoirs. As an artist, Brackett was well respected by his peers and in demand as a sculptor of portrait busts for important cultural and political figures. He was in Boston at the moment when the abolitionist movement was colliding with the defenders of slavery. His associations with many of the leading abolitionists made it possible for him to create an iconic portrait of John Brown. Brackett was mentor to Edmonia Lewis, the first African American woman artist to achieve international recognition. When the Civil War broke out, he put his convictions to the test and served as battalion quartermaster of the First Massachusetts volunteer cavalry. After the war, he became deeply involved in spiritualism, holding séances in his house and writing tracts defending the reality of "materialized apparitions" – those spirit guides summoned by mediums to give reports to the living from the other side of death. At a time when science and spiritualism were not so far apart, Brackett keenly followed the scientific debates of his times. In texts still available today, he commented on the debates surrounding psychic phenomena, evolution and germ theory.

Brackett was also a published poet, a horticulturalist and an animal breeder whose estate was overrun with Mongolian pheasants, Belgian hares, quail and grouse. As an amateur architect he adapted a do-it-yourself plan for octagonal houses to build a unique home that is today on the National Register of Historic Houses. His final decades were spent as the Commissioner of the Massachusetts Fish and Game Commission, during which time he led efforts to replenish populations of fish and game depleted by years of overfishing and hunting.

Today Brackett merits our attention as a fascinating, idiosyncratic and multifaceted figure who lived in an era when borders between disciplines were more porous and specialists had not yet cordoned themselves off behind a wall of professional degrees. He represents a moment when it was still possible for inspired amateurs to influence newly emerging fields. But he is also significant because his life opens a window into a foundational period in American history. Brackett's America was searching for a cultural identity that would distinguish it from what it viewed as a decrepit and decadent Old World. It was being pulled apart by the battle over slavery. It was also on the cusp of scientific and technological changes that would radically reshape society. These forces ignited political, cultural and social revolutions whose repercussions continue to be felt today.

This book offers a picture of that world from the inside. What did it take for an ambitious young man without schooling or connections to find his way into the cultural milieu of antebellum New York and Boston? How did the issue of slavery awaken the moral consciences of white northern abolitionists and inspire them to life threatening acts of courage? Why did so many intelligent and reputable people fall under the spell of spiritualism? How did it feel to be torn between faith and science at the dawn of the 20th century? Such questions were all part of the lived experience of Edward Brackett.

I might never have heard of this extraordinary man if he were not my great-great grandfather. As a child, I was aware that Brackett was a sculptor and I recall hearing from my grandfather that his mother's early life as an artist's child was an ever-oscillating financial see-saw between "feast and famine." But it all seemed too long ago and far away to carry any real interest. However, after pursuing a career as art critic and art historian for forty years, I decided at long last to delve into this seemingly arcane bit of family history. Initially, information was sparse. The gulf between my grandfather's grandfather and the present day was too wide for any first hand recollections or memorabilia. My starting points were my memory of a sculpture of a woman in my great aunt Edna's house and a bust of painter Washington Allston by Edward Brackett which is in the collection of the Metropolitan Museum in New York. From there, I began to pick up the other threads of Brackett's story. My researches were to take me far beyond the confines of family lore and into the fascinating complexities of 19th century America.

Over the four years that I spent researching and writing this book, I came to be completely beguiled by this witty, generous and inspiring man. I also found myself in constant dialogue with him regarding various issues that remain contentious today. We argued about art, politics, spirituality and science. His life and thoughts have led me to rethink many of my own assumptions. They have also made me aware of the debt we all owe to history and of the degree to which the present is the child of the past.

I have tried to write Edward Brackett's life as he lived it, immersed in a complex and shifting milieu. This biography traces his life through the record of his multifarious activities and writings. Put into context, these give us access to the passions of his time and to the fascinating cast of characters with whom he came in contact. His story is thus both a personal and a social history. Like any well lived life, it ripples outward, spilling into the larger world and continuing to lap at the shores of our own time.

Chapter 1
The Struggles of Early Genius

The photographs of Edward Augustus Brackett that have come down to us reveal an imposing patriarch with a broad forehead, a faraway look and a chin buried in a wild morass of graying whiskers. In an undated studio portrait he appears as a man in his seventies or eighties sitting before a photographer's painted backdrop in a three-piece suit. (fig 1) He twists to the right as he leans his arm against the back of his chair with feigned casualness. His untamed white beard reaches almost to the watch chain that droops over the front of his over-tight waistcoat. The stiffness of the pose cannot hide a certain rumpled grandeur. He seems well suited to the role of artistic eccentric assigned him by many of his contemporaries.

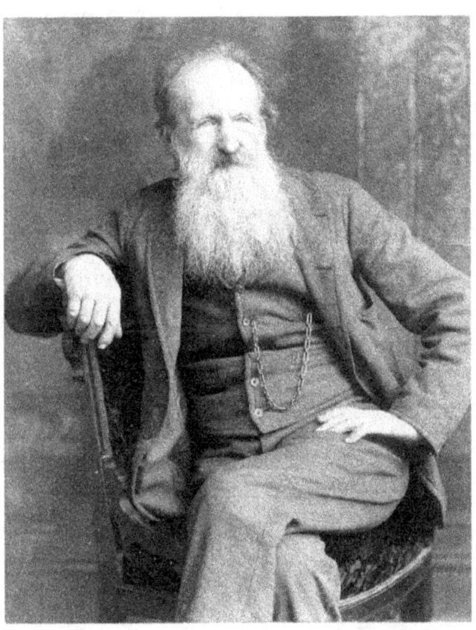

fig. 1 An undated photograph of Edward Augustus Brackett taken by Carleton E. Shorey of Lynn, MA, Courtesy of the Winchester Massachusetts Archival Center.

Brackett's impressive mane in this late photograph bears a striking resemblance to that of his most famous artistic subject, the abolitionist John Brown. To create his powerful marble portrait of Brown, Brackett eschewed the bland neo-classical style that governed the portrait bust industry of his day. Looking more like Michelangelo's Moses than Phidias' idealized gods, Brackett presents Brown as a doomed revolutionary who stares fiercely forward, his gaunt face encircled by rippling hair and a thick flowing beard. However, the similarities between creator and creation end with their coiffures. Brown's arched brows overhang eyes that flash with fire and brimstone while Brackett's aspect is kindly and gentle. One can almost detect a suppressed twinkle of amusement at the role the photographer has induced him to play.

By the time this photograph of Brackett was taken, he was a well-established and respected figure in Massachusetts, recognized for such diverse activities as sculptor, poet, naturalist, abolitionist, amateur architect and spiritualist. We have no photographs of the youthful Brackett, and so must imagine a farm boy with a clean chin and unlined face, poor, indifferently schooled and brimming with ambition. Born in 1818 into a Quaker family whose patriarch had little sympathy for the extravagances of art and culture, young Edward nevertheless seems to have been drawn from an early age into a fascination with sculpture. This coexisted with a deep love of the natural world. These two interests, as we shall see, would play vital roles in the shape of his future life.

Official records of Brackett's life prior to his twentieth year are sparse, telling us little more than the circumstances of his birth and the peripatetic nature of his family's life. However, we do have a document that brings the young man, or at least a version of him, to life with remarkable detail. This is a lightly fictionalized account of Brackett's first twenty years written by Joseph Holt Ingraham, one of the most prolific novelists of his day. It offers a blow by blow account of Brackett's childhood and emergence as an artist. The existence of this account – a serialized novel spread out over twelve issues of a short-lived literary magazine - is a curious fact. Its author was more given to dramatic tales of romance and derring-do than to the professional struggles of young unknown artists. To understand why Ingraham devoted so much attention to the as yet unknown Edward Brackett, it is necessary to take a detour into antebellum America's literary world.

Brackett in fact and fiction

In mid-19th century America, Ingraham was more popular than his contemporaries Edgar Allan Poe, Herman Melville and Nathaniel Hawthorne. According to his biographer Robert Weathersby, during his most prolific writing period in the 1840s Ingraham accounted for ten percent of all fiction titles published in the country.[1] Ingraham specialized in stories about the swashbuckling adventures of pirates, soldiers and American renegades. Published in two volume sets by the prestigious publisher Harper and Brothers or serialized in weekly papers and monthly magazines, his works were loved by readers but excoriated by critics. Poe described an early effort: "We are surfeited with unnecessary detail. . . . Not a dog yelps, unsung. Not a shovel-footed negro waddles across the stage . . . without eliciting from the author a vos plaudite, with an extended explanation of the character of his personal appearance—of his length, depth and breadth,—and, more particularly, of the length, depth and breadth of his shirt-collar, shoe-buckles and hat-band."[2] Another critic put in more succinctly "Had he written less, he would have been appreciated more."[3]

Ingraham was born in 1809 to a prosperous family in Portland, Maine. Though a poor student, he was a keen observer and spent much of his early adulthood traveling throughout the southern and western (what we would now call mid-western) United States as well as such then exotic locales as Buenos Aires, the Caribbean and Cuba. These experiences provided color for his melodramatic tales. Among his most read efforts were highly embellished histories of Captain Kyd, the Pirate Jean Lafitte and the disgraced statesman Aaron Burr. He also published historical romances, Revolutionary War sagas, tragic tales of miscegenation and moral parables featuring fallen women and undeserving wastrels. Eventually Ingraham threw over these secular thrills for religion. He became an Episcopalian minister serving various congregations throughout the South. This change of profession was accompanied by a complete change of manner. Shortly after his ordination in Jackson, Mississippi in February 1852, a reporter for the *Mississippi Free Trader* remarked on the change: "We noticed a somewhat unusual longitude of countenance and the white cravat, very much at variance with the former jaunty, dashing, imposing, mustachioed, half-bandit air of the same gentleman years since on the paves of Philadelphia and New York, with silver-mounted pistol and jeweled attaghan in belt."[4] But even his new flock could not keep Ingraham from writing, though this now took a biblical turn. He gained his greatest fame from a series of historical novels that explored the rise of the Hebrew people and the emergence of Jesus Christ. Ingraham's death at age 51 in 1860 seemed an echo of his more rabble-rousing days. He died from an accidentally self-inflicted gunshot wound as he removed a loaded pistol from a drawer in the vestibule of the church.

Though he no doubt merits his own extended consideration in the history of American eccentrics, Ingraham intersects with our story because, between April 1841 and March 1842, he departed from his standard practice. Over the course of twelve installments in the equally forgotten literary magazine *The Baltimore Phoenix and Budget*, he set aside his usual bloodcurdling tales of murder and mayhem to present *THE JUVENILE GENIUS; or, Five Eras in the Life of a Sculptor*. By the third installment the title of this artistic bildungsroman was amended to *The Struggles of Early Genius*. Ingraham evidently realized that his readers might be taken aback by his change of subject and tone. In an aside in installment two, he noted, "This may be regarded as a very simple story, but it is not the writer's intention to amuse by a brilliant romance; but to unfold the progressive steps by which inborn genius breaks the shell of its humble condition, expands its eagle-like wings, and, overcoming every obstacle cast in its path, rises superior to circumstances and accomplishes its lofty destiny."[5]

Edward Brackett, the real life subject of this novel, never gained the lofty success awarded by Ingraham to his literary counterpart. In fact, his life offers a study of the vagaries of fate that beset the self-taught artist in mid-19th century America. Ingraham's narrative follows the twists and turns of Brackett's life from his childhood in Maine to his arrival New York in 1839 at age 21. He ends the tale on a triumphant note, implying that from this point on the young sculptor's fame was assured. Though setting out on a similar trajectory, the real Brackett continued to struggle in New York and departed after two years for the more welcoming cultural milieu of Boston. There he attracted some important patrons and achieved modest success as a sculptor. However he was unable to provide for his growing family and eventually he closed his studio to throw himself into other interests. He spent his last three decades serving as Massachusetts Commissioner of Fish and Game.

The fictionalized Edward Brackett portrayed by Ingraham is a young, often uncertain boy-man who bounces from one failed trade to another while quietly longing to devote himself to art. It is clear that Ingraham was very familiar with Brackett's actual circumstances. (For purposes of clarity, I will refer to the fictional Brackett as Edward and the historical one as Brackett.) The novel's dedication reads: "Inscribed to Edward Brackett, esq. on the events of whose early life are founded the incidents composing this series of tales."[6] Ingraham's narrative was written shortly after the last events it chronicles. The story's culminating event, Edward's arrival in New York, appeared in an installment published just two years after the real twenty one year old Brackett traveled by steamship to New York in October 1839.

While it is not clear how Ingraham met Brackett, they were both in New York in 1839 and 1840, just prior to the time the novelist would have been penning his story. It seems likely that this is where they became acquainted. Ingraham's text follows Brackett's early life so closely that I was able to use it to track down additional leads about Brackett and his associates. Many of the people his Edward encounters are figures who offered support or encouragement to the real Brackett. Occasionally Ingraham quotes reviews from fictional publications that crib from the notices published in actual newspapers and journals. There are literary flourishes, of course. Brackett's younger sister Jane has been transformed into Mary and given a central role. Because Edward lacks the kind of romantic entanglements characteristic of most Ingraham heroes, Mary provides an almost creepy surrogate love interest. (In fact, the real Brackett had a sweetheart, Amanda Folger whom he would later bring to Boston after somewhat establishing himself. He also had three brothers, unmentioned by Ingraham, including a younger brother Walter who became a painter and would prove a stalwart supporter of his older sibling). Ingraham also devotes whole sections to travelogue-like descriptions of the sights and sounds as Edward journeys by canal boat, steamer, rail and stagecoach through the Northeast and Midwest. There is an extended set piece about Edward's failed efforts as a schoolteacher that seems drawn from Ingraham's own experiences since nothing suggests that the real Brackett pursued this profession. And Ingraham seems to have somewhat exaggerated the bumpy road of Brackett's pre-artistic life, giving him a series of early apprenticeships under masters of Dickensian stupidity and cruelty.

The Struggles of Early Genius was published on the heels of several of Ingraham's most successful early novels. Why did he shift gears so dramatically to focus on the life of this very young and obscure artist? Clues can be found in some of the narrator's asides, as well as several places in the novel where Edward encounters an Ingraham-like figure who, from the lofty age of thirty, offers advice to the aspiring sculptor. Ingraham frames Edward's saga as the story of a brilliant but impecunious creator who is driven from the city of his first success by lack of financial support. One sees parallels to Ingraham's own situation. Even though he was publishing prolifically at this time, he was barely able to make ends meet. In 1841, while writing this and eighteen other serialized novels, he was forced to declare bankruptcy. This novel gave him a forum to complain about his own financial struggles as a writer.

Thus for instance at one point the narrator lambasts the "patrons who lounge around the studio" praising the sculptor's work but offering no material support. He adds, "'Geniuses' see a great many such patrons! They belong to the class of those patrons of an author who honor him by condescending to send and borrow his 'last works' to read!"[7] Underscoring the point further, he recounts how Edward is being showered with acclaim at the same time that he is "secretly toiling till midnight carving blocks on a bench beside his statue to get bread to put into his own mouth! Reader, this is no fiction which I am writing, though I have put it in the guise of a romance!"[8]

He also has the Ingraham surrogate, a "literary friend" by the name of Mr. T___complain about copyright law, noting, "Confound these English novelists that are stealing the bread out of our mouths. If we don't have an international copyright law, our native literature will go to the d____l."[9] At one point, Edward and Mr. T___ discuss the nature of fame and immortality. Edward remarks, " . . my greatest ambition is to achieve something in imperishable marble, the labor on which shall afford me daily gratification while I live, and which after I am dead shall carry my name down to posterity! I should exist miserably if I thought I should be forgotten dead!" Mr. T___ in what might be a prescient comment on Ingraham's own future status, remarks, "That's the devil of authorship. We are like seeds, we must be put under the ground before we can show atop of it. Posthumous reputation isn't worth a fig."[10]

Such passages suggest that Ingraham, though ten years older and more established than Brackett, identified strongly with his ambitious young friend. From this perspective, the ultimate triumph of the fictional Edward represents a form of wish fulfillment for a writer who also was longing to reach a state of financial success and professional acclaim. *The Struggles of Early Genius* is thus a hybrid narrative, mingling fact and fiction by focusing on a hero who is a mix of Brackett and Ingraham. Because we have no account in Brackett's own voice about this early period of life, Ingraham will serve as our guide to the story of Edward Brackett's emergence as an artist.

Antecedents

Both stories – fictional and real - begin in Vassalboro, Maine where Brackett was born in 1818 to Reuben Brackett, a farmer, clockmaker and nurseryman and his wife Elizabeth (née Starkey). A voluminous 1000 page family history published in 1907 by Herbert Ierson Brackett attests to the Brackett family's colorful history in America. [11] The *Brackett Genealogy* is written in lively prose. Its author, a lawyer and the historian of the Brackett Family Association, was clearly more interested in the dramatic deeds and reversals of the earliest generations of Bracketts than in the humdrum activities of later generations after they had established themselves in the now tamed wilderness. He does however devote several paragraphs to the diverse activities of Edward Augustus Brackett. In the end he traces more than six hundred Brackett descendents going back to the 17th century.

The Brackett family history begins around 1640 with a figure known in the *Genealogy* as Anthony the Selectman who may have emigrated from Scotland (Herbert Brackett also suggests possible English or Welsh origins) to Portsmouth, New Hampshire. Portsmouth was then a port just recently wrestled from the native Abenakis by English colonists. Settlers cleared land, built houses, farmed, traded and set up fisheries and established businesses for the manufacture of salt, potash, lumber and pipe staves. Already political intrigue and conflict were rife between the officials of the Massachusetts Bay Colony and the new landowners. Perhaps even more frightening were skirmishes with the displaced indigenous inhabitants who had been driven from their lands, hunted down, deprived of means of hunting for food and occasionally sold into slavery. Once peaceful relations between natives and immigrants were now marred by raids, massacres, kidnappings and at times all-out war.

Anthony, having acquired status and land through marriage, was a prominent figure in the newly established community. He was elected a selectman, one of three men responsible for collecting taxes to pay the salary of the local minister. There were run-ins with the Colony officials over religious differences. (Brackett was an Episcopalian while the officials were Congregationalists, and Herbert Brackett makes much throughout his narrative of the clash between censorious Puritans and the more free-thinking Bracketts.) Despite these tensions he sums up his hero's life thus: "It is safe to venture that the life of Anthony after he settled in America was happy, far happier and easier than the lot of any of his ancestors of whom he had knowledge. Right fortunate he could consider himself in being the possessor and owner of fertile land, part in natural meadow, near to the sea and in the midst of a growing settlement."[12]

This equanimity was to be sorely tested by subsequent events. Anthony had five children. His sons were awarded land as children of settlers. The two eldest boys, Anthony Jr. and Thomas, decided to strike out on their own and moved in the early 1660s north to Casco, later renamed Falmouth, and now the site of Portland, Maine. It was a wilder area just being settled by a small community of farmers. All seemed well until August 11, 1676. Responding to an attack on his cows, Anthony Jr. engaged a local Native American named Simon to track down the perpetrators. Unbeknownst to him, Simon was the infamous "Yankee Killer" who, along with Wampanoag chieftain Metacomet (also known by his nom-de-guerre King Phillip), had been staging raids in a last ditch effort to chase the settlers out of New England. Simon and the culprits returned with a full-scale war party. Thus began a two-month assault on the new settlers. In the first foray Anthony Jr.'s brother-in-law Nathaniel Mitton was killed and Anthony Jr., his wife, five children and a Black slave were captured. The raid continued with the killing of Anthony Jr.'s brother Thomas in the next farm, and the capture of his wife and children. Eventually the toll reached thirty-four colonists killed or captured. Anthony Jr.'s family managed to escape in a leaky purloined canoe repaired, legend says, by the needlework of his wife. The family of the slain Thomas fared less well. His wife died in captivity within a year. The children were finally ransomed from the natives by their Grandfather Anthony Sr. six months later following the fatal shooting of Metacomet by a "praying Indian," the term for a Native American who had converted to Christianity.

One of Thomas' children, Samuel, is the direct ancestor of our Edward Brackett. He was two years old at the time of the raid, and after being orphaned and ransomed, was sent to live with his aunt Martha and her husband John Grove in Kittery, Maine. This is an important development for our story because they raised Samuel as a Quaker, insuring that this line of the Brackett family would be brought up in a tradition of religious tolerance and opposition to slavery. Meanwhile grandfather Anthony Senior was himself killed in an Indian raid in 1691 along with his wife and at least fifteen other people. His grandson Samuel married Elizabeth Botts, whose father had also been a victim of the Indian Wars. Herbert Brackett comments in his *Genealogy*: "Certainly she and young Samuel could relate doleful tales of harrowing times. Indian wars meant sorrow and affliction for them; they meant to them in their married life, not death nor captivity it is true, but the living in block and garrison houses in times of peril, and a narrow escape from death by the young husband on one occasion, owing to his being fleet of foot." He reports that Samuel served bravely as a soldier in the Indian Wars, but nevertheless was harassed by the Puritan leaders for the crime of "not frequenting the public worship of God on the Lord's day." In a foretaste of Edward Brackett's resistance to organized religion, Herbert Brackett concludes, "The solace of a poverty-stricken, war-desolated home far excelled the consolation which that church could afford, though its minister lived to preach for a century the promises to come." [13]

After early tragedies worthy of Ingraham in his more bloodcurdling mode, the Brackett chronicle quiets down. The Treaty of Portsmouth, signed on July 13, 1713, ended the Indian wars between the Abenakis and the British provinces of Massachusetts Bay and New Hampshire. That same year saw the birth of Samuel Brackett Jr. who followed in the family footsteps as farmer and selectman. He and his wife produced six daughters and eight sons, one of whom was again named Samuel. A farmer, he is described by Herbert Brackett as "a strong advocate of the cause of the colonists in their struggle with Great Britain."[14] His ten children included Rueben, again a farmer, who begat yet another Rueben who was the father of our Edward Brackett. The younger Reuben Brackett was a farmer and watchmaker. The *Genealogy* describes a peripatetic life as he bounced around Maine and Massachusetts before moving to Cincinnati, Ohio and finally dying in Denmark, Iowa. His eldest son, Edward, was born during an eight-year stint in Vasselboro, Maine.

Early Life

We are now back in the territory of Ingraham's narrative. Ingraham, with what seems to be good deal of veracity, follows his hero Edward's early life as he moves with his family and attempts to satisfy his father's desire that he take up a trade. There is a pivotal early scene in which fifteen year old Edward's artistic leanings are stifled by his mother, who quotes to him the biblical injunction against the creation of graven images. Edward's hopes are revived when Reverend Dr. Gillet of Hallowell, an itinerant preacher, comes to Vasselboro. He preaches a sermon on Deuteronomy that distinguishes between idol worship and art. Reverend Gillet maintains, "The true and scriptural signification of this command has been singularly perverted by certain recently risen Christian sects. . . God here has forbidden nothing, that like the Arts of Painting and Sculpture, contributes to the intellectual elevation and moral dignity of the human race."[15] This message so overwhelms Edward that he falls into a fever and then joyfully resumes making little sculptures out of clay.

There was a real Congregationalist Reverend Eliphalet Gillet from Hallowell, Maine, who did in fact speak at the dedication of the Meeting House in Vasselboro in 1817. This doesn't exactly jibe with the real Brackett's chronology, as our Brackett was born in 1818 and there is no indication that the Vasselboro sermon dealt with iconoclasm. However, Ingraham's habit of pulling in real people and events helps illuminate the larger issues that shaped Brackett's world. This anecdote suggests the religious ferment that characterized early 19th century New England. Though begun as a theocracy, by the 19th century the new country was becoming a cauldron of different and often warring belief systems. The state-supported Congregationalists, descendants of the original Puritans, clashed with newer groups like Quakers, Unitarians and Universalists who replaced the Puritan's vision of humanity's innate depravity and doctrine of predestination with a more optimistic belief in human perfectibility and spiritual equality. Meanwhile evangelicals were challenging both of these groups with their embrace of an ecstatic conversion experience that emphasized the believer's personal relationship with God and downplayed the state's role in religion.

As a result there were striking differences of opinion about doctrinal matters. The dour view of art espoused by Edward's mother echoes that of Cincinnati minister Joshua L. Wilson, an Old School Calvinist who maintained in his 1820 Commonplace Book: "An artist may form a knife, a spoon, a table, bureau and be not only an innocent but an estimable workman. But should he give to the handle of the knife the form of a serpent or fix on his spoon the likeness of an eagle or cause his table to stand upon the feet of a bear or mount his bureau with the heads of lions, be becomes, in my opinion, a transgressor of this moral law."[16] Wilson's old style Calvinism shared with mainstream Presbyterianism an aversion to frivolity that was rooted in their mutual abhorrence of Catholicism, then seeping into the country by way of working class immigrants. Wilson characterized Catholic churches as "the houses of spacious and splendid idolatry," and "places of resort for the idle, the superstitious, the deluded."[17] He regarded Catholics as anti-democratic and un-American for their allegiance to the Pope. Almost as iniquitous, in his view, were the Unitarians and Universalists who did not believe in the divinity of Christ or the doctrine of the Trinity and professed that all souls were destined for heaven.

The more generous interpretation of the Second Commandment attributed by Ingraham to Reverend Gillet represents a softening of this iconoclastic position. As the 19th century progressed and Americans began to travel to see the artistic glories of Europe, perceptions of art in the New World were changing. By the mid century, art was no longer considered by definition a decadent throwback to the Old World or a sinful assertion of parity with God. Increasingly writers and artists made the argument that art could be a useful tool to illuminate the glory of God and the secular achievements of the new society. Nathaniel Hawthorne, who thought deeply about the relationship of art and religion in the Old and New Worlds, lamented Puritan America's aversion to art. He made Hester Prynne, the adulterous heroine of his 1850 *The Scarlet Letter*, an embroiderer whose passion, love of beauty, and honesty lift her far above the cramped morality of her Puritan accusers. And in his 1860 novel *The Marble Faun* which deals with the adventures of three young American artists and an Italian Count in Rome, Hawthorne's narrator defends the idea of sculpture as a kind of sacred Trust. He remarks, "{marble} insures immortality to whatever is wrought in it, and therefore makes it a religious obligation to commit no idea to its mighty guardianship, save such as may repay the marble for its faithful care. . . Under this aspect, marble assumes a sacred character; and no man should dare to touch it unless he feels within himself a certain consecration and a priesthood. . ."[18]

The real Bracketts were Quakers and one biographical note reveals that during the peripatetic family's stay in Providence, Rhode Island, young Edward was sent to a Friend's school. The Quakers espoused a philosophy of simplicity that made them suspicious of art forms that encouraged vanity or pleasure for its own sake. However, all indications are that the objections raised by Brackett's father to his son's desire to be an artist were more practical than theological. In Ingraham's fiction and in real life, Reuben Brackett attempted to interest his son in some sensible trade. In the novel, these options included shoe making, tailoring, calico block printing and tombstone carving. As for the real Brackett, a contemporary biographer notes that "His father wished him to acquire a good trade, and for this purpose placed him at six different trades; but perceiving at length that he made no progress in either, he gave up the point, and suffered him to consult his own inclination, which was to be an artist."[19]

In Ingraham's account, various apprenticeships coincided with the family's moves across the country. From Vasselboro, the Bracketts migrated to Lynn, Massachusetts, then the shoe capital of the world, where Edward is unhappily apprenticed for three years to a shoemaker. Ingraham has the aspiring artist create a sculptural caricature of his humorless master that not only entertains his fellow apprentices, but draws public crowds when placed in the shop window. Following his inevitable dismissal, he is next apprenticed to a tailor, who relegates him to domestic tasks and treats him like an indentured servant. Again Edward escapes the yoke and moves with his family to Westbrook, Maine where he is able to use his artistic talents carving patterns on wooden blocks for his father's calico fabrics manufacturing business, a skill also attributed to the real Brackett.

A New Start in Cincinnati

Finally, the Brackett family, including seventeen-year old Edward, relocates to Cincinnati, Ohio. Ingraham recounts an exciting and complicated trip by covered wagon through the White Mountains, Bennington, Vermont, Troy and Schenectady, New York, on canal boat to Buffalo, by steamer to Cleveland, and finally sailing down the Ohio River to Cincinnati. He describes such restlessness as a national trait, remarking, "Americans are locomotive; and their rivers and railroads afford to them such inviting facilities for moving from place to place, that, from the way they avail themselves of them, it would seem that they believed they were despising Nature's bounty by staying at home."[20]

According to *Artists in Ohio*, a biographical dictionary of Ohio artists, the real Brackett family was lured to Cincinnati in 1835 by Reuben's brother Oliver who had already established himself there as an oilcloth manufacturer.[21] To make this material, cloth was treated with linseed oil to waterproof it and then printed with patterns for use in such items as capes, luggage, tablecloths, and satchels. Oliver may have employed his nephew in cutting patterns onto blocks used to print the cloth. The fictional Edward is employed in this business by his father before throwing it over to work for an old school friend in a foundry.

Whichever account is true, it is a fact that Cincinnati gave Brackett his start as a sculptor. Cincinnati was fertile ground for an aspiring artist. Located on the confluence of the Licking and Ohio rivers, Cincinnati was an agricultural mecca, a manufacturing center and an important shipping port connecting North to South by way of the Ohio River's link to the Mississippi. Because of its natural advantages, the city experienced spectacular growth in the first half of the nineteenth century. Americans from the Northeast and the South as well as immigrants from Ireland, Germany and England flocked to Cincinnati and its population nearly doubled every ten years.

As a trading center and the nation's third largest manufacturing city, Cincinnati was touted by its leaders as a cultural model for the rest of the country. Ebenezer S. Thomas, editor of the *Cincinnati Daily Advertiser*, preened in his 1840 memoir, "But it is not in the number and architectural beauty of her private dwellings, and public buildings, that Cincinnati alone excels; it is in all that constitutes refinement and taste. It is in her Literature, her Authors, her Arts, her Artists, and her numerous Literary, Scientific and benevolent institutions, that has given her a name, not only among the cities of the great Valley, but of the civilized world, that will go down to the most remote posterity."[22] Alexis de Tocqueville, who passed through in 1831, was less effusive. He mused, "Cincinnati presents an odd spectacle. A town which seems to want to get built too quickly to have things done in order. Large buildings, huts, streets blocked by rubble, houses under construction; no names to the streets, no numbers on the houses, no external luxury, but a picture of industry and work that strikes one at every step."[23]

Boosters like Thomas regarded their city as an outpost of gentility and civilization in the Wild West and anointed it the *Queen City*, or *The Athens of the West*. A less elevated nickname for Cincinnati was *Porkopolis*, highlighting its status as the pork-processing center of the country.

Although the main business of Cincinnati was business, it was beginning to attract a coterie of artists and intellectuals around the time of Brackett's arrival. Cincinnati was the most important publishing center in the west, with dozens of daily, semi-weekly and weekly newspapers. The city hosted numerous museums, libraries and academies. There was a lively artist community that included a number of nationally recognized sculptors. Like Brackett, none were native Cincinnatians, but the town's welcoming atmosphere attracted them, at least for a while, before most of them headed off to Italy to complete their artistic education.

Only ten years earlier, it had been quite a different situation. The English novelist Mrs. Francis Trollope found herself in Cincinnati in 1828 after the failure of a utopian community she had hoped to help establish. She painted a dim picture of the artist life there. In a biting report on the state of American culture, she focused on the provincialism of her adopted city. She remarked, "With regard to the fine arts, their paintings, I think are quite as good, or rather better, than might be expected from the patronage they receive; the wonder is that any man can be found with courage enough to devote himself to a profession in which he has so little chance of finding maintenance. The trade of a carpenter opens an infinitely better prospect; and this is so well known, that nothing but a genuine passion for the art could beguile any one to pursue it."[24]

Art and Patronage in Cincinnati

But by 1839, prospects were far brighter, at least for sculptors in Cincinnati, thanks to the emergence of a substantial patron class. For the most part these patrons were wealthy businessmen who looked upon art as a means to promote the moral and social edification of society. As practical men, they were more interested in skill and verisimilitude than in any attempts at visual poetry, originality or imagination. Those who had traveled abroad used the art of the past as touchstones for their patronage. For painting, they looked to the Old Masters of the Renaissance and Baroque era for models of great art. In the case of sculpture, classical Greek and Roman statuary were the ideals. However, James Jackson Jarves, one of the most influential critics of the day, remarks dismissively that such patrons' taste ran to works which were "a weak echo of the third rate classical manner after it had abandoned beauty for prettiness."[25]

In Cincinnati, as back East, aspiring sculptors quickly learned that portrait busts were the currency with which to attract financial support. Both historical and contemporary subjects were popular and more than one young carver (Brackett included) discovered that representations of George Washington were the ideal passport to recognition. As a result, the oeuvres of all these sculptors were bursting with plaster heads, the most popular of which were recreated in marble multiples and can still be found in museums around the country. Looking askance at this tendency, Nathaniel Hawthorne has his narrator in *The Marble Faun* remark, "Posterity will be puzzled what to do with busts like these, the concretions and petrifactions of a vain self-estimate; but will find, no doubt, that they serve to build into stone walls, or burn into quicklime, as well as if the marble had never been blocked into the guise of human heads." [26]

Among the most important patrons in Cincinnati was Nicholas Longworth. The second richest man in the United States (his obituary notes proudly that in 1850 his tax bill was second only to that of William B. Astor), he was a self-made millionaire who embodied a classic American rags to riches story. His father, once a successful merchant, had lost everything after backing the Tories in the American Revolutionary War. Young Nicholas, originally apprenticed in his native New Jersey to a shoemaker, made his way to Cincinnati where he swiftly rose from law clerk to land speculator. His obituary notes, "He foresaw, at an early period of his residence in the West, the future greatness of the then insignificant village of Cincinnati; and though unsustained in the new community, took advantage of their unbelief, and began a series of systematic investment of every thing he could make by his services as lawyer and land agent. . ."27

He was so canny that by age thirty-six he had acquired a real estate fortune vast enough to allow him to retire and pursue his interests in horticulture and gardening. He made a second fortune as a vintner. With the cultivation of the Catawba grape which grew prolifically in the Ohio Valley he managed to establish the first American wine industry This enterprise was memorialized by Henry Wadsworth Longfellow in his poem "Ode to Catawba Wine," which reads in part:

"For richest and best
Is the wine of the West,
That grows by the Beautiful River;
Whose sweet perfume
Fills all the room
With a benison on the giver ..."

Longworth also gained renown as a philanthropist. He was famous for his support of those he termed, "the devil's poor," namely individuals so downtrodden and unlucky that no one else would give them money. He was also a generous patron of artists and art institutions. One of his beneficiaries remarked, "It may be said with entire truth that there was never a young artist of talent who appeared in Cincinnati, and was poor and needed help that Mr. Longworth, if asked, did not willingly assist him."28

This assistance took a variety of forms – he purchased art, he gave artists money to travel back East for further study, or in a few cases, to establish themselves in Italy, then seen as the mecca for aspiring American artists. He also wrote letters of introduction and provided living expenses for needy artists. His motivation seems, at least in part, to give cultural legitimacy to the city that had made him so rich. Despite all this he was not universally liked. Some artists resented his insistence that they extend their training by returning East or going abroad. The painter James Henry Beard refused Longworth's offer to send him to Philadelphia for further study because Longworth insisted that Beard leave his wife behind. Painter Lilly Martin Spencer refused a trip to Italy because Longworth wanted her to spend the year copying works by other masters. And the painter John P. Frankenstein resented Longworth's worship of the Old Masters and his stinginess when paying for art so much that he memorialized the businessman as "Nick Littleworth" with a poem titled "American Art: Its Awful Altitude". Frankenstein quotes his anti-hero:-"Give artists work!" he cries, 'I'm no such fool!G-d d-n em, starve em! that's my rule!..."
29 Most artists, however, were happy to accept Longworth's patronage.

By all accounts Longworth cut an eccentric figure. (fig 2) His obituary describes him thus: "He was small in stature, probably about five feet three, thin in figure, and moved with a shambling gait. He was very careless in his costume. He unfailingly wore a white cravat, with a shirt collar sometimes reaching to his ears, sometimes falling over on his neck. His hat was hapless, old, and discolored; his clothes fitting loosely about him; his shoes, or brogans rather, were large and unblacked, with the thongs, if they had any, straggling about."[30] A famous anecdote has Abraham Lincoln coming to admire his grounds and initially mistaking Longworth for the gardener. When Lincoln realizes his mistake, the businessman tells the future president, "You are the first to find me out so soon … Sometimes I get 10 cents and sometimes as much as a quarter for showing visitors my grounds." [31]

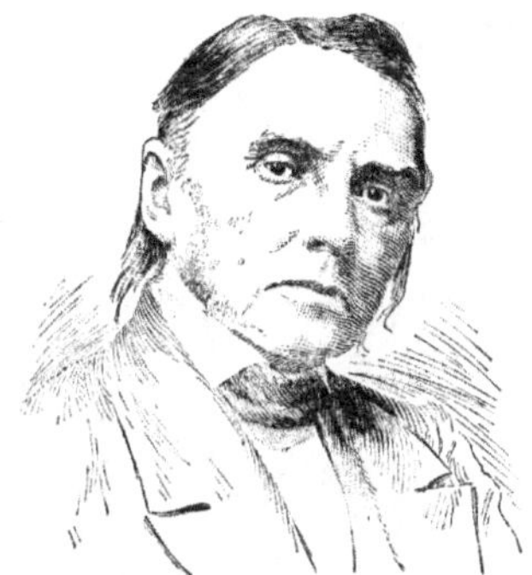

fig. 2 *Nicholas Longworth*, engraving by an unknown artist,
Historical collections of Ohio Vol 1. Centennial Edition, 1908,
Courtesy Creative Commons.

Longworth makes a notable appearance in Ingraham's novel where he is described in equally unflattering terms: "He was a short, little man, slovenly dressed in black with stout soiled boots, and a very much worn low-crowned broad brimmed hat. . . His beard was thick and not recently shaved, and his brows were very thick, dark and projecting, beneath which shone a pair of restless eyes that expressed mingled penetration and good nature."[32] He commissions a portrait bust from Edward but advises him to look beyond portrait busts to grander subjects, advice that leads to his first real masterpiece. There is no evidence that Longworth sat for the real Brackett but he did provide him with encouragement and letters of introduction.

As there was no art academy in America at this time, the artists nurtured by Longworth and other culturally minded businessmen came to their vocation from various artisanal or mechanical backgrounds. Of them the most famous was Hiram Powers, who would later gain international fame for his *Greek Slave*, a sculpture of a nude woman demurely hiding her privates with her shackled

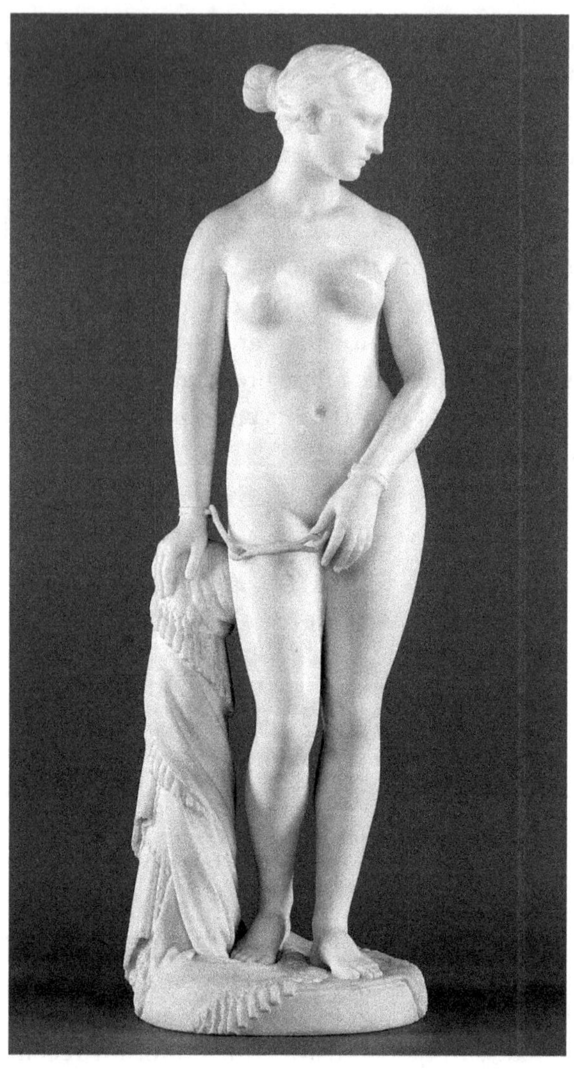

fig. 3 *Greek Slave* by Hiram Powers, marble, modeled 1841-1843, carved ca. 1873, Smithsonian American Art Museum, Gift of Mrs. Benjamin H. Warder, Courtesy of Creative Commons.

hand. (fig 3) Carved in marble in 1844 from a plaster model Powers produced in 1843, it was exhibited to great acclaim in the 1851 Crystal Palace Exhibition in London. While saccharinely innocuous by modern standards, the work was embroiled in controversy in those more conservative days by American viewers who regarded it as salacious. Men and women were required to view it separately, which only added to its allure. The sculpture's defenders argued that, however titillating, this paragon of victimhood was chastely clothed in virtue.

The popularity of the *Greek Slave* made the work susceptible to a variety of interpretations. In the years running up to the Civil War some abolitionists embraced the sculpture as an emblem of the evils of slavery. Poet Elizabeth Barrett Browning made the case for a larger reading in a poem from 1850 which concludes:

" . . . Pierce to the centre,
 Art's fiery finger! and break up ere long
The serfdom of this world. Appeal, fair stone,
From God's pure heights of beauty against man's wrong!
Catch up in thy divine face, not alone
East griefs but west, and strike and shame the strong,
By thunders of white silence, overthrown."

Powers was not alone in his adoption of the slave motif. According to art historian Albert TenEyck Gardner, "There was certainly a discernable preoccupation with chains, shackles, and slaves which found expression in American sculpture. Perhaps it was not only the effect of the burning slavery question of the day, perhaps it was symbolic of the sculptors' bondage to materialism and inexperience. In any case, this concern with chains amounted almost to a national mania."[33] But for all the popularity of this subject, representations of African slaves were rare. This may in part be due to artists' dependence on white marble as a symbol of purity and classical pedigree. The fetishization of this material would have hindered any representation of the blackness of America's enslaved population. But equally problematic from the sculptors' point of view was the potential controversy that might surround direct references to the conflict that was soon to tear the country apart. Powers could inoffensively reference slavery by presenting his shackled victim as a white Christian woman who has been enslaved by the swarthy Turks. A far more potent sculptural symbol of the abolitionist movement, as we shall see, would take the form of Edward Brackett's John Brown. However, at the time of Edward Brackett's arrival in Cincinnati, Powers was transitioning from engineer to artist. He came to sculpture by way of *The Infernal Regions,* an exhibition in Cincinnati's Western Museum, where he was the chief maker of automata. An adjunct to the museum's collection of western curiosities, (offerings included such items as the tattooed head of a New Zealand chief, various Native American artifacts, a kaleidoscope, and "enchanted mirrors,") *The Infernal Regions* was a life size model of Hell. Power's contribution included a group of wax effigies inspired by Dante's *Inferno* that groaned, emitted smoke and rattled chains. As with his later, chastely erotic *Greek Slave,* Powers here was able to render potentially scandalous material palatable to a "respectable" audience. The profane pleasures that attracted crowds to *The Infernal Regions* were lightly disguised by a veneer of religiosity.

Powers worked for the Museum from 1829 to 1834, after which he abandoned fun-house entertainments for marble sculpture. Like all the sculptors of his day, he focused on portrait busts. Having gained attention for a bust of Andrew Jackson, Powers was doing a brisk business in portrait busts at the time of Brackett's arrival, and hence served as a good model for an aspiring sculptor. He combined artistic skills with a hardnosed sense of commerce. Albert TenEyck Gardner notes, ". . . successful businessmen . . . have always been inclined to be suspicious of artists. But they could understand Hiram, especially when he kept raising his prices until he could demand and get a thousand dollars for a portrait bust."[34] In 1837 Powers moved to Italy to set up shop in Florence with a workshop manned by less successful Italian carvers. He was to remain in Italy for thirty-six years, never returning home, and building renown as the "Praxiteles of the Western World." This reputation, sadly, has not stood the test of time.

Another sculptor gaining attention during Brackett's Cincinnati sojourn was Shobal Vail Clevenger. The fictional Brackett is introduced to the possibilities of sculpture by a chance encounter in a stoneyard with a young man whom he sees carving a stone cherub. Noticing Edward's interest, he offers him the chisel, whereby Edward, though totally untrained in stonecutting, finishes the wing of the cherub so beautifully that the young man says, "let us be friends and not rivals."[35] His new acquaintance introduces himself as Clevenger. He brings Edward into a studio full of clay and plaster busts whereupon Edward is overcome with emotion and resolves to become a sculptor.

Whether or not this encounter actually happened, the real Brackett was undoubtedly acquainted with the real Clevenger. Their time in Cincinnati overlapped, both shared a patron in Nicholas Longworth and both moved East to pursue their careers in 1839. As Ingraham suggests, Clevenger came to sculpting by way of tombstones. From 1829 to 1833 he was apprenticed to stonecutter David Guion, where he became a master carver of decorative figures for buildings and tombs. His first portrait bust was the likeness of E. S. Thomas, editor of the *Cincinnati Evening Post* who was also a great champion of Brackett's work. Thomas, who was never short of superlatives, described Clevenger as "the future Canova of this country." As was the custom of the time, Clevenger built his reputation with busts of famous Americans, among them William Henry Harrison, Daniel Webster, Martin van Buren, Henry Clay, and Washington Allston.

After a sojourn to New York, Washington and Boston where he further solidified his reputation, Clevenger moved, with the support of Nicholas Longworth, to Italy in 1840. There he translated a number of his plaster busts into marble with the help of local artisans. He also tried his hands at more literary subjects, among them the head of *The Lady of the Lake* and an *Indian Warrior*. Sadly, he was not to match Powers' success. Instead, Clevenger became ill with tuberculosis, dying shipboard in 1843 while en route home.

Other members of the class of Cincinnati artists are largely forgotten. They enjoyed varying degrees of success in their lifetimes. Sculptor John L. Whetstone is best known now as one of the founders of the Cincinnati Academy of Fine Arts. Painter Thomas Buchanan Read was employed as Clevenger's assistant when he caught the eye of Nicholas Longworth, who provided him with a studio and connections. He is remembered today (if at all) as a poet whose patriotic poems drew on his experiences as a major in the Union Army during the Civil War. John P. Frankenstein was a double threat as portrait painter and sculptor. However Longworth declined to offer him support, which may have exacerbated the mental troubles that embittered him against the art world. After penning his satirical poem, "American Art: Its Awful Altitude" in 1864, he ended his life in squalor in New York City. His younger brother Godfrey N. Frankenstein had a happier career. He was a landscape painter whose "Panorama of the Niagara," was to enjoy a successful tour of the country from 1853 to 1854. Meanwhile, painter James Henry Beard established himself as a portraitist and genre painter, but gained his greatest success with his portraits of dogs and cats.

These were the shining stars who elicited this assessment from a writer for the *New York Star* in 1840: "Cincinnati! What is there in the atmosphere of Cincinnati that has so thoroughly awakened the arts of sculpture and painting? It cannot surely be mere accident which gives birth to so many artists, all of distinguished merit, too; what must be quite gratifying to that city — all possessing high moral worth."[36]

An American Culture

The dollop of righteousness that concludes this quotation is a reflection of the mid-19th century expectation that art should serve as a tool of moral uplift and civic education. Art historian Albert TenEyck Gardner has provided an extremely entertaining account of this development in his 1945 book *Yankee Stonecutters: The First American School of Sculpture 1800 -1850*. Originally commissioned as a catalogue of the early nineteenth century American sculpture collection of the Metropolitan Museum of Art in New York, this text metastasized into a social history of this fascinating period. Gardner puzzles over the sudden emergence out of the American frontier of a surfeit of classically inspired sculpture in the 1830s and 40s. He remarks, "From the histories of American sculpture, one would gather that for no apparent reason young men were suddenly seized with an irrepressible yearning to become sculptors."[37]

The reality, he suggests, hinged more on politics and economics than mystical inspiration. He recounts a national drive to establish a "Classico-Jacksonian" school of sculpture that would rival the greatest productions of the Old World. The term conjures a strange forced marriage of the elitist and populist elements in American culture. Cultural leaders argued that American sculpture should draw on antique prototypes to emphasize the classical roots of American democracy. The rebuilding of the Capital after War of 1812 revealed the embarrassing fact that there were no American artists with the skills to create the desired heroic statues. Instead commissions went primarily to Italians. Gardner remarks, "One of the main forces in creating an American school of sculpture was apparently the wounded national pride."[38]

Perceptions of American sculpture began to change with the emergence of Horatio Greenough, who defined the neo-classical style with his 1832 *Enthroned Washington*. (fig 4) This work, originally intended for the Capital rotunda but eventually relegated to the National Museum of American History, presented the founding father as a bare chested Greek god who raises his right index finger heavenward while he clasps a sword in his left hand. The pose was largely based on the now lost statue of *Zeus Olympios* by the ancient Greek sculptor Phidias. Greenough had gained his skills by settling in Florence in 1828 where he learned the trade from Italian artisans. Many other sculptors were to pursue his example, though not, as it turns out, Edward Brackett. Following Greenough, the approved style for official sculpture hewed closely to classical models, however inappropriate to the subject matter.

The rush to emulate and surpass the ancient masters was fueled by an infusion of cash from government coffers and patriotic businessmen. City, state and the federal officials were willing to pay what were then considered astounding sums for monuments to great men and important moments in American history. Private commissions followed the same path, with an emphasis on the memorialization of great (or at least wealthy) men or the realization of grand literary subjects in pristine white carrara marble. Patrons enriched the most successful artists who were then celebrated as the heroes of the age. By 1856, poet Walter Savage Landor could write with pride to Emerson that, "Sculpture in the present day flourishes more than it ever did since the days of Pericles; and

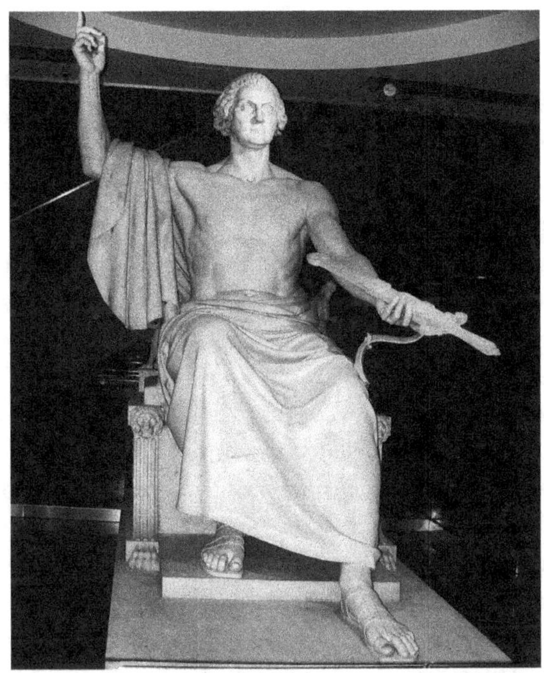

fig. 4 *Enthroned Washington* by Horatio Greenough, 1832, marble, National Museum of American History, Courtesy of Creative Commons.

America is not cast into the shadow by Europe." [39]

Not all observers were so enthralled. The critic James Jackson Jarves decried the appropriative impulse, noting that the demand for sculpture in public monuments had brought forth "a bounteous call for costly busts, portrait-statues, cheap copies of classical marbles and dear at any price originals of Eves, Judiths, white Slaves, and other crude fancies of second-hand sentiment, or bland effigies in stone of imperfect nudity in the flesh." This quote appears in Jarves' 1882 book *Art Thoughts*. Jarves wends his way through the glories of French and Italian art before stopping short with a discussion of American art. This section begins: "If this chapter were to be limited to what actually exists in America of indigenous art, it would be almost as brief as that on snakes in a certain History of Ireland."[40]

Jarves, like many of the culturally enlightened connoisseurs of his day, was enthralled with the art of Europe. His commentaries are amusingly acerbic, but many of his calls have failed the test of time. He writes disparagingly of some of the 19th century artists who are most revered today, among them Whistler, whose paintings he found incomplete, and Hudson River School Painters Albert Bierstadt and Frederick Church who were "cold and untruthful."[41] Among the few American sculptors whom he could countenance was Edward Brackett, whose bust of John Brown was to earn his highest approbation.

On the other hand, many of his comments on the relationship of art and money have a very contemporary feel. Jarves was highly critical of the materialist basis of the fledging American art scene. Once derided by the Puritans as ungodly and frivolous, art was quickly becoming, in his view, too popular. He sniffed, "The anti-respectable notion of art, the joint offspring of the utilitarian habits of a country new to civilization and the religious tenets of Puritan settlers, has given place in the common mind to a notion almost as one sided and ignorant in the opposite direction. It inclines to take a sentimental view of the functions of an artist and his works, as of an exceptional being not amenable to the usual rules of criticism, and, covering them with poetical haze, allows the imagination to accept the promise for the fulfillment."[42]

The reality, he suggested, was far more prosaic. Decrying the commercialization of art, he complained: "An increasing number of persons engage in art for no sincere purpose except to speedily become rich; their credit, like that of merchants, being based on the amount of business they do."[43]

Jarves' Eurocentric views suggest the obvious contradiction in the drive to create a genuinely American school of neoclassical sculpture. Unlike the Hudson River School painters who turned to the American landscape to celebrate the Edenic beauty and freedom of the New World, ambitious American sculptors sought to emulate the ancient masters. They aimed to rise above their peers and satisfy the classicizing taste of their patrons by taking off for Italy. There they hoped to learn to follow and even surpass the classical and renaissance masters. In reality, many of them merely produced lifeless and generic busts and anatomically questionable figures, sometimes composed, like Frankenstein's monster, of disparate elements cribbed from less well-known antique statues. Rarely did they actually carve the marble themselves, instead handing their plaster casts off to third rate Italian sculptors who churned them out with machine-like regularity. Hawthorne took a dim view of such emigres, noting acerbically, "For the sake of such brotherhood as they can find, more than for any good that they get from galleries, they linger year after year in Italy, while their originality dies out of them, or is polished away as a barbarism."[44]

Brackett Begins

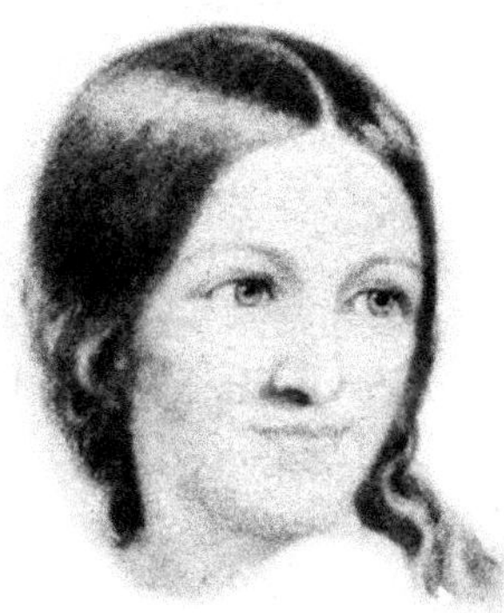

fig 5. *Jane Brackett Field,* by Edward Augustus Brackett, n.d.. Brackett's *The Poetess* is lost but this drawing of his sister may suggest Brackett's approach to her bust. Courtesy of the Winchester Massachusetts Archival Center.

Entering into this milieu, Brackett was as well, or, one might argue, as ill prepared as any of his compatriots. Like his peers, he was essentially self-taught. One biographical sketch says that he studied the works of Powers, another has him enthralled by the works in Clevenger's studio, while others describe him as sui generis. It seems likely, as Ingraham suggests, that he was introduced to his trade as an apprentice tombstone carver. Commentators on his early artistic career tend to marvel at how quickly he broke into the scene. Having arrived in Cincinnati at age seventeen with his parents in the spring of 1835, he first tried his hand at sculpture in 1838. By 1839 he was producing works that were garnering high praise. Among the first were a medallion of Washington and a bust of his sister Jane that he titled *The Poetess.* (fig 5) Neither survives, but the latter is mentioned both by commentators and by Ingraham, who says of it, "It looked like an ideal classic head, but it was but the perfect likeness of a lovely American girl."[45] In Ingraham's novel, the bust is effusively praised by a "Mr. Thomas, Editor of the Gazette," who becomes one of Edward's most stalwart supporters.

This character's real life counterpart was the aforementioned Ebenezer Smith Thomas, a Cincinnati newspaperman with a great interest in art. Here again we see how Ingraham only lightly fictionalized real events. Before arriving in Cincinnati in 1828, Thomas had experienced a peripatetic career in which he had bounced around the South working as a bookseller, editor, farmer, member of the Maryland State Legislature and real estate investor. Having lost a fortune in the latter, he settled in Cincinnati as editor of first, *The Commercial Daily Advertiser* and then the *Evening Post.* All of this is recounted in his lively 1840 memoir *Reminiscences of the Last Sixty-five Years,* which contains an entertaining discussion of the Cincinnati art scene at the time of Brackett's sojourn there.

By his own account, Thomas was one of the first to recognize Brackett's talent. In his memoir he proudly quotes from a description of his critical acumen written in the *Louisville News Letter,* "It was he [Thomas] who first discovered and encouraged Powers, Clevenger, Beard, and Frankenstein, and to him belongs the honor of fostering the dawning genius of the young and highly gifted Brackett."[46] Ingraham has Thomas write a glowing report about Edward in the *Gazette* that finally convinces his father that he may have prospects as an artist after all. The review opens: "It would be quite honor enough for any place to claim *one* eminent sculptor or painter, but this favored spot has sent forth a number. Powers is actually astonishing all Europe: Clevenger is preparing himself for Florence, where he will receive his share of admiration; and Brackett is a new candidate for the honors of a Praxiteles and a Canova. Who is Brackett? He is a youth scarcely nineteen whose parents reside in this city, and who though highly respectable, have not sufficient wealth to educate him to that rank for which his genius has evidently destined him."[47]

The fictional review goes on at great length to laud Edward's brilliance and promise. The opening lines of this text are taken verbatim from a much shorter notice written by the real Thomas for the *New York Star* in April 1840 after Brackett's departure from Cincinnati. This review is far less effusive and erroneously predicts the young sculptor's imminent departure for Italy. It does however reveal Thomas' admiration for the young sculptor. The review by the real Thomas, reprinted in his memoir, reads, "It would be quite honor enough for any place, to claim one eminent sculptor, or painter, but that favored spot has sent forth a number. Powers is actually astonishing all Europe; Clevenger is preparing himself for Florence, where he will receive his share of admiration; and Brackett who is now in New York, is steadily working his way to favor. As soon as circumstances will permit, he also will go to Italy. The greatest difficulty with sculptors, is to embody expression, particularly when it is a mixed one; Brackett has been eminently successful in this way, and it is that which has brought him so immediately before the public."[48]

The first reports of Brackett's appearance on the Cincinnati art scene date from 1839. His biography in *Artists in Ohio* notes that was the year he set up a studio in Foote's Row, an artists' haunt. It was also the year he exhibited several busts as well as *The Poetess* at the Cincinnati Academy of Fine arts and the Ohio Mechanic's Institute, a center for the education of workingmen. Like his fellow sculptors he was kept busy with commissions for busts for, among others: vintner Henry Ives, writer Rufus Dawes, and phrenological lecturer James Stanley Grimes. However, this did not ensure a steady income. As Ingraham complains, "But there is a certain class of persons who are very ready to patronize rising genius, especially of painting or sculpture, and who deem it a sufficient honor to condescend to sit for the artist for bust or portrait, and permitting him to have it to exhibit in his rooms. This they call patronage, and no doubt it is, for we don't like to quarrel with terms; but Dr. Johnson has another word for it in his dictionary."[49]

The real Brackett, like his fictional counterpart, was considered a very talented sculptor, but he was evidently not a brilliant businessman. He struggled to make ends meet, and unlike some of his more fortunate peers, never put together the funding for the expected trip to Italy. (Gardner suggests that this may have been to his benefit, as he never acquired the classical gloss that rendered the works of his more traveled compatriots so generic.) Brackett's departure from Cincinnati came on the heels of his disappointment with the City's failure to raise funds to purchase his first major work. His financial struggles were to continue throughout his art career, leading him finally to eschew sculpture altogether for the security of a full time government job.

Nydia, Blind Girl of Pompeii

While busts brought sculptors patrons (and also, as Ingraham indicates, hangers on), real respect required works of the imagination. These were literary or historical subjects that allowed the artist to compete with the ancient masters. In his Cincinnati years, Brackett created one such sculpture. His 1839 work *Nydia, Blind Girl of Pompeii* was based on the then wildly popular novel, *The Last Days of Pompeii,* published by Edward Bulwer-Lytton in 1834. In that story, Nydia is a blind slave girl who burns with unrequited love for her master, Glaucus. Her blindness becomes an asset when Mount Vesuvius erupts, as she is able to lead Glaucus and his ladylove through the ash covered streets because she knows them by feel. Upon delivering them to safety, she drowns herself in the sea because she knows her love is unrequited. The subject was an appealing one, not only for its soapy plot, but because it fed into the new Republic's vogue for all things classical. Interest in the story was heightened as well by the popularity of the ruins of Pompeii and Herculaneum as tourist sites.

This sculpture plays a pivotal role in Ingraham's tale. Edward is motivated to create this work by Nicholas Longworth, who remonstrates, "Have you no imagination? Can't you conceive a statue and employ your leisure in working upon it. You will never do anything worthy of your powers if you confine yourself to the lowest order of your Art – copying heads of fat citizens. Let me see you commence some great work – something that will be identified with your name."[50]

Edward turns for inspiration to the story of Nydia, fixing on the passage in which Nydia is interrupted by Glaucus as she waters flowers: "'Nydia, my child,' said Glaucus. At the sound of his voice she paused at once -listening, blushing, breathless; her lips parted, her face up-turned to catch the direction of the sound!" Ingraham describes Edward's creative ferment: "'He sees Nydia, the blind girl! He is beside her as she flies! Nay, he identifies his spirit with hers!"[51] He works in a frenzy and when he is done he steps back and weeps. His friends all gather around and acclaim his genius and then take up a campaign to have the city buy the work. In his memoir, the real Thomas confirms this reception. He quotes a *Louisville Newsletter* account of the sculpture that notes that, "during a brief exhibition in his studio, it has excited the admiration of connoisseurs, who have wafted most acceptable incense to the genius of the gifted sculptor."[52]

Nydia's current whereabouts are unknown. At the time, the sculpture engendered considerable comment from the Cincinnati Press. The Brackett Collection in the Archival Center of Winchester, Massachusetts contains a trove of clippings in which unidentified writers wax ecstatically over the sculpture and exhort readers to support the effort to keep it in the city.[53] One colorfully describes a visit to the studio in which "We made our bow to the lady a day or two since and were agreeably surprised to find no creation of heathen gods and goddesses – of Diana with her 'cutty sark'[54] or Venus in the costume of a Frenchy dancer – no Centaur of the 'half horse and half alligator' breed, but as pretty a little 'Buckeye' girl as ever 'toted' water from the spring in a *yearthen* (sic) pitcher. . . With a face upturned, and parted lips which look as if they had hitherto been a "sealed fountain", who looks for all the world like the pretty girls we have seen at apple cuttings, waiting for a kiss, afore now."

Other reviewers are less titillating, but repeat the encomiums to Brackett's youth and genius. One of these notices is quoted verbatim by Ingraham and attributed to a Mr. Hammond. The identical review in the archive is unsigned, but given Ingraham's penchant for appropriating real life figures, is presumably newspaper editor Charles Hammond of the *Cincinnati Gazette*. The review maintains that Nydia is "the first statue ever executed in the great Valley of the Mississippi" and includes a plea to the city for financial support. The writer declares, "Mr. Brackett has fixed his mind upon the pursuit of the sculptor's art, and has no other resource; and from our knowledge of him, we unhesitantly say that he possesses the genius, industry and stability, which cannot fail to carry him to the very height of perfection in the art that he has chosen to pursue; provided, that patronage is afforded him, to which his merits as a *man*, and an artist, so justly entitle him. Let all remember that, as 'without rain from Heaven, the corn will wither on the stalk,' so without patronage, the fine arts must wither and fail. Let that never be said of a city which is supplying the whole nation with artists."

There is however in the archive one dissenting view. It is from a writer for the *Cincinnati Daily Gazette* who signs himself O. P. Q. He (we assume it is a he) takes issue, not so much with Brackett's talent, but with the exaggerated claims of the city's cultural boosters who appear oblivious to any shortcomings in the works of their chosen genius. He remarks, "Unless a reformation take place they soon will rival in the *art of puffing*, the makers and vendors of quack medicines." He praises the statue as a good start for a very young, untaught artist, but points out some flaws: "The figure is too large and in the form of the chest, the hips and the limbs, there is a want of that soft, graceful, founded outline – which marks the young, expanding girl. The face is too old for its prototype, and the body, partaking in some degree of that flabby appearance which is a better representation of forty than blooming sixteen. . . the vase is transformed into a large, long-necked pitcher, standing by her side – such a pitcher too as the infantile Nydia of Bulwar, could hardly raise from the ground, much less carry in her head, as with "graceful motions she hovered from flower to flower' and the young and delicate little Thessalian becomes a stout woman of thirty, who, with a sober face, and far from a graceful position of the body, is quietly preparing to make her way to the side of Glaucus."

He also takes issue with the much repeated – to this day – claim that this is the first full size statue completed in the Mississippi Valley. He argues, "Is this not a mistake? If I am correctly informed, Powers, before setting off for Italy, spent nearly a year on a statue, and then threw it aside because he could not please himself; and Clevenger, before starting to Boston, made a statue of one of his children. Both of these were executed prior to the statue of Nydia." O.P.Q concludes, "I would say this to Mr. Brackett, go ahead. He has made a capital beginning, and with patient industry and diligent study, may in despite of his puffers, become a distinguished sculptor."

It is impossible to know how much this dash of cold water influenced the city fathers. However, both the real and fictional Brackett failed to secure the funding that would have allowed the sculpture to remain in Cincinnati. Disappointment with the city fathers led Brackett to leave Porkopolis for the greener art pastures of New York City. Meanwhile, twenty years later, Nydia was to be the subject of a much better known sculpture by Randolph Rogers. (fig 6) This work was replicated a reputed one hundred and sixty seven times and versions can be found in such prestigious venues as the Metropolitan Museum in New York, The Art Institute of Chicago and the National Gallery of Art in Washington D.C. Interestingly, Rogers' sculpture also depicts a listening Nydia,

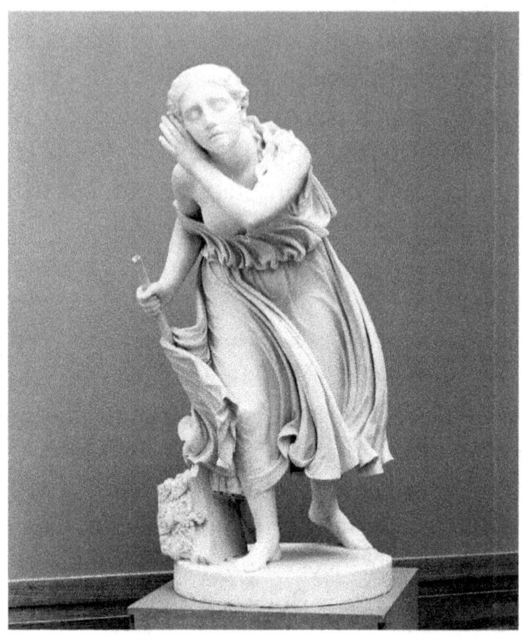

fig. 6 *Nydia, the Blind Flower Girl of Pompeii* by Randolph Rogers, marble, 1858, Metropolitan Museum of Art, Gift of James Douglas, 1899, Courtesy of Creative Commons.

who twists gracefully as she cups a hand to her ear. Instead of a pitcher, there is a staff signifying her blindness. How much did this representation owe to Brackett's lost earlier representation? In the absence of any visual documentation of the work, we will never know.

Moving On

Ingraham's narrative ends with Edward's travel by canal boat and train to New York City, where he discovers that he is preceded by his reputation as the sculptor of *Nydia*. The account is rather drawn out, with a great deal of material that seems more suited to a travelogue and leads one to suspect that Ingraham needed to pad the story in order to achieve the necessary twelve installments. Surprisingly, however, he fails to include an anecdote recounted in a biography of Brackett that would seem to lend itself to exactly his style of fiction.

The story is told in *Familiar Sketches of Sculpture and Sculptors*, an anthology of art and artist biographies published by Hannah Farnham Sawyer Lee in 1854.[55] Sawyer Lee was a prolific writer whose novels have a proto-feminist quality and whose nonfiction works include biographies of Martin Luther and Pierre Toussaint. *Familiar Sketches* is a two-volume work that chronicles the lives of various artists from the early Egyptian period to the present. Her biography of Edward Brackett passes very quickly over his life in Cincinnati, but gives a long account of his departure for New York. She reports that he had set aside $150 for the trip and invested it in notes from the United States Bank. This was before the days of a central banking authority, and banks were autonomous entities. After taking a canal boat to Cleveland, he boards a boat for Buffalo. But when he presents payment for his passage, he is told that the bank has failed and that his money is worthless. (This was a consequence of the Panic of 1837, a financial crisis that led to numerous bank failures between 1837 and 1844 and initiated a major depression throughout the United States.) Brackett wraps himself in his coat on the deck and attempts to sleep, only to be interrupted by an old gentleman who has observed his plight and bought him a ticket. The man turns out to be a prosperous farmer in upstate New York. He says, "Give me twenty-five dollars of your bad money, and I will give you good for it. I can afford to lose it, and am in the habit of giving away a few hundreds a year, to worthy objects who need assistance." Brackett accepts his help, and according to *Familiar Sketches*, they afterward maintained a correspondence for many years. One can only imagine that Ingraham neglected this story because it did not jibe with his tale of triumphant genius. *Familiar Sketches* goes on to chronicle Brackett's difficult years in New York before he manages to establish himself in Boston. This will be the subject of our next chapter.

The Slavery Question

But before moving on, another, more important lacuna in Ingraham's narrative needs to be addressed. Ingraham makes no mention of political upheavals in Cincinnati that must have exerted a vital formative influence on the real Brackett. In the first half of the 19th century, the slavery question was roiling both the city of Cincinnati and the nation at large. Ohio was a free state, meaning that slavery was prohibited there, but it bordered Kentucky, which was a slave state. The fact that Ohio was a free state didn't mean that fugitive slaves or even free Blacks found a warm welcome in the Queen City. Because of the economic, cultural and social ties that flowed both ways across the border, many in Cincinnati were unsympathetic to the abolitionist movement. Even many of the more "enlightened" citizens favored Colonization, a movement endorsing the return of the nation's Black population to Africa. (Brackett's patron Nicholas Longworth was of this opinion.) Thanks to the "Black Laws" enacted by the Ohio State Legislature in 1807, free Blacks living in Cincinnati had far fewer rights than their white counterparts. They could not testify in court, they were taxed for the support of schools they could not attend, there were restrictions on gun ownership and marriage, and they were required to produce two white people who would offer a surety of $500 to ensure their good behavior.

In Ohio, as throughout the rest of the country, fugitive slave laws based on the states rights provisions in U.S. Constitution mandated the return of enslaved people who escaped from one state into another. At the same time there was a small but growing membership in the Cincinnati Anti-Slavery Society. As a local chapter of a national organization, it called for the abolition of slavery and urged influential citizens to break off all ties with slaveholders. It also argued that slaveholders passing through free territories had abdicated their rights to their "property." Many members of the Anti-Slavery Society were also active in the Underground Railroad, the route by which fugitive slaves fled from the South to freedom in Canada. Between 1810 and 1850 40,000 slaves passed through Ohio. Many of them passed through Cincinnati, which was considered the Southern terminus of the railroad because of its position across the Ohio River from Kentucky.

By 1836, the year after Brackett's arrival in Cincinnati, conflicts over slavery had turned the city into a powder keg. The ensuing conflagration was given the name the "anti-abolitionist riots." Their immediate cause was the arrival of James Birney, a former slaveholder turned publisher from Kentucky who was now an adamant abolitionist. In April 1936 Birney brought his abolitionist newspaper, *The Philanthropist* to Cincinnati. A committee of citizens, Longworth among them, advocated closure of the paper, arguing that it was undermining the interests of business and property. There were meetings and discussions, but things remained quiet until July when a white mob attacked the offices of the paper and dismantled the press. A public meeting was called to discuss the situation. It was dominated by anti-abolitionists who compared their position to the attempts of the patriots of the Boston Tea Party to throw off the yoke of tyranny. Stoked by such sentiments, a second riot ensued several weeks later. A well-dressed crowd of eminent citizens with the unofficial sanction of the Mayor ransacked the printing office again. They then roamed the streets looking for abolitionists to tar and feather. They burned several Black shanties as well as buildings where the races were known to commingle. Disturbances continued without sanction for the next three nights. Finally public opinion began to turn against them, and there were rising condemnations of mob rule. Eventually several instigators were indicted and convicted. In 1837, following high profile case in which he was fined for harboring a fugitive slave, Birney left Cincinnati to become an officer in the American Anti-slavery Society in New York. *The Philanthropist,* meanwhile continued to publish under Birney's chosen successor until 1843.

None of this is even hinted at in Ingraham's narrative. This is no doubt due at least in part to the fact that his focus is on the cultivation of artistic genius rather than the social and political tensions of Cincinnati. But he also had little sympathy for abolitionists. This became evident in his later life when he moved to the South, married a plantation owner's daughter and penned a defense of the accusations against the slaveholding class found in *Uncle Tom's Cabin*. Ingraham's 1855 novel is titled *The Sunny South* and takes the form of a series of letters written by a northern woman who has come to Nashville to be a governess. Typical of her observations of Southern slavery is this passage: "There are many things to admire and to interest one in the social and domestic condition of the slaves, and I am almost ready to acknowledge that the African is happier in bondage than free! At least one thing is certain: nearly all the free negroes I have ever seen in the North were miserable creatures, poor, ragged, and often criminal. Here they are well clad, moral, nearly all religious, and the temptations that demoralize the free blacks in our northern cities are unknown to, and cannot approach them."[56]

What impact did the abolitionist turmoil in Cincinnati have on young Edward Brackett? I have found no documents explicitly linking him to Birney, *The Philanthropist* or the riots. This is not really surprising because at the time he would have been a young man of eighteen. However, he could not have been unaware of the disturbances, as they engulfed the city. As a Quaker he belonged to a sect that was deeply involved in the Underground Railroad. His later strong convictions about abolition and his close ties to important abolitionists argue for a significant influence on his thinking. And in the context of the furor over slavery during his years in Cincinnati, one wonders if his Nydia is a covert statement, created two years before the model of Power's *Greek Slave*, on the injustice of the slave's lot.

We can observe the effect of these events on another impressionable young mind from the reaction of Harriet Beecher Stowe, who lived in Cincinnati from 1832 to 1850. She was twenty-six and newly married at the time of the riots. Like Brackett, she had a front seat to the uprising. She describes it in great detail in a daily journal that she sent to her husband who was away at the time. After the public meeting following the first attack, she writes, "The mob madness is certainly upon this city when men of sense and standing will pass resolutions approving in so many words of things done contrary to law, as one of the resolutions of this meeting did. It quoted the demolition of the tea in Boston harbor as being authority and precedent."[57] She cites Nicholas Longworth as one of those who, "meant to go as revolutionists and support the mob. . ."[58]

Following the eruption of the second riot, she reports, "The mayor was a silent spectator of these proceedings, and was heard to say, 'Well, lads, you have done well, so far; go home now before you disgrace yourselves;' but the 'lads' spent the rest of the night and a greater part of the next day (Sunday) in pulling down the houses of inoffensive and respectable blacks."[59] After things finally calmed down, she concludes, "Another time, I suspect, such men as Judge Burnet, Mr. Greene, and Uncle John will keep their fingers out of such a trap, and people will all learn better than to wink at a mob that happens to please them at the outset, or in any way to give it their countenance. . . They are justly punished, I think, for what was very irresolute and foolish conduct, to say the least."[60]

The memory of the riots stayed with Stowe and mingled with her growing awareness of the horrors of slavery. The following year she mused in a letter to her husband, "Pray what is there in Cincinnati to satisfy one whose mind is awakened on this subject? No one can have the system of slavery brought before him without an irrepressible desire to do something, and what is there to be done?" [61]

What indeed? Stowe went on to write *Uncle Tom's Cabin*. Edward Brackett went on to produce an iconic sculpture of John Brown.

Chapter 2
A TALE OF TWO CITIES

NEW YORK: A Commercial Cauldron

Now we bid goodbye to Ingraham and his triumphal fantasy of the artist's life and follow the real Edward Brackett back east. In October of 1839 Brackett traveled by steamboat to New York and remained there until the summer of 1841, with side trips to Washington D.C., Philadelphia, and back to Ohio. In doing so, he joined an exodus of fellow Cincinnatians, most notably, Hiram Powers, Shobal Clevenger and painter Thomas Buchanan Read, all of whom made New York a stop on the way to Europe. The latter was to become a good friend. Read and Brackett shared exhibition space in New York, as well several prominent portrait subjects, and when Read began to gain notice as a poet, he published verses inspired by Brackett's sculptures.

But for all the presence of familiar faces, New York presented a new experience for the newly minted sculptor. Then as now, it was a city of vast wealth. As the center of the national art market, it had a large population of nationally and internationally recognized artists, a well-heeled patron class and a very pragmatic attitude toward art. In contrast to the high-minded principles about art's social role professed by Cincinnati's cognoscenti, New York's power brokers regarded such sentiments as mere window dressing to the business of making money. For the many artists drawn to New York by the promise of patronage and fame, this unvarnished commercialism could be disconcerting.

This is evident in comments by artists struggling to make it in New York in the mid-nineteenth century. In a letter to his wife, painter Samuel Morse wrote that New York City is "wholly given to commerce. Every man is driving at one object – the making of money – not the spending of it."[62] Sculptor Henry Kirke Brown complained to a friend, "You don't know how changed man I am since I came to this bedlam of a city. I have lost my quick way of doing things, and have become . . . drawn into the vortex and confusion of business. . . The sound of B'way is like a distant thunder, it is the most unartistlike city on the face of the globe in my opinion.[63] A similar lament was expressed by attorney Peter Augustus Jay to James Fenimore Cooper. Remarking on the poor reception of his friend Horatio Greenough's sculpture *Chanting Cherubs*, he concluded, "I must continue to consider my townsmen as a race of cheating, lying money getting blockheads."[64] Echoing this language, an unnamed journalist writing for the *New York Herald* framed the problem as a matter of ignorance. He noted, "The Fine Arts in this city, like politics, finance and religion, are too much in the power of *cliques* of miserable pretenders. When a young man of genius makes his appearance here, he is hunted down by these packs of blockheads."[65]

In such a climate, it must have seemed to ambitious artists that their primary job was marketing. In the all-important matters of attracting patronage and generating profit, publicity was the indispensable tool. Like Cincinnati, New York had a bewildering number of newspapers and journals that regularly reported on the art scene. An artist navigating today's critical field would find the tabloid interest in art in antebellum New York surprising and enviable. Brackett's personal files in the Winchester Archive are full of short and extended notices about his sculptures. Some are merely brief mentions encouraging readers to come to his studio during viewing hours, while others offer critical judgments, comparisons with other artists and more general remarks on the state of art in New York City. Most, unfortunately, have been clipped without the date, name of the publication or name of the writer, though it seems that the latter were often anonymous. However, the varieties of format and writing style indicate that Brackett was being watched by writers across the political and social spectrum.

The Politics of Portraiture

In her study of the politics of art criticism in antebellum New York City, Wendy Jean Katz evokes a journalistic wild west akin to our own unregulated and uncensored internet.[66] For every shading of political opinion, it seemed, there were corresponding publications. She describes the antipathy between the "penny papers" and the "six penny papers" in terms of class and privilege. The penny press comprised cheap mass circulation newspapers that catered to populist sensibilities – she describes them as the favored forum for "socialists, working class men, bohemians, and utopianists."[67] They stood as a challenge to the older subscription based "sixpenny" dailies that were seen as supporting established politics and interests.

Within these publications, art often served as a proxy for larger political battles. Artists who were simply trying to attract an audience tried not to be pulled into these conflicts, though often neutrality was nearly impossible. Katz describes a lawsuit over the value of a plaster statue damaged in shipping to which Brackett was called as a witness. The creator of the sculpture, James Varick Stout, was favored by James Gordon Bennett, editor of the populist *New York Herald*, while Brackett's fellow witnesses were representatives of the Mechanic's Institute and the National Academy, two art institutions perceived as representatives of elitist taste. Katz speculates "Perhaps to prevent Bennett from turning against Brackett, who until now had enjoyed the Herald's favor, a letter writer explained that Brackett declined to give any opinion as to the merits of the sculpture but only said that he thought a plaster statue could be repaired."[68] Apparently this prevarication was to no avail, as Brackett's next review in the *Herald* deemed his work a "poor affair."[69]

Such were the pitfalls facing the new arrival. In New York, as in Cincinnati, artists sought entry into the art world through the creation of sculpted portrait busts. Even art critics of the time held a jaundiced view of this practice. As a writer for the *New York Mirror* put it: "When an artist is aspiring after fame, there is no other way of making himself known in this country than to take the likeness of some man well known in the community, for the dullest perception can trace resemblances. A young man will therefore be compelled to wait until full patronage is obtained before he can indulge himself in embodying those rich *thick coming fancies* with which the soul of genius is gifted. . . It is only busts of those who are distinguished for great virtues or great talents which are thought worthy of preservation; the rest is rubbish and are suffered to crumble away."[70]

New York's heated political atmosphere turned the selection of portrait subjects into a statement of loyalties that often overwhelmed the artistic merits of the work. This was particularly the case if the bust in question presented a portrait of a politician. Katz notes the keen interest taken by the populist papers in depictions of "great men." She maintains, "But in contrast with the suspicion of aristocratic privilege that the penny press directed at most artworks, sculpted portraits, copies of which were arrayed in fire-company rooms, political meeting halls, etc., often escaped the stain of class precisely because they acted like ancient Roman busts to inspire civic virtue."[71] As a result, portrait busts provided occasions for political brawls. She adds, "One praised a statue's likeness, its truthfulness, or else contemptuously knocked it over and broke its nose."[72]

This may explain the lively commentary surrounding Brackett's bust of General and future President William Henry Harrison. Only months after his arrival in New York, Brackett returned to Ohio at the behest of sponsors to create a bust of the Ohio based war hero. In 1840, at the time of Brackett's bust, Harrison was living in North Bend, Ohio and running as the Whig candidate for President. He was campaigning on the strength of his record as a military leader who had fought in the Indian Wars and the War of 1812, and as a statesman who had served in the Ohio State Legislature and the U.S. Senate. As a Whig, he was the standard bearer of a new party formed in opposition to the rabble-rousing Jacksonian Democrats who, under Jackson's successor Martin van Buren had presided over the disastrous economic crisis of 1837. After a short existence, marked by infighting over the policies of Harrison's successors on issues like western expansion and slavery, the Whig party would dissolve in 1856 as many of its former members formed the core of Lincoln's Republican Party.

Brackett's bust is lost although an engraving based on it exists.[73] (fig 7) Writers in both the Cincinnati and New York press praised it for its accuracy and nobility. One reviewer enthused, "The resemblance is perfect as though the features had been moulded by the magic of the Daguerreotype. . . The face beams with the same high resolves of the patriot and statesman as are developed in the life and actions of the original."[74] Another reports, "The General, in a letter to Mr. N. P. Tallmadge says his friends deemed the bust the best likeness ever taken of him."

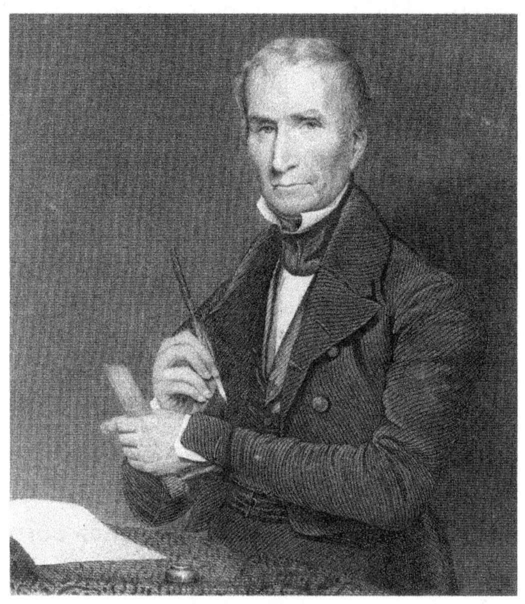

fig. 7 *William Henry Harrison*, by G. Parker, n.d. This engraving
is based on Brackett's lost bust of William Henry Harrison.
Courtesy of Indiana Historical Society.

A Cincinnati publication (the clipping is identified only by the date May 27, 1840,) provides context for this work. "The city is overrun by artists, who have come from distant parts, commissioned by bodies of Whigs to take the portrait of Gen. Harrison; some from Illinois, some from Boston, and some from New York," it reports, adding, "A young Mr. Brackett has taken a very exact bust indeed." The article goes on to describe the passions swirling around Harrison's candidacy. "Gen. H. is sadly beset. Letters pour in upon him through the daily mail by the *hundred*. Some of them most shamefully insulting, signed 'A Democrat,' or 'A Locofoco,'[75] postage not paid. Sometimes a large packet, with two or three dollars postage upon it, will arrive, with nothing but coarse blank paper, and in the centre a letter with such words as 'You are a d____d old granny. Yours, &c. a Democrat,' or something of that sort. There are some men who make it their business to send such letters to distinguished men. But the old General is daily growing in the respect and veneration of his country, from his disinterested goodness of heart, and his inestimable services to the West, which are rapidly becoming known and understood. His popularity will surpass that of Gen. Jackson himself; and will be far less dangerous, because he will use it, as he has used every other gift, to nobler purposes."[76]

One of the commentators on Brackett's bust of Harrison notes that "casts will be taken to supply orders," and another remarks, "We do not doubt that every true Harrison man who can afford it will procure a copy of the bust."[77] Such comments indicate that Brackett's bust, paid for by "an association of individuals in New York," was part of a larger program to promote Harrison's candidacy. Many historians maintain that Harrison's greatest impact on the Presidency was not his tenure, (which lasted only thirty one days as he died from pneumonia contracted during his long winded inaugural address,) but in his introduction of modern campaign methods. It is possible to trace the celebrity orientation and circus atmosphere that surrounds the contemporary political campaign to Harrison's innovations. To appeal to the electorate, Harrison transformed himself from a sophisticated, classics loving blue blood into a rustic representative of the common man. He posed as the candidate of "log cabin and hard cider" and pioneered the distribution of campaign paraphernalia, including whiskey in log cabin-shaped bottles, cups, plates, flags, and sewing boxes emblazoned with the campaign's slogan "Tippecanoe and Tyler too." (The reference was to Harrison's role in a decisive battle in the Indian War and to his running mate John Tyler.)[78] Brackett's bust, along with a painted portrait of Harrison by his studio-mate Thomas Buchanan Read, put art in the service of this effort.

Brackett presented his Harrison bust, along with other works, in his studio and most of the notices include the street address along with visiting hours. This was a common practice in the days before the emergence of the gallery system. Although reviews and newspaper notices were in generous supply, places to exhibit art were scarce. So artists rented spaces, installed work and took out notices in newspapers encouraging visitors to view their work. New York's premiere exhibition space, the National Academy of Design, was seen as elitist and exclusive, and at any rate, had little commitment to sculpture. At the time of Brackett's arrival in New York, however, the things were beginning to change. Records of the National Academy indicate that he was able to exhibit a pair of busts there, identified only as *Bust of a Lady* and *Bust of a Gentleman* in 1841. It was apparently at this time that he also met Emma Stebbins, a well connected young woman who aspired to be an artist. He provided her first lessons in sculpture. These were to bear fruit in Stebbins' successful Rome based career whose crowning achievement was the *Angel of the Waters* (1873), the centerpiece of the Bethesda Fountain which continues to be a major draw for visitors to New York's Central Park.[79]

More important for Brackett's professional exposure was the 1838 inception of The Apollo Association. This membership organization, which soon morphed into the American Art Union, would become a significant force in the nation's cultural life. The Art Union's mission was to promote and educate American artists and to cultivate patronage and audiences for the nation's struggling creators. This innovative organization supported itself through memberships, initially set at five dollars a year. For this members received an annual engraving of a work in the Art Union's collection as well as the chance to win a work by a contemporary artist through what became an eagerly anticipated annual lottery. The Art Union also held exhibitions of the works of member artists and published a journal. In its early days the membership roster comprised 800 New Yorkers. By 1849, this had swelled to a membership of 19,000 from almost every state in the country. The Art Union was dissolved in 1852 when the New York State Supreme Court ruled that the lottery was a form of illegal gambling.

In its heyday controversy surrounded the Art Union over the question of whether it exploited struggling and emerging artists and whether it promoted mediocrity in art. A typical complaint, aired in the *New York Day Book* in 1852, charged breathlessly, "We are tired of those exhibitions, too numerous at all times, which are got up for ostensibly charitable or liberal purposes; and which borrow works from struggling and suffering artists, use them and often damage them; never pay for the use of damage; and rarely invite the lenders to enjoy the oysters and punch and tobacco smoke with which they tempt great men of dollars, and editors, and reporters and other notables, whom the works alone could not attract, to visit, praise, puff and speechify, for the benefit of the party that gets up the ostensibly liberal movement at the expense of the unpaid and often crippled artists, without even thanks to them, or honorable or respectful mention of them."[80]

Brackett defended the Art Union's policies, noting, that while some of its money may have been spent poorly, it helped rising young talents and, in contrast to other organizations, focused on art at home.[81] He spoke from experience – he himself had been quick to take advantage of the exhibition opportunities offered by the fledgling Art Union. In 1840 he exhibited his Harrison sculpture along with three other busts in its annual exhibition and the next year he presented three more. These sculptures were available for sale but the association's records reveal no takers, perhaps reflecting the bias of the Art Union's audience toward painting. However, it seems likely that this presentation of Brackett's portrait busts helped bring him other commissions.

A Pantheon of Portraits

The subjects of the portrait busts by Brackett mentioned in newspaper notices and the Art Union exhibition list represent a cross-section of New York's political and literary elite, along with a few representatives of the scientific and religious communities. Most of the busts themselves do not survive, or if they do, they share the fate of countless similar "heads" by other artists. Without signatures and often nearly indistinguishable from each other, such plaster and marble busts gather dust today in attics, museum storerooms and auction houses or serve as decorative accents in Victorian inspired domestic interiors. Nevertheless, the list of Brackett's portrait commissions help us chart his professional and social progress through New York's cultural milieu. Politically, as the Harrison bust suggests, he gravitated toward the Whig Party, whose anti-slavery members would eventually form the core of Lincoln's Republican Party.

Several notices mention his bust of New York Senator Nathaniel P. Tallmadge, a former Jacksonian Democrat who jumped over to the Whigs in 1839. Another powerful subject was Charles A. Stetson. He is described in one of the newspaper notices as "Brackett's generous friend" and may be the shadowy patron whom Brackett wished to thank publicly but who resisted being identified.[82] Stetson was the manager of the Astor House, New York's first luxury hotel. Its stylish curving bar and dining rooms provided a gathering place for some of New York's most distinguished residents and visitors. Mathew Brady lived there in the 1840s and William James was born there in 1842. Astor House patrons included Henry Wadsworth Longfellow, Daniel Webster, Henry Clay, Rufus Choate, and William H. Seward. Brackett created busts of Longfellow and Choate, then U. S. Senator from Massachusetts, and it seems likely that his introduction to these figures came by way of Stetson and the Astor House. His bust of Stetson received praise from a reviewer who noted, "The likeness is good, and the execution artist-like." The writer argued, apparently unsuccessfully, that "It should be copied in brass or marble, that the handsome and hospitable features of Stetson may be perpetuated while the Astor House shall stand." [83] Brackett's bust of Longfellow, now at the Longfellow House in Massachusetts was less favorably received. The portrait presents the young clean shaven Longfellow who contrasts sharply with the older bewhiskered image

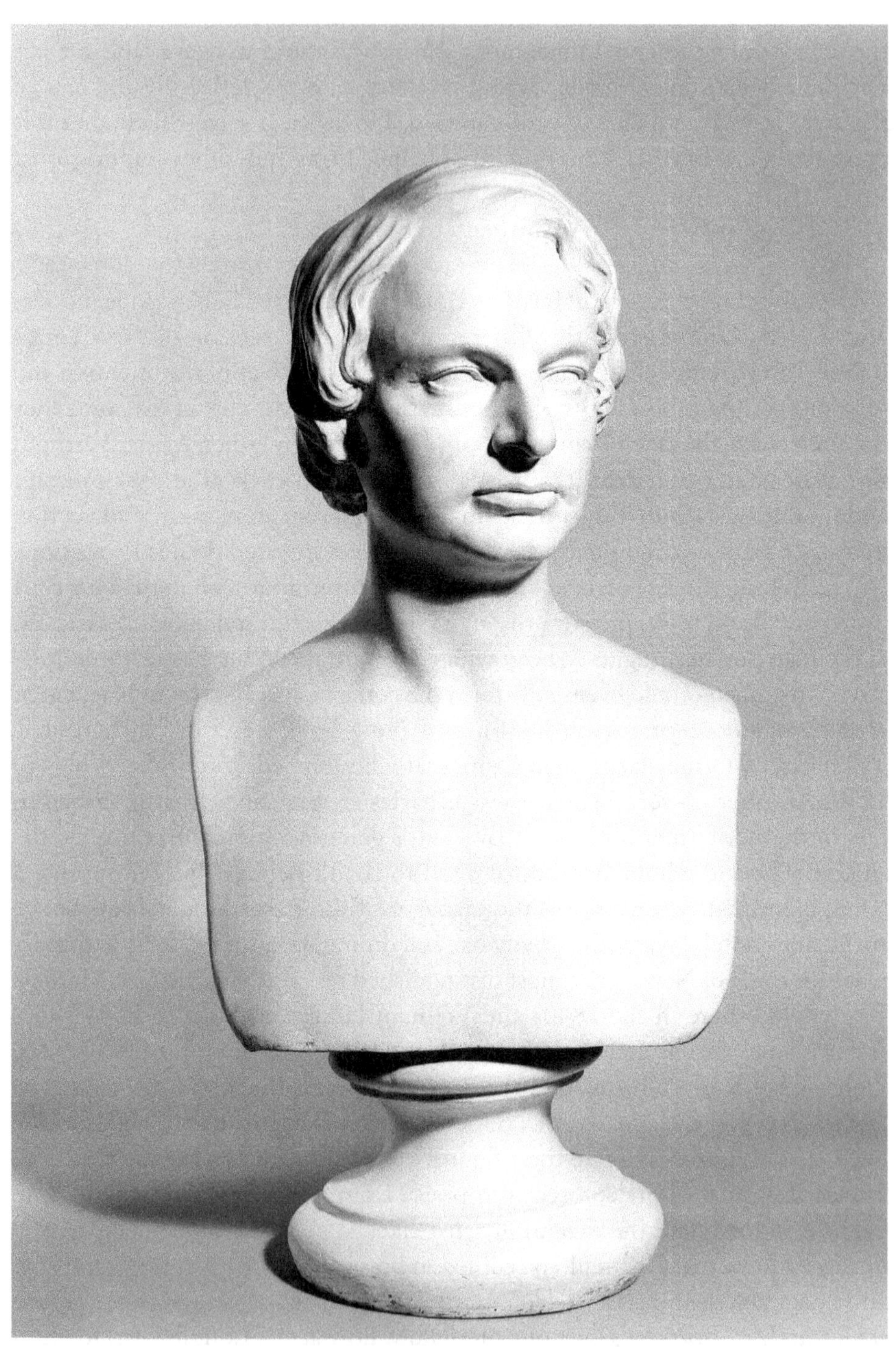

fig. 8 *Henry Wadsworth Longfellow* by Edward August Brackett, 1844, plaster cast after early 1843 original. Courtesy of the National Park Service, Longfellow House-Washington's Headquarters National Historic Site. object # LONG 4398.

of the poet more familiar to us today. Reportedly, Longfellow felt it was a bad likeness, though it compares well to photographs taken of Longfellow around this time. (fig 8)

Many of Brackett's New York subjects came from the literary world. One particularly interesting and influential one was Mordecai Manuel Noah, playwright, editor of various newspapers and the first Jew born in the United States to reach national prominence. Noah occupies a somewhat equivocal place in history. An ardent utopian Zionist, he was also an anti-abolitionist. In 1825 he attempted to set up a colony that was to serve as a refuge for Jews of all nations in Buffalo New York. He named it Ararat after the mythical resting place of Noah's Ark in the Book of Genesis. His plans advanced sufficiently to lay a 300 pound cornerstone in Grand Island, New York following a parade of Christians and Jews through the city. Ultimately the project failed from lack of financial support. Noah pursued his ideas in essays like his 1837 *Discourse on the Evidences of the American Indians being the Descendants of the Lost Tribes of Israel* and his 1840 *Discourse on the Restoration of the Jews* which called for the rebuilding of a homeland for the Jews in Palestine.

Brackett's lost bust of Noah garnered praise from a writer for the *New York Mirror* who exclaimed, "The artist could not have chosen a better subject for the exercise of his talent and for his future fame. Mr. Noah is not only well-known in this city and throughout the United States, but in Europe also. . . We owe a large debt of gratitude to Mr. Noah, for in times of danger and gloom there is no man living who so unwearedly, and it may be said, effectually exerts himself to prevent the spirits and energy of a whole community from sinking. . . " In a reference to Noah's heritage, he continues, "Mr. Brackett has been so fortunate as to hit off the entire expression, both of the man and of the nation to which he belongs. It is the expression of the ancient Hebrew when his head was erect, his body free, his heart warm, his step firm and he was the man *after God's own heart.* This is a master-stroke of the artist, for, since the persecution of that race, art has endeavored to give a sordid and ignoble expression to the Jewish features which never belonged to them."[84]

Noah's aspirations for the freedom of the Jews contrasts with his position on slavery. He wrote that "To emancipate the slaves would be to jeopardize the safety of the whole country." In his capacity as playwright and theater reviewer he was known for scathing reviews and legal harassment of plays by Black authors produced at the African Grove Theatre, an operation founded by William Alexander Brown, a free Black man in New York City. *The Freedom's Journal,* the first African-American owned and operated newspaper published in the United States, called Noah "the black man's bitterest enemy."[85]

Though Brackett was later to throw himself wholeheartedly into the abolitionist movement, his bust of Noah, done early in his stay in New York, suggests a more pragmatic approach to politics. It seems he was willing to overlook Noah's views on slavery in order to cultivate a powerful journalistic figure. This calculation was to bear fruit in the favorable notices he received from Noah's *Evening Star*. Many of Brackett's other friends and patrons were more progressive by modern standards. Several sources cite his friendship with Mary Ann Delafield DuBois, an American sculptor and philanthropist who was co-founder of New York Nursery and Child's Hospital, and who, during the Panic of 1837 opened an empty warehouse to accommodate men left homeless by the economic downturn. Another friend, Mrs. Seba Smith, aka Elizabeth Oakes Prince Smith, was a poet and feminist who is known now for writings like "Woman and Her Needs." This series of essays in the *New York Tribune* was published between 1850 and 1851 and advocated for women's rights. Smith was to commemorate several of Brackett's sculptures in verse.

Brackett also made the acquaintance of William Cullen Bryant, poet and the powerful editor of *The Evening Post*. Bryant would prove to be a pivotal figure in Brackett's life, making important introductions following his move to Boston and facilitating the selection of one of his busts for the Art Union lottery. Bryant is less well regarded today than figures like Edgar Allan Poe, Walt Whitman and Emily Dickinson, but in his day he was among the country's most celebrated poets. Despite his passion for poetry, however, he was forced to practice law and eventually drifted into journalism to feed his family. As Editor of *The Evening Post*, a job he held for fifty years, he evolved from a Jacksonian Democrat into a staunch abolitionist. Meanwhile he continued to publish volumes of poetry, which eventually made him enough money that he could have retired from journalism were it not for his commitment to his editorial career. By the time Brackett met him in the early 1840s Bryant was a powerhouse in the New York political world. But he was also deeply involved in the worlds of art and literature. He served for several years as President of the American Art Union. In that capacity he was well positioned to offer support to young artists and he flexed his muscles to make sure that Brackett received the then princely sum of $300 for his inclusion in the Art Union lottery.

Other bust commissions show Brackett making inroads in the realms of literature, religion and science. He sculpted a bust of Rufus Dawes, a poet with an impeccable pedigree but a less fortunate career. Dawes had disappointed family expectations for a legal career when he was thrown out of Harvard College for insubordination. His poetry career actually began as an act of retaliation, taking the form of a poetical satire lampooning members of the faculty. Besides poetry, he dabbled in spiritualism, politics and philosophy. At the time that Brackett sculpted him, Dawes was beginning to make a name in the literary world. However, his major works, little remembered today, were excoriated by Edgar Allan Poe, who remarked in an 1841 review, "'Athenia of Damascus' is pompous nonsense, and 'Geraldine' a most ridiculous imitation of Don Juan, in which the beauties of the original have been as sedulously avoided, as the blemishes have been blunderingly culled. In style, he is, perhaps, the most inflated involved, and falsely-figurative, of any of our more noted poets."[86] Still smarting from this invective eight years later, Dawes advised a younger writer to steer clear of poetry. In a letter he noted with a certain amount of prescience, "There will certainly be a great social revolution in the course of this passing century - in our country probably of a gradual and peaceful character. But come it will." He adds, "…I like some of your verses very much - but if you were my own brother and you wrote even better than you do, I could not advise you to enter on a career which I myself have almost entirely abandoned…the poetic faculty may be turned into more useful channels, at present, than in the composition of verses."[87] Dawes' history underscores how precarity pervaded the literary as well as the artistic life. After his early blast of glory, he ended his career as a clerk in a government office.

Other commissions brought Brackett into contact with men of science, an augur of the deep interest he would take such matters in his later life. He sculpted a bust of Alban G. Smith, a pioneering surgeon who is remembered for introducing lithrotrity, a technique for removing kidney and gallstones, to the United States. Brackett also created a bust of James Stanley Grimes, who had recently published a treatise on phrenology, the now discredited study of bumps on the skull as an indicator of mental traits. As a "science" that attempted to align the inner and outer worlds, phrenology was closely associated with spiritualism, a practice that would deeply engage Brackett in his later life.

Similarly, Brackett's drift toward Unitarianism was a foreshadowed by his bust of Orville Dewey, an American Unitarian minister who was also a member of the National Academy of Design. Dewey's freethinking ideas about the unity of God, the dignity of human nature, and the eternal progress of mankind towards virtue and happiness were controversial in Calvinist circles, but must have resonated with the young Brackett as he worked out his own philosophical beliefs. Dewey was a representative of what historian Neil Harris describes as "new types of ministers ascend[ing] American pulpits, particularly among Episcopalians, Congregationalists and Unitarians" in the middle third of the 19th century. They were "cultivated men of the world, liberally educated in European philosophy. . . Accustomed to intensive reading and extensive writing, they formed a natural corps of lecturers, eager to spread news of the nation's cultural achievements and the relationship between taste and morals"'[88] Dewey had studied the great religious masterpieces in Europe and came home to advocate for the arts as incubators of Republican virtue. He maintained, "There is need among us of objects that kindle up admiration and enthusiasm, that awaken the sense of delight and wonder, that break up the habits of petty calculation and sordid interest, and breathe a liberal and generous soul into the people: and this need the arts would supply."[89] He put these ideas into practice by supporting art institutions and artists, Brackett among them.

The Binding of Satan

This survey of Brackett's portrait work gives us the picture of a young sculptor kept busy with commissions from important citizens. However, as in Cincinnati, this did not translate into financial security. The problem seems to have been Brackett's inability to charge the same rate as artists who had made the trek to Europe and were able to boast of their first-hand study of the great Greek and Roman masters. Patrons may have claimed that they wanted to support American sculpture, but they wanted it served up with an aura of classical antiquity. Unable or unwilling to travel across the ocean, Brackett remained, in their eyes, merely a hometown provincial. The result of this disadvantage is revealed in a letter from his Cincinnati admirer Nicholas Longworth to Hiram Powers following Brackett's move to New York. Longworth inveighed against "the *stupid Gothamites* [who] let him starve whilst they give Clevenger 500$ for Busts. I understand he has got but 2 busts, at 40$."[90]

Equally detrimental to the pursuit of financial success was Brackett's desire to make a mark with uncommissioned imaginative works. Unwilling to be seen as a mere portrait maker, he again threw himself into a project that he hoped would showcase both his technical skill and the depth of his philosophical ideas. This work, a sculptural group, depicted the binding of Satan, was to be the most ambitious creation of his New York years. The theme comes from a moment in *The Book of Revelation* when an angel descends from heaven with a chain and a key to the bottomless pit and binds Satan for a thousand years. The subject might have seemed fit for the hellfire and brimstone theatrics of the *Infernal Regions* display designed by Brackett's hero Hiram Powers for the Western Museum in Cincinnati. But in fact, Brackett took a much more understated approach. In a letter to his friend G. Forrester Barlow, Brackett laid out his conception: "I have endeavoured in the one figure to express the *apparent* superiority of evil, and in the other the *actual* superiority of goodness; hence the spiritual or moral character of the one figure, contrasted with the natural or physical character of the other."[91]

The work has disappeared, no doubt because it was never realized in marble, but we can get a sense of it from contemporary accounts. One was published in *Arcturus*, a short-lived journal of books and opinion that existed from 1840 to 1842. The writer notes, "His [Brackett's] subject is not, however, as he supposes, the first two verses of the twentieth chapter of Revelations. That has given him the first thought – all the rest are his own: abandoning the angelic and fiendish characters, as suggested by the inspired writer, he has chosen to represent the spirits of evil and good in a merely human guise, and to familiarize his moral by reducing its representations to standards known or discoverable in actual life."[92]

Another account, published in the *Boston Post* on July 21, 1841 shortly after Brackett's move to that city, gives a more explicit description. This unnamed writer also remarks approvingly on the work's lack of histrionics. The text describes the archangel Michael, shorn of sword and breastplate, brandishing a chain over the prone Satan. "Satan lies stretched upon the earth, thrown upon his left arm and side, his shield beneath him, his spear broken beside him, with every muscle in his frame strained to its utmost, while his face is half turned to Michael, and breathes the utmost impotent hate and scorn."[93] Michael, we are told, looks on with pity and majesty, "and his whole appearance conveys at once the idea that his conquest has been one of the Spirit alone." A pair of sketches in Winchester Archives may present Brackett's preliminary thoughts on the

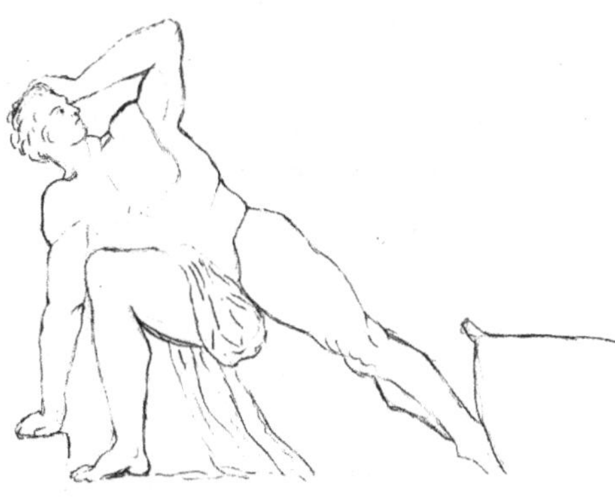

fig 9 (above) Pencil drawing by Edward Augustus Brackett, presumably of the Satan figure from his lost sculpture of *The Binding of Satan*, c. 1841.

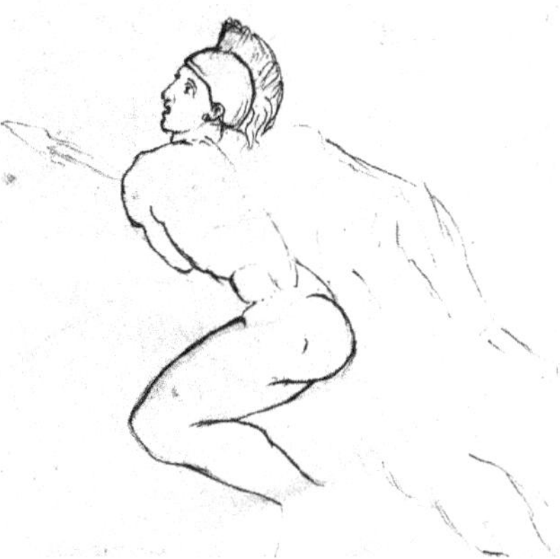

fig 10 (below) Companion pencil drawing of the Archangel Michael figure. This and fig 9 are included in a Friendship album dated from 1834 through 1838, along with articles on The Binding of Satan, c. 1841. Courtesy of the Winchester Massachusetts Archival Center.

figures. Satan is largely as described here, though Michael still brandishes a sword. (fig 9) (fig 10)

The descriptions of the two antagonists are in keeping with the Quakers' optimistic vision of human perfectability as opposed to the Calvinist belief in human nature's innate depravity. Evil, in the Quakers' view, is the absence of good rather than an inevitable and unstoppable force in itself. By reducing both figures in the sculpture to human scale, Brackett seemed to be asserting the need to discover our moral compass in the world of human experience rather than in the transcendent realm of angels and devils. We see him here moving closer to the Unitarian philosophy with its stress on ethics and human responsibility.

In an intriguing coincidence, sculptor Horatio Greenough, who had just completed his bare-chested George Washington, also embarked on a bust of *Lucifer* in 1841. This was ultimately to find a home at the Boston Public Library along with a later pendant sculpture, a bust of Christ. Greenough was a Unitarian and like Brackett presented Lucifer as a man rather than a demon. His Lucifer, depicted just after his expulsion from heaven, is a beautiful youth with flowing locks and an arrogant expression. The only indications of his supernatural identity are the serpent and pair of small winged devils upon which the bust rests. What led both men to simultaneously create humanistic representations of the devil - a conception much at odds with the prevailing Puritan conception of the "Evil One"? It seems unlikely that either would have seen the other's work, as Greenough was at his studio in Florence while Brackett was working in New York. The two sculptures are evidence of a larger cultural turn against rigid religious conceptions in the mid-nineteenth century. The affinity between the two artists was confirmed ten years later Greenough provided moral and material support for the unsuccessful effort to sell Brackett's 1851 sculpture, *Shipwrecked Mother and Child* to the Wadsworth Athenaeum.[94]

Like *Nydia* in Cincinnati, *The Binding of Satan* was widely commented on with mostly favorable notices. One reviewer remarked, "It is one of those bold flights of genius, which occur rarely, and we do verily believe has not before occurred in this country. The angel in this group is of exquisite beauty, and we are rather glad the artist has not provided him with wings, for we would not have such a figure fly away. Satan himself is a surly old scoundrel just fit to be manacled as he is."[95]

Another writer uses the sculpture to make the case for support of American artists: "This is the first group of any considerable size ever executed in this country. This fact alone should be sufficient to call our attention to it, even were its artistical merits less than they really are. We are very sensitive to foreign sneers at our devotion to the 'almighty dollar,' and our deficiency in taste and genius for the fine arts, and yet when the sacred flame shows itself among us, we let it expire for want of fuel. . .Thousands are wasted in useless and tasteless display by those who will do nothing to assist in the creation of works of art which will live forever, and confer honor on their country. We hope that some gentlemen who are so fortunate as to combine wealth and taste, will engage the artist to execute this group in marble, or by other commissions enable him to give his powers that cultivation, which alone they need, to enable him to attain a lofty eminence."[96]

Reviews were not uniformly positive, though it seems that some of the negative reactions were infused with the politics of religion. A review in the conservative *Commercial Advertiser*, a six penny paper that was a stalwart defender of the Protestant Bible, condemned the non-metaphysical nature of Brackett's description. The writer, William Leete Stone, the publication's editor, argued "The conception we think defective. Both figures lack elevation of character, nothing in either to indicate the grand and awful nature of the subject, nor without explanation could one discover what they represent. All that appears to the eye is a powerful man lying on ground his limbs drawn up as if in pain and a scowling expression, while a youth stands over him looking down in compassion."[97]

In a volume of poetry published many years later, Brackett offered a more personal interpretation of this work. He spun off the struggling figures in a poem titled "The Group," published in a collection of writings under the title *My House, Chips the Builder Threw Away* in 1904. This Gothic tale, somewhat in vein of Edgar Allan Poe, relates an artist's possession by the fiendish creature he is fashioning from clay. After working feverishly on a sculpture of a wicked sprite,

"The statue moved, and writhed and turned;
It grew to wondrous size;
Cheeks lank and thin, with fiendish grin;
Fierce gleamed those sculptured eyes."[98]

The artist is chased by this creature through a wild ride across a stormy sea and is ultimately saved by the Angel of Truth and Nature. The experience becomes a lesson in the nature of art:

"The artist hath an inward power.
The visions of his mind
Will never let him rest until
Some outward shape they find."[99]

A note accompanying the published poem relates, "This ballad was written soon after completing a life-size group of the "Archangel Chaining Satan," and was intended to express something of that obsession which every artist or actor feels while absorbed in his work." Brackett adds this curious addendum: "As no one wanted the Devil chained, the group was broken up."[100]

The *Brackett Genealogy* suggests that this work was destroyed by the artist, as "it was not to his liking."[101] However, a more likely explanation was Brackett's usual shortage of funds. The letter to Forrester Barlow that describes his intentions also includes this plaintive complaint, "It is indeed a rapid production, thrown off in the excitement of the moment, under peculiarly embarrassing and restricting circumstances."[102] The critical encouragement Brackett received for this and other works was evidently not enough to keep him gainfully employed. Soon after, Brackett left New York to seek greener pastures in Boston, using the *Binding of Satan* as a calling card.

BOSTON: The Shining City

In the opening scene of *The Bostonians,* Henry James' not very sympathetic novel about the nascent feminist movement, the New York based Mrs. Luna describes the acquaintances of her Bostonian sister Olive Chancellor thus: " . . . they are all witches and wizards, mediums, and spirit-rappers, and roaring radicals." Elaborating on the last point she continues "She's a female Jacobin – she's a nihilist. Whatever is, is wrong, and all that sort of thing."[103]

From the perspective of hard-nosed New York, Boston was a melting pot of irrational passions and fancies. But what was a drawback for the "cheating, lying money getting blockheads," of the so-called Empire City was balm to an idealistic young artist. Boston was, after all, the original site of John Winthrop's shining "city on the hill." This phrase eventually came to stand for "American Exceptionalism" and was used by politicians as different as John F. Kennedy, Ronald Reagan and George W. Bush to hail the United States as a beacon of democracy and enlightenment in a benighted world. But in 1630 Winthrop was speaking about the Massachusetts Bay Colony, a community newly established by Puritans fleeing England. He produced this memorable phrase in a sermon aboard the *Arabella* as he preached to the settlers who were setting foot in the New World for the first time. Adapting a passage from Matthew 5:14, Winthrop invoked their special mission, telling his fellow colonists, "For we must consider that we shall be like a city upon a hill, the eyes of all people are upon us."[104]

Two centuries later, the Colony had become part of a new independent nation and the Puritan theocracy had given way to a more diverse religious landscape.

But greater Boston retained its aura of singularity. If New York was America's commercial center, Bostonians argued, their city was its spiritual heart. At the time of Brackett's arrival, Ralph Waldo Emerson was promoting his influential new philosophy of Transcendentalism. Henry David Thoreau was living in Emerson's house, four years away from his move to Walden Pond. Margaret Fuller was editing the *Dial*, Emerson's Transcendentalist journal and working on her seminal feminist book, *Woman in the Nineteenth Century*. George and Sophia Ripley had just founded Brook Farm, a utopian community nine miles outside of Boston that, during its short life would attract such seekers as Fuller, Nathaniel Hawthorne, Horace Greeley and Elizabeth Palmer Peabody. And William Lloyd Garrison, publisher of the widely-read anti-slavery newspaper *The Liberator*, had just given a talk on abolition which galvanized a young former slave named Frederick Douglass.

This was the world that Brackett entered in 1841 when he made his move to Boston. He found a city composed of interconnected worlds, several of which would become part of his life. Most important for him was the institutional art world. At the time of his arrival this centered on the Boston Athenaeum, a public library and gallery that had initiated annual sculpture exhibitions in 1839. However, 1841 also saw the formation of the Boston Artists' Association. Founded by Washington Allston and other artists, it for ten years organized social meetings, presented exhibitions of members' works and held art classes. Brackett is listed as a signer of the charter membership list and was to argue unsuccessfully for the formation of a Boston Artist Union along the lines of the institution he had left behind in New York. [105]

As in New York, the artist community was closely connected with the literary crowd. This association proved very helpful for artists. Fashionable journals tracked art and poetry closely, reviewing new works and debating their relative merits. Writers helped publicize the work of their artist friends through prose and poetry, while many artists, Brackett among them, also wrote poetry. Many of his friends published poems about his sculptures. In a letter to his mentor William Cullen Bryant, the young sculptor remarked that he knew "from experience" how much young artists benefited by associating with writers.[106] As in New York, art criticism and journalism in general were rife with politics. But the raucous battles between Whigs, Republicans and Democrats and the politics of class that consumed New York took a different tone in Boston. The literary world was associated with progressive political ideas, among them abolition, woman's suffrage and the plight of Native Americans. Brackett and many of his artist friends shared such ideals.

Brackett established a studio on Tremont Row, an artist enclave that was not far from the newly formed Boston Artists' Association. He was joined there two years later by his brother Walter who shared his older sibling's artistic leanings and had become a painter. He and Walter would remain close, with Walter providing crucial support at needed moments. Brackett also brought his sweetheart Amanda Folger from Cincinnati and married her in 1842.

While we have little information on Amanda Brackett, she seems to have been a sensible woman who was able to ground her idealistic husband in the practicalities of life. An undated carte-de-visite in the family album presents a pleasant young woman with intelligent eyes and a serious expression.(fig 11) Amanda would in 1848 purchase four acres of undeveloped land in South Woburn (soon to become Winchester) and supplemented these with adjoining acreage in 1855. This would eventually become the site of The Crow's Nest, Brackett's famous Octagon House, now on the National Register of Historic Houses. Interestingly, the deed stipulates that the land was to be ". . . for her sole and separate use, and free from the interference or control of her said Husband in any manner."[107] Historian James A. Newton speculates that, "some felt more sympathetic to the wife of the artist than to the artist himself".[108] A more likely explanation can be found in changes to property law in the wake of the financial crisis of the late 1830s that allowed estates to insulate wives' property from their spouses' creditors.

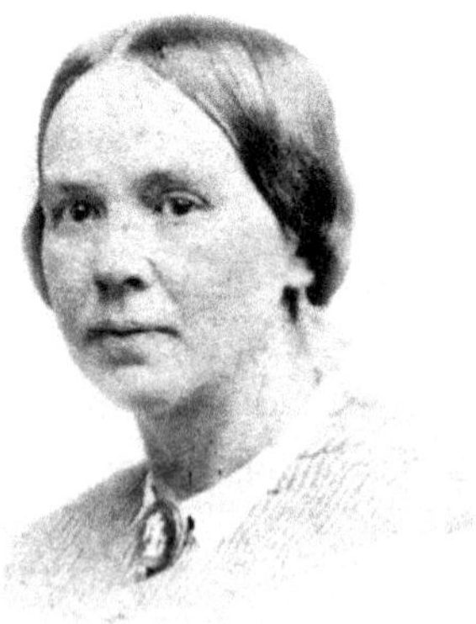

fig 11 *Amanda Brackett,* undated photograph. Courtesy of the Winchester
Massachusetts Archival Center.

An Important Introduction

Brackett's confidence in his new life was no doubt bolstered by the support he received from poet and publisher William Cullen Bryant. Bryant provided him with a letter to his friend Richard Henry Dana, Jr. requesting an introduction to the painter Washington Allston.

Dated New York May 21 1841, it read:

My dear sir,

This letter will be put into your hands by Mr. Brackett whose Binding of Satan you have seen, and of which I am glad you think so well. Might I ask of you for a meritorious and modest young artist the favour to give him an introduction to Mr. Allston?"[109]

Brackett was to eventually sculpt portraits of all three of these correspondents. To parse this introduction is to catch a glimpse of the complex web of inter-relationships between artists and writers in nineteenth century America. Bryant, as we have noted, was a powerful New York based publisher, poet and patron of the visual arts. His central role in the cultural worlds of the young country is suggested by his appearance in Asher B. Durand's iconic 1849 painting *Kindred Spirits*. (fig 12) The canvas depicts two men, one holding a sketchbook and the other a walking stick as they engage in conversation on a rock ledge overhanging a spectacular landscape. The scene is an amalgam of two actual vistas: Kaaterskill Clove and Kaaterskill Falls in upstate New York. The painting presents a dramatic waterfall cutting through a stony gorge. The rushing water is framed by a pair of steep stone cliffs and nestled beneath a receding set of mountain peaks. The shifts of space and perspective underscore the wild beauty of the Catskill landscape. The two men overlooking it are Thomas Cole, the recently deceased leader of the Hudson River School of painting and Bryant, his close friend and eulogist. As the title suggests, the painting pays tribute to a friendship rooted in a love of nature and art. But it has also come to symbolize the intertwining of the literary and visual arts.

Richard Henry Dana Jr., to whom Bryant appeals in the letter above, was a Boston based writer, lawyer and abolitionist and a member of a prominent Boston family. He is best known today as the author of *Two years before the Mast*, a memoir of his youthful adventures as a merchant seaman during an interregnum between his studies at Harvard College and Law School. A genuine Boston Brahmin, as members of the Boston elite are known, Dana gained sympathy for the experience of the common man through his time at sea. This was to fuel a lifelong interest in the downtrodden and enslaved. Dana and Bryant became friends in 1840 after Bryant, as a favor to Dana's father,

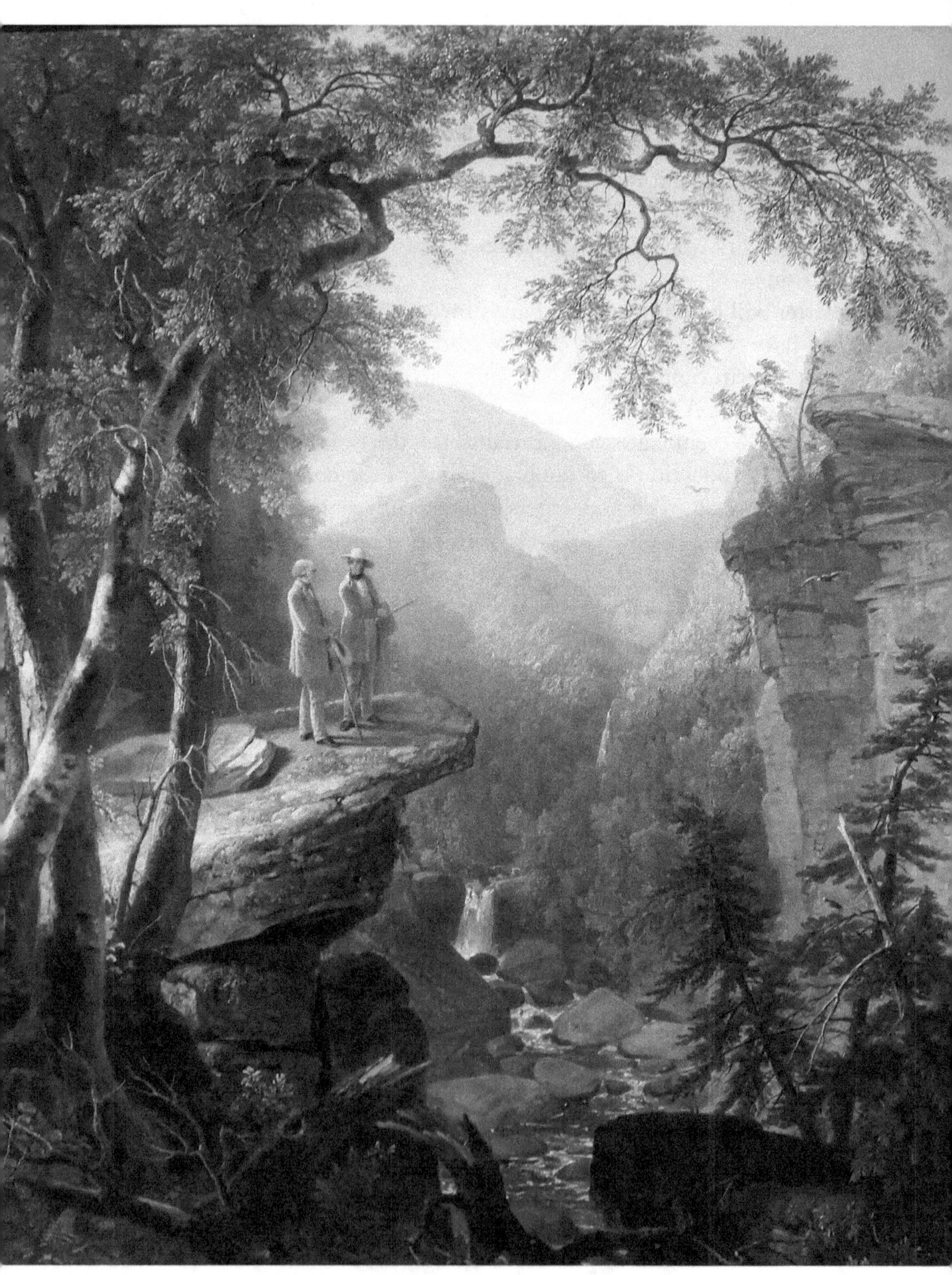

fig. 12 *Kindred Spirits* by Asher B. Durand, 1849, oil on canvas,
Crystal Bridges Museum of American Art, Courtesy of Creative Commons.

managed to secure a publisher for his tale of the sea. Bryant followed up this support with a lengthy review of the book in the *Democratic Review* and a notice in his own *Evening Post*. The two men corresponded frequently thereafter about literary and artistic matters and visited each other's homes when traveling to each other's respective cities. As a result of this letter, Dana was also to become a friend and champion of Brackett's work.

Washington Allston, the object of the letter of introduction, was Dana's uncle by marriage, having married his aunt Martha in 1830. He was also something of a cult figure in the American art community. With his long curling hair, luminous eyes and air of sensitive detachment, he might have fit well within the counter-cultural world of the 1960s. In nineteenth century Boston, he was revered for his disdain for the materialism that drove so much of the art world and for his devotion to the call of the artist's imagination. Allston was the first important painter of the American Romantic movement, and was a major influence on younger artists like Thomas Cole, Albert Pinkham Ryder and Ralph Blakelock. He also had a considerable reputation as a poet and was known for melancholy verses on death, nature and loss. He authored a Gothic novel that chronicled the tragic life of an Italian artist destroyed by the machinations of his villainous friend. A set of *Lectures on Art and Poems,* edited by Dana, was published posthumously. In an appreciation written shortly after his death, writer and diplomat C. Edwards Lester extolled Allston's dual talents: "While the painter held the pencil it spoke the language of the soul—when he took up the pen he was a poet—and poetry and painting are only two breathing forms of the same spirit."[110]

While this kind of breathless praise was typical of much art writing of the day, it also captures the aura of spiritual transcendence that surrounded Allston during his life. He gave the impression, according to Brackett's Cincinnati friend, Thomas Buchanan Read, "of a being whose mind was too pure to mix in the groveling things of Earth."[111] The son of a distinguished southern family from Charleston, South Carolina, Allston had been sent north for a Harvard education. Determined to be an artist, he spent his paternal inheritance on extensive travels in Europe during the first two decades of the nineteenth century. There he was exposed to the wonders of Northern Renaissance painting and met such leading writers of the Romantic Movement as William Wordsworth and Samuel Taylor Coleridge. The latter was to become a lifelong friend and encouraged Allston's ideas about the primacy of the imagination and the divinity of the artist.

Allston's painting career began in London, where he attempted to rival his Renaissance heroes with ambitious narrative paintings of biblical subjects. In keeping with his fascination since childhood with, as he put it "the wild and marvelous",[112] these works tended to present scenes of miracle, mystery or revelation. One of his most celebrated works was *The Dead Man Restored to Life by Touching the Bones of the Prophet Elisha*, painted in London between 1811 and 1813. The painting depicts a ghostly white figure throwing off his shroud as the soldiers, bystanders and family members surrounding him stand in amazement. The work contains deliberate references to Raphael, Michelangelo and Sebastiano del Piombo and helped earn Allston the appellation the American Titian. It received an important prize in England and was ultimately acquired by the Pennsylvania Academy of Fine Art, whose directors mortgaged the building to pay for its purchase.

Returning home to take up residence in Cambridge, Massachusetts in 1818, Allston found a less favorable environment. The American art world favored realism, didactic representations of scenes from American history and portraits of leading citizens over the kinds of heroic subjects that had worked so well for him in Europe. He turned increasingly to landscape, imbuing his scenes with the same kind of imaginative drama that marked his narrative works. But he still nursed the ambition to compete with the old masters.

In what one writer describes as a project that was "part Holy Grail, part albatross"[113] he embarked in 1817 on a massive 12 x 16 feet canvas that was to depict *Belshazzar's Feast*, an incident in the Old Testament in which the Prophet Daniel interprets divine writing that has appeared on the wall of the decadent Babylonian king Belshazzar. It was a subject that had been dramatically realized by Rembrandt and was to be the subject of a hugely popular work three years later by Allston's fellow painter John Martin.

Allston had high hopes for this painting, whose subject he described in a letter to his friend Washington Irving in 1816: "I know not any that so happily unites the magnificent and the awful. A mighty sovereign surrounded by his whole court, intoxicated with his own *state*, in the midst of his revelings, palsied in a moment under the spell of a preternatural hand suddenly tracing his doom on the wall before him; his powerless limbs like a wounded spider's kept from vanishing by the terrified suspense that animates it during the interpretation of his mysterious sentence. His less guilty, but scarcely less agitated, queen, the panic struck courtiers and concubines, the magicians, the holy vessels of the temple (shining, as it were, in triumph through the gloom), and the calm solemn contrast of the prophet, standing like an animated pillar in the midst, breathing forth the oracular."[114]

Alas, this work was to be one of the most famously unfinished would-be masterpieces of the American canon. Allston struggled for twenty-five years with this painting. At one point, a group of ten friends raised $10,000 to assist in its completion, which apparently only heightened his painter's block. In 1829 he set it aside, to return to it only a few months before his death. He was working on one of the figures the day that he died. There are multiple explanations for his failure to complete the work. One story is that the artist Gilbert Stuart, famed for his portrait of George Washington, faulted its perspective, shaking Allston's confidence and leading him to rework the whole composition. Another is that John Martin's far more spectacular version of the scene stole his thunder. For whatever reason, it was never finished, although another Boston artist, Thomas T. Spear, would later present a completed version of the painting based on what he claimed were Allston's intentions according to indications on the original canvas.

The sad history of this work only enhanced the mythic aura surrounding Allston. Reflecting on the unfinished work in a biographical sketch published several years after Allston's death, C. Edwards Lester remarks, "But we cannot suppress a burst of indignation when we think that the sordid soul of some sordid wretch, who weighted dollars against Allston's Art, and could see nothing in Belshazzar's Feast but three hundred yards of canvas, should have locked up that half formed vision, when a few more weeks of the master's magical pencil would have given the world a creation that our countrymen three hundred years hence would speak of as the Italians now speak of the Last Judgment of MichaelAngelo."[115]

At the time of Bryant's letter, Allston was sixty-one and had two years to live. The painter was well known for his support of younger artists and it is likely that he found the metaphysical ambitions of Brackett's *The Binding of Satan* particularly appealing. He welcomed the young sculptor, made more introductions and declared his admiration for Brackett's now lost bust of his friend Richard Dana. He reportedly commented that, with the exception of one head by Hiram Powers, he had never seen anything modern or antique that pleased him as well.[116] When Allston died unexpectedly after a day in the studio, Brackett was the family's choice to create a memorial bust from a death mask. The family was extremely pleased with Brackett's plaster cast, reportedly preferring it to one created five years earlier by Shobal Clevenger, Brackett's fellow Cincinnatian.

A comparison of the Allston busts by Clevenger and Brackett suggests why the latter's sculpture was favored. Both capture the painters famous flowing locks, but Clevenger's Allston has a lined and weary face and tips his head slightly downward, as if worn by the cares of life. (fig 13)Brackett's Allston head is tilted upward, as if gazing toward some unseen inspiration. (fig 14)The ravages of time have been subtly smoothed, giving him a more youthful and

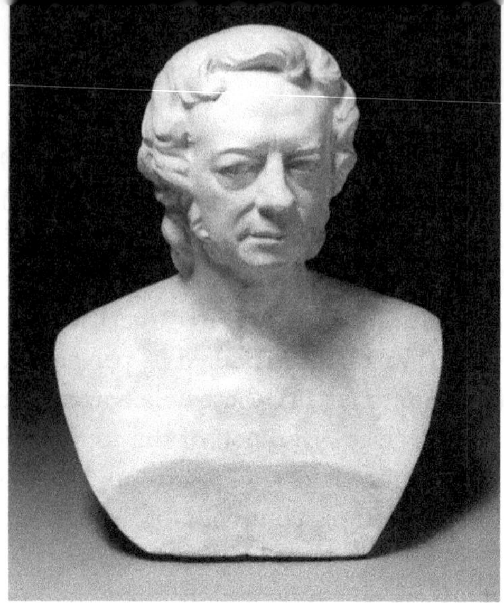

fig. 13 *Washington Allston* by Shobal Vail Clevenger, 1840, marble. Courtesy of Pennsylvania Academy of Fine Arts.

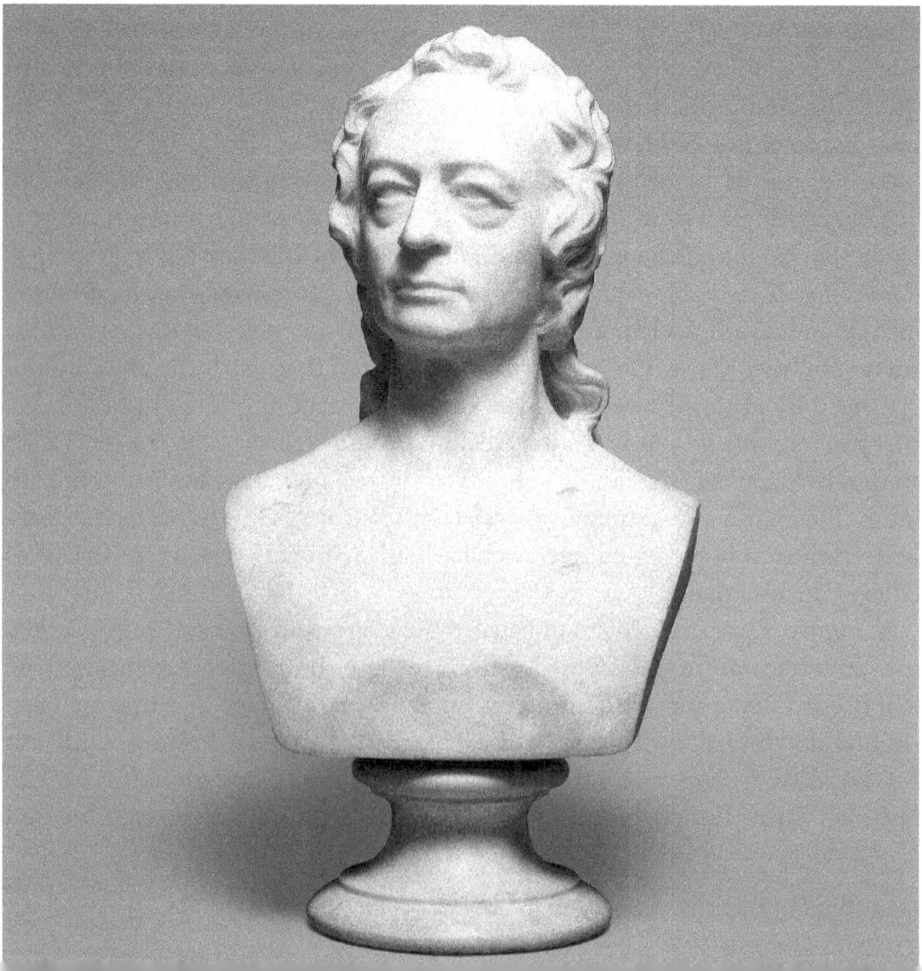

fig. 14 *Washington Allston* by Edward Augustus Brackett, 1843–44, marble, Metropolitan Museum of Art, Gift in memory of Jonathan Sturges by his children, 1895, Object Number: 95.8.2. Courtesy of the Metropolitan Museum of Art

vital aspect. Clevenger's commission came just after Allston had recovered from a severe attack of neuralgia, and the face he sculpted reflected that struggle. Creating his bust after Allston's death, Brackett felt free to idealize the painter for future generations. Ironically, some observers felt that Clevenger's bust from life suggested death and mortality, while Brackett's death mask evoked the living legacy of poetic genius that was so much a part of Allston's myth.

An exchange of letters between Dana and Bryant reveals the efforts both made to have the plaster model carved in marble for distribution in the lottery of the American Art Union, of which Bryant was the President.[117] There is some back and forth on the price, and ultimately Brackett was paid $300 for his work. Bryant hoped that the bust would stay in the organization's permanent collection, but it was included in the lottery of ninety-two works of art for 1844. Passing through several hands, it ended up in the collection of the Metropolitan Museum of Art in New York where it is sometimes on display in the American wing.

As with *The Binding of Satan*, Brackett was moved to compose a poem in the sculpture's honor. He titled it *Lines Suggested on Finishing a Bust of Allston*. The poem describes the unearthly gaze he has imparted to his subject and recounts how the artist "poured the strength of my full soul" into the work in his effort to give it life. The poem concludes with words of praise,

"Thou who wast kind, and good, and great,
Thy task on earth is done;
Of those that walked in beauty's light,
Thou wast the chosen one."[118]

The Artist as Poet

Brackett's tendency to versify his sculptures was not unusual and it underscores the interpenetration of poetry and visual art in the nineteenth century. Artists were poets, poets were art critics, and individual works of art were frequently honored with celebratory verses. The friendship of William Cullen Bryant and Thomas Cole celebrated in Asher Durand's painting *Kindred Spirits* echoed numerous other close writer/artist relationships, among them James Fenimore Cooper's friendship with Samuel Morse and Washington Allston's lifelong bond with Coleridge.

So it is not surprising that Brackett, who like Allston was an artist/poet, should gravitate toward literary figures. As in New York, he associated with writers and created busts of well-known writers like Dana, Bryant and Longfellow and remained close to his Cincinnati friend Thomas Buchanan Read who also oscillated between art and poetry. Read painted portraits of such luminaries as Abraham Lincoln, Henry Wadsworth Longfellow, Alfred Tennyson, Elizabeth Barrett Browning, Robert Browning and William Henry Harrison but gained more popular attention for his poems, among them the still read *Sheridan's Ride*. Brackett's work was also celebrated by poet Elizabeth Oakes Prince Smith, now better known for her work as an activist for female rights.

In 1845 Brackett published his own small book of verse. In his introduction to *Twilight Hours: Or Leisure Moments of an Artist*, he noted modestly, "The enthusiasm which every artist brings to his profession, not unfrequently finds vent in other things. These outbreakings may be termed his waste thoughts, and he should be thankful that they take no worse direction than that of writing verse, though ever so humble its character."[119]

The poems take on a variety of subjects – some are moral tales, others offer reflections on life, death and the sustaining power of nature, yet others pose the poet and artist as romantic figures inspired by sorrow and burdened by the cruel demands of an unreasonable world. Several have autobiographical origins. *To Amanda* is a brief but heartfelt love poem to his wife, praising her as " the bright star in the cold cold world." *The Dream* describes recognizing his dead mother's features in his sister Jane's face. (The elder Mrs. Brackett had died in 1837 in Cincinnati at age thirty eight, not long after her son had begun his study of art.) Another poem, mentioned above, is a reflection on his own bust of Washington Allston. One of the most affecting works in this collection is titled *The Wreck of the Slave Ship*. It tells the story of a slave ship that is shattered by a storm, tossing its unfortunate prisoners into the jaws of a ravenous shark. The final verse offers a condemnation of the slavers' cruelty to their fellow men:

"The storm-lit sea, that angrily
Now swallows up the dead,
Is yet more kind than they who bind
On man a yoke of lead,
Till, like a serf, he licks the turf,
Where ruthless tyrants tread."[120]

This poem may have been inspired by an actual incident, the wreck of the Spanish slave ship Trouvadore in 1841 in the Caribbean, killing as many as 100 of the captives aboard. *The Wreck of the Slave Ship* is interesting for several reasons. It signals again Brackett's abolitionist leanings. And the shipwreck theme would reappear several years later in one of his most celebrated sculptures, *Shipwrecked Mother and Child*.

The poems in *Twilight Hours* tend to be sentimental and by today's standards somewhat saccharine. (Brackett's poetry would get more original later when he used it to explore his idiosyncratic interests.) The tone of melancholy, the recurring references to death and the turn to nature as metaphor owe a great deal to a circle of popular nineteenth century American writers dubbed the Fireside Poets. As the sobriquet suggests, these were the creators of verses that could be read aloud as the family gathered around the hearth.

Poetry in the nineteenth century had none of the elitist connotations that surround it today. David Reynolds' biography of Abraham Lincoln, for instance, details the important role poetry played, both in Lincoln's personal pleasure reading and as a tool with which to connect to his countrymen.[121] Like many of his countrymen, Lincoln's taste ran to simply written poems that expressed a range of emotional states. His reading stretched the gamut from morbid meditations on death to works of comic absurdity. In the dark days of the Civil War, he was buoyed by works like Julia Ward Howe's stirring verses in the *Battle Hymn of the Republic*, Henry Wadsworth Longfellow's *The Building of the Ship* which provided a metaphor for the construction of the Union, and William Cullen Bryant's epic poem *Thanatopisis* which presents a Wordsworthian vision of the inseparability of nature and human mortality. Lincoln was known to quote poetry, as well as the lyrics of popular songs and bawdy jokes in his conversations and speeches, enhancing his reputation as a man of the people.

Lincoln's literary affinities point to the outsized role that poetry played in America's cultural life in the antebellum era. Not confined to lyric expressions, poetry was a medium for satire, narrative, philosophy, drama, history, and even, as we shall see in some of Brackett's later verses, scientific speculation. It was also an important educational tool for molding the values of ethics, leadership, piety and good citizenship. As historian Carl Bode remarks, "The extent of the audience for poetry [in the early nineteenth century] is almost inconceivable to the present-day American. Accustomed as he is in this Age of Prose to eyeing any poet suspiciously and dismissing his poems as either too difficult or too easy, the average man finds it hard to believe that housewives, merchants, ministers and clerks often had a little volume of verse handy at their table or bedside. They read poetry for pleasure and profit both, and much of the poetry popular in the two decades before the Civil War gave them exactly what they wished."[122]

The Fireside Poets comprised Henry Wadsworth Longfellow, John Greenleaf Whittier, Oliver Wendell Holmes, James Russell Lowell, and Brackett's mentor William Cullen Bryant. Brackett had personal ties to several members of the group, two of which (Bryant and Longfellow) he sculpted, and one of whom (Holmes) was the subject of a portrait painting by his brother Walter. He shared with them an abiding love of nature, a streak of melancholy and convictions about the evils of slavery.

The contemporary appeal of the Fireside Poets stemmed not only from the accessibility of their works, but also from their public personas. All the Fireside Poets took stands on the political issues of the day. William Cullen Bryant, often seen as the leader of the group, used his position as Editor in Chief and co-owner of the *New York Evening Post* to promote the right of workmen to strike, to defend religious minorities and immigrants and to call for the abolition of slavery. Longfellow, now remembered for works of Americana like his *Song of Hiawatha* and *Paul Revere's Ride*, helped draw attention to the cruel and inhumane nature of slavery both through his 1842 *Poems on Slavery* and by secretly spending money he earned from his best-selling poems to buy enslaved people their freedom. John Greenleaf Whittier, meanwhile, was a founder of the American Anti-Slavery Society, and was involved with the Boston Vigilance Society that aided fugitive slaves. James Russell Lowell served for a time as the editor of an abolitionist newspaper and was active in a variety of social reform movements. Oliver Wendell Holmes was a physician, professor, medical reformer and author as well as poet. He was also the father of famous jurist whose opinions on civil liberties and American constitutional democracy helped shape the progressive wing of the nation's judiciary.

Historian James H. Justus attributes the impact of the Fireside Poets partly to the simple fact that they were all very long-lived. However, he adds "perhaps more important is the fact that not one was simply a poet. These men led conspicuously public lives – as editor, professor, linguist and translator, diplomat, doctor, novelist, lecturer, essayist – whose careers defined at an upper level the dominant public values of America at mid-century: an ethical idealism that for all its failure in specific instances directed the sense of national mission."[123] The popularity of their poetry, cemented by easily remembered rhyme schemes and simple rhythmic cadences, allowed them address divisive issues in an engaging way.

As we shall see, Brackett shared the Fireside Poet's sense of social responsibility. He also emulated their immersion in multiple roles. In part this was dictated by necessity. Between 1847 and 1862, the Bracketts welcomed four children into the world. To meet the needs of this growing family, Brackett supplemented his sculpture commissions with various side jobs. In a biographical sketch published in 1854, Hannah Farnham Sawyer Lee reports, "At one time he had recourse to drawing heads in crayon, and added something by this employment to his means of subsistence."[124] The *Brackett Genealogy* adds that he started a nursery, noting, "In this he was more or less successful; he added several varieties of strawberries and grapes, and was the first in his vicinity to successfully raise cucumbers under glass."[125] This is confirmed by an 1862 report from the Massachusetts Horticultural Society that praises Brackett's Seedling Grapes, remarking, "This year, when it bore many bunches, Mr. BRACKETT presented a bunch to the Committee; those of them who tasted of it formed the highest opinion of its value, and it seemed to them the best and by far the most promising new hardy grape that had been brought to their notice."[126] Brackett also, various biographers note, raised Belgian hares and Mongolian pheasants, experimented with fish breeding, studied bees and cultivated specialty fruits and roses in a hothouse.

Edward and Amanda seem to have provided a boisterous and happy, if financially precarious, home. It is clear that they eschewed the example of Brackett's father, instead encouraging their children's creative pursuits. The Winchester archive contains carefully preserved drawings by Brackett's daughters Bessie and Lena Rose. His son Walter, named after Edward's painter brother, carried this interest further. He would study art, and made a career as an art teacher and director of art programs in Cambridge's public schools.

The Shipwrecked Mother and Child

In 1848 Brackett embarked on what would be his most ambitious sculpture - a life size depiction of two figures titled *Shipwrecked Mother and Child*. (fig 15) The sculpture presents the naked corpses of a mother and child flung up on the shore. The inspiration, according to Hannah Farnham Sawyer Lee, was the wreck of the SS President, a British passenger liner that sank in 1841, killing all 136 onboard.[127] Later, by coincidence of its date of presentation, the sculpture became identified with the tragic death of feminist Margaret Fuller in 1850.

Lee presents a lively account of the sculpture's creation. She reports that Brackett was able to begin this work thanks to financial help from an unnamed benefactress and from his friend Richard Dana who raised a subscription in the amount of $140. It was slow going. Brackett molded the clay figures in the attic of his Tremont Row studio. "To preserve it in a proper state," Lee tells us, "it was necessary to keep it damp by sprinkling it with water every evening, and by covering it every night with India-rubber cloth."[128] In a foreshadowing of the difficulties involved in the conservation efforts of the Worcester Art Museum one hundred and seventy two years later, she describes problem of removing it down the stairs to the room below. "It was very heavy, the stairs difficult of descent, and the apprehensions of the poor sculptor, lest a misstep should ruin

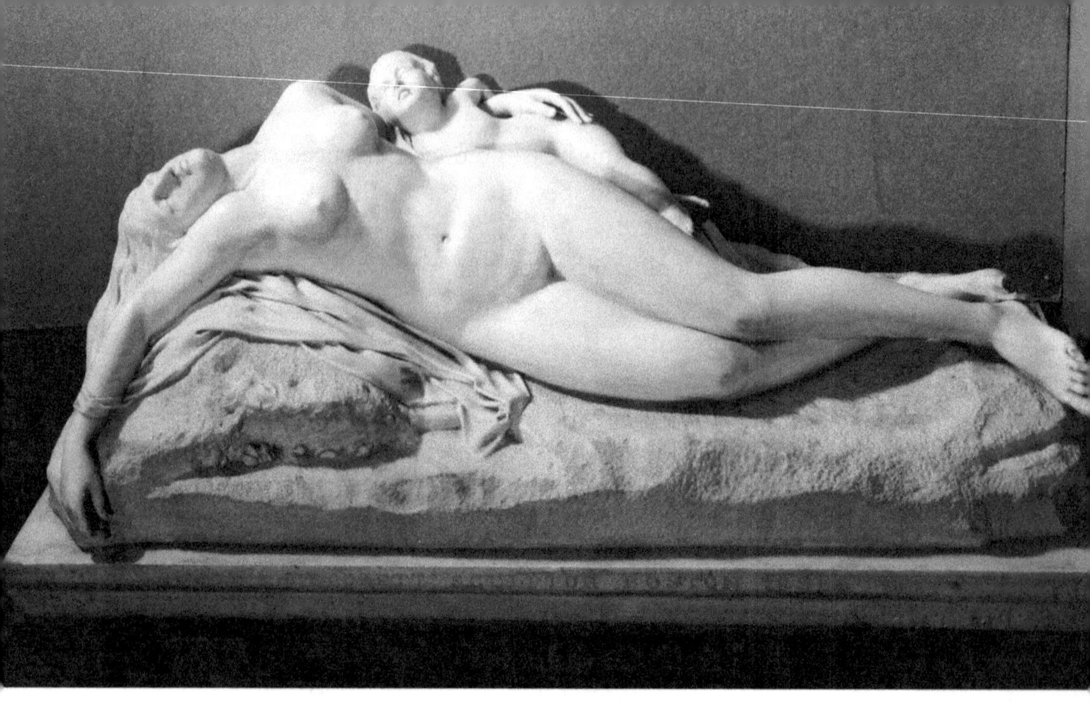

fig. 15 *Shipwrecked Mother and Child* by Edward Augustus Brackett, 1850, marble, Worcester Art Museum. Courtesy of Bridgman Images.

the work of years, amounted to nervous derangement."[129] The clay model was cast in plaster and exhibited to great praise in Boston and Philadelphia.

Lee reports that this positive reception, along with promised aid from an unnamed source, encouraged Brackett to transfer his *Shipwrecked Mother* to marble. However, once the block of marble arrived from the Vermont quarry, the aid failed to materialize, leading to a financial crisis. "With what distress must he have looked on his wife and two children, who were to be supported during the progress of the work!" she exclaims.[130] Brackett's brother Walter came to the rescue, arranging a loan of a thousand dollars "from the leading men of Boston." For a year, Brackett worked all day on the sculpture. Each evening Walter joined him, pitching in for another five or six hours after having already spent a full day painting in his own studio. Lee estimates that Brackett clocked an average of sixteen hours of work a day over a period of twelve months, interrupted only by one short trip to the country with Richard Dana. Upon completion in January 1851, the marble version was presented at the Wadsworth Atheneum. Lee, writing in 1852, concluded hopefully, "It has the commendations of our first poets; and we trust the artist's ten years of study are to be remunerated by substantial benefits from a generous public."[131]

Following a now familiar pattern, acclaim from critics and intense public interest did not translate into financial success. Dana, aided by sculptor Horace Greenough, attempted unsuccessfully to drum up support for the purchase of the work in various Boston and New York papers. With the purchase price not forthcoming, the *Shipwrecked Mother* remained in limbo at the Athenaeum. One report suggests that the sculpture was installed for several years at Mount Auburn cemetery where it sustained water damage. The sculpture did not find a permanent home until 1904, when Brackett donated it to the Worcester Art Museum in Worcester, Massachusetts. Following an initial showing, it was relegated to the museum basement. It remained there until 2019, when the museum received a large grant from the Henry Luce Foundation to restore the now stained and damaged sculpture.

In Love with Death

What prompted Brackett to expend so much time and energy on a depiction of this rather morbid subject? For an answer we might look to Brackett's affinity with the Fireside Poets and to more general antebellum attitudes toward death. It is striking, when perusing the poems in Brackett's *Twilight Hours*, to discover how many turn on the theme of death and mortality. At the time of the volume's publication in 1845, Brackett was a grand old man of twenty-seven. His mother had died in 1837 when he was nineteen, but he otherwise had not experienced the kind of massive familial losses that plagued many of his contemporaries in this era of widespread epidemics of cholera, scarlet fever and typhus. Nevertheless, the poems are full of expressions of grief, ennui and mourning. A boy and his father think they see the dead mother's face reflected in a stream. A beautiful woman weeps over the family grave. The flowing of the Kennebec River stirs memory of those gone. A beggar boy, refused help by a rich man, dies and is lifted heavenward by angels. A child longs to see his dead mother again and an old man, grieving for his dead wife, finds solace in the turning of the seasons and the knowledge that he will soon join her.

Such verses carry echoes of one of the most famous poems by Brackett's mentor, William Cullen Bryant. *Thanatopsis*, written when Bryant himself was only seventeen, eschews the pieties of religion. Instead he advises the reader chilled by thoughts of mortality to seek solace in the fact that death means reunion with all the humans who have gone before. The poem ends with the exhortation:

> "Thou go not, like the quarry-slave at night,
> Scourged to his dungeon, but, sustained and soothed
> By an unfaltering trust, approach thy grave,
> Like one who wraps the drapery of his couch
> About him, and lies down to pleasant dreams."

According to Philippe Aries, author of a monumental history of the idea of death, the nineteenth century ushered in the desacralizing of death. No longer overhung with the fearsome specter of final judgment, death held the promise of reunion with departed loved ones. It became, for many, a state to be desired. In this new conception, death was no longer frightening or ugly. Instead, Aries says, "Death has started to hide. In spite of the apparent publicity that surrounds it in mourning, at the cemetery, in life as well as in art and literature, death is concealing itself under the mask of beauty."[132] This attitude would flower, in the second half of the century, into a burgeoning interest in spiritualism and the belief that the spirits of the dead were still with us, ready to communicate through the voice of the medium.

Brackett's *Shipwrecked Mother and Child* can be seen in the context of the Beautiful Death. The work recall's Poe's dictum that "The death [of] a beautiful woman is, unquestionably, the most poetical topic in the world. . ."[133] When the death occurred in horrific circumstances, it become even more compelling. For its contemporary audience, Brackett's sculpture evoked the terrors of untamed nature and the violence of the shipwreck – a fate that was not far-fetched at a time when every sea voyage was fraught with danger. Viewers found themselves identifying with the tragic pair and even reliving the event. One reviewer conjures the scene: "We were on the sea shore with the artist, the storm was raging far out, the ship was laboring, the blow was struck, the mother and the child engulphed, the rugged shore received them – the mother and child – twins of affection, immortally united by the sweet tie of art."[134]

But in fact, Brackett has eschewed the drama of the wreck itself. Instead he depicts the dead mother apparently beautifully at peace. She lies naked, stretched across the rocky shore as she cradles her dead child with one arm. She is voluptuous and graceful, assuming a pose that might recall the odalisques of Renaissance art were her head not flung back at a slightly unnatural angle. Much was made at the time of the clinical accuracy of her bloated body, with reports that medical students were studying its representation of the corporeal effects of death. Some viewers objected to the sculpture's realism. However, to a contemporary eye, it offers a highly aestheticized vision of death. The pair could simply be asleep, lying languidly on the rocks with dreamy expressions on their faces. In this the sculpture echoes the sentiments in a poem about the death of a child that Brackett wrote several years before embarking on this work. It concludes:

"Death and Sleep twin brothers are;
Death is folded to the breast;
Gentle Sleep he soothes life's care,
Death doth give eternal rest."[135]

For many viewers it was precisely this paradox that gave the work its power. The sculpture is a masterful blend of the beautiful and the poignant, an image of life tragically cut short and of a maternal love that transcends death. In his study of American popular culture in the antebellum period, Carl Bode remarks on the era's general preference for a sentimental depiction of death. "The accent would seldom be on the tragic, frequently on the pathetic. The dying little girl, as opposed, say to the dying warrior, would be the perfect subject for pathos. She could expire in tinkling rhyme almost as effectively as Dickens' Little Nell managed it in prose."[136]

As if to reinforce this point, Brackett did create a now lost sculpture of Little Nell, Dickens' doomed heroine. He evidently sculpted it in 1842 and it was still in his possession at the time of his death. A newspaper report gives us a sense of it: "Brackett, the Sculptor, is engaged upon a statue of Dicken's Nell, the finest and sweetest creature of modern fiction. It represents her in the church yard seated upon a rough stone, pondering over her sorrows and her coming death."[137] In 1843, he created another work that suggested the sweet sadness of premature death when he sculpted a portrait bust of Francis Dana, the young son of his friend Richard Dana's cousin, also named Francis. Brackett created the work following the boy's death at age 7. (fig 16) The bust is now in the collection of the Boston Museum of Fine Arts. It endows the child with a beatific expression, offering at once a memory aid for the grieving family and a suggestion of the heavenly serenity which Francis has now achieved.

With the *Shipwrecked Mother* Brackett went the next step, creating an image that made physical death itself seductive. Or so it seemed to its viewers. In a letter from New York, Grace Greenwood, a correspondent for *The National Era*, remarked, "There is death in every limb, in every muscle, in every line of that grand figure. There is something indescribably mournful and expressive in the fall of the head, and the drift of the long, wavy hair. . . But though mournful beyond what words may tell, there is a beautiful fitness in such a death, for one of God's most glorious creatures. There is grandeur in the thought, that such beauty, unwasted by disease and undarkened by sorrow, should yield itself to 'that mighty minister of Death,' the sea."[138]

The affinity of sorrow and beauty is also evoked in a letter by Horatio Greenough published first in the *Boston Daily Advertiser* and then reprinted in

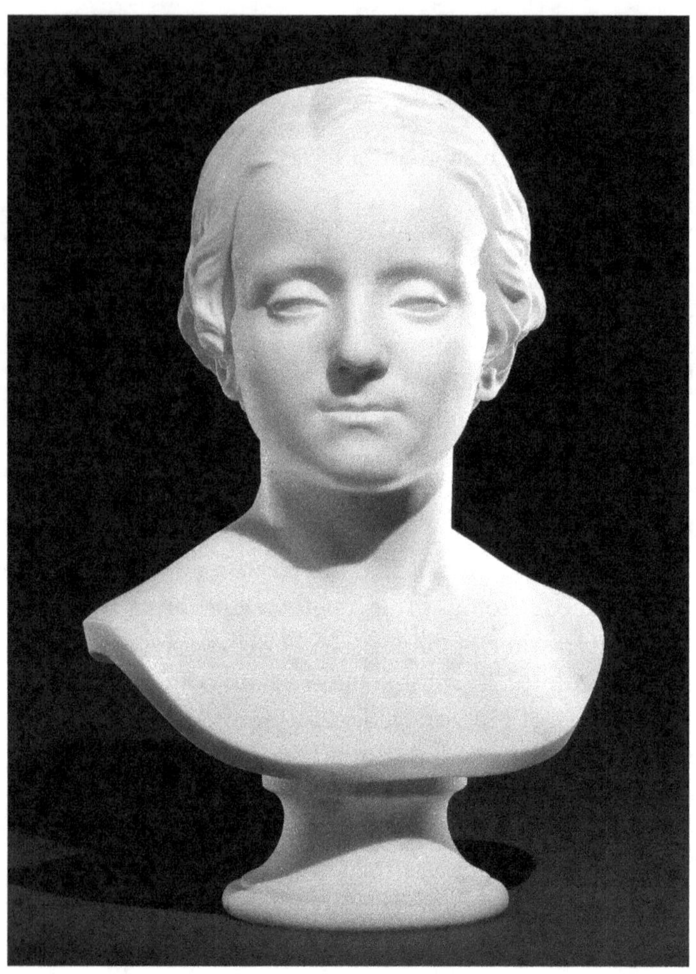

fig. 16 *Francis Dana* by Edward Augustus Brackett, circa 1843, marble, Museum of Fine Arts, Boston. Gift of Miss I. H. Dana. object number 19.120. Courtesy of Museum of Fine Arts, Boston.

the Athenaeum catalogue of 1852. He reports, "I have several times sat for an hour in the same room where Mr. Brackett's group, the "Wrecked Mother and Child," is exhibited, and always with a new sense of power which has made that block of stone the vehicle of so many sad and tender thoughts, expressed in the language of beauty. I have admired the art by which he has so placed the head, that a glance tells us her sufferings are passed, and so swept every limb and tress, that we see the surge has lodged her there, and there left her".[139]

There was as well an element of national pride in the reception of the work. Grace Greenwood remarked, "I felt, when looking on this noble group, a patriotic pride in the fact that its creator was an American – a young man, self-taught, and one who has never even wintered in Italy."[140] Another unidentified writer noted with pride that the sculpture was hewn from Vermont marble and concluded, "It has proved to be all that was expected of it, and inferior to none in the world. Indeed, we may safely say, that the time is not far distant when Vermont will supply most of the statuary used both in England and America."[141]

As always, of course, there were dissenting voices. One of the most strident, published in the *Sunday Courier*, questioned the unelevated nature of the subject. The unnamed reviewer complains, "If he had been embodying a popular legend, or perpetuating an article of religious faith, his subject would have been sanctified, like the crucifixion or the Laocoon in the mind of the spectator and he would have no choice but to be true to his text. But a naked woman lying lifeless upon the rocks, with all her limbs and members offensively exposed, without story or faith to aid the imagination in throwing a nimbus of sanctified sentiment around her is a subject wholly unfit for art."[142]

But in fact, for another critic, Charles G. Leland, it was precisely this lack of literary pretense that gave the work its value. He saw in "the elevated naturalism of this work, which is of a much higher grade than the average type of the English school, . . . the presentiment of a coming school of American art, which shall be something new, glorious and beautiful."[143]

The commentaries on *Shipwrecked Mother and Child* illuminate many of the issues surrounding American art at mid-century. It became a bellwether for debates over the virtues of naturalism versus idealism, the relative importance of technique versus conception and the propriety of adherence to classical models versus home-grown originality. And of course, the work encapsulated the era's romantic conception of death – an attitude that would sharply change in the face of the carnage soon to be wreaked upon the nation.

Brackett never again attempted an imaginative sculpture on this scale, likely because of its failure to attract financial support. Over the next two decades he continued to sculpt portrait busts, and in one case was commissioned to create a full-scale portrait figure of Reverend Hosea Ballou for a funerary monument in Mount Auburn Cemetery. At the same time, he dug more deeply into his non-art pursuits, among them horticulture, animal husbandry and architectural design. Meanwhile, he was about to be swept into the raging political currents pulling America toward Civil War.

Chapter 3
AN ABOLITIONIST AND A SPY

In 2015, Laura McDonald, registrar for the Tufts University Art Galleries, made a startling discovery. A student intern going through the gallery archives presented her with a letter written in 1950 by Tufts President Leonard Carmichael to an art conservation firm. Carmichael was inquiring as to whether a new nose could be fabricated to repair the museum's damaged bust of John Brown. A light bulb went off. McDonald recalled that when she was poking through the museum's storage facility several years earlier she had come upon a pair of heavy sculptures in a corner of the gallery storeroom. They were wrapped in plastic, strapped to a pallet and covered with dust. Curious about these mystery objects, McDonald had pulled away the plastic to reveal a pair of rust stained and damaged marble busts, one of which was missing its nose. Even in the absence of any identification, she had been impressed. "The piece had clearly been through some difficult times," she says, "but you could see that it had been quite spectacular."[144]

The new information allowed McDonald to identify the damaged bust as Edward Brackett's portrait of the notorious abolitionist John Brown. A bit more digging revealed that the other bust was the work of Samuel Morse and presented a posthumous likeness of George Stearns, the abolitionist whose money funded Brackett's sculpture. In life the two men had been united in their efforts to push the nation toward Emancipation. Then for many decades their busts had been united in neglect, ignominiously lost to history in the bowels of the storage room. Using a plaster copy of the bust that had ended up in the collection of the Boston Athenaeum, McDonald was able to recast and repair Brown's broken nose. Today both busts, cleaned and restored, are on proud display in the Tufts Gallery, after having served as centerpieces for a historical exhibition detailing the remarkable circumstances surrounding Brackett's most perilous creation. (fig 17) (fig 18)

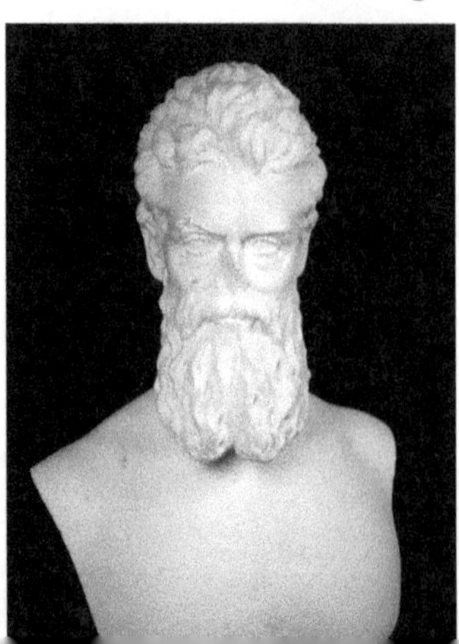

fig 17 *John Brown* (prior to recent repair) by Edward Augustus Brackett, 1860, marble, Tufts University permanent collection. Courtesy of Tufts University.

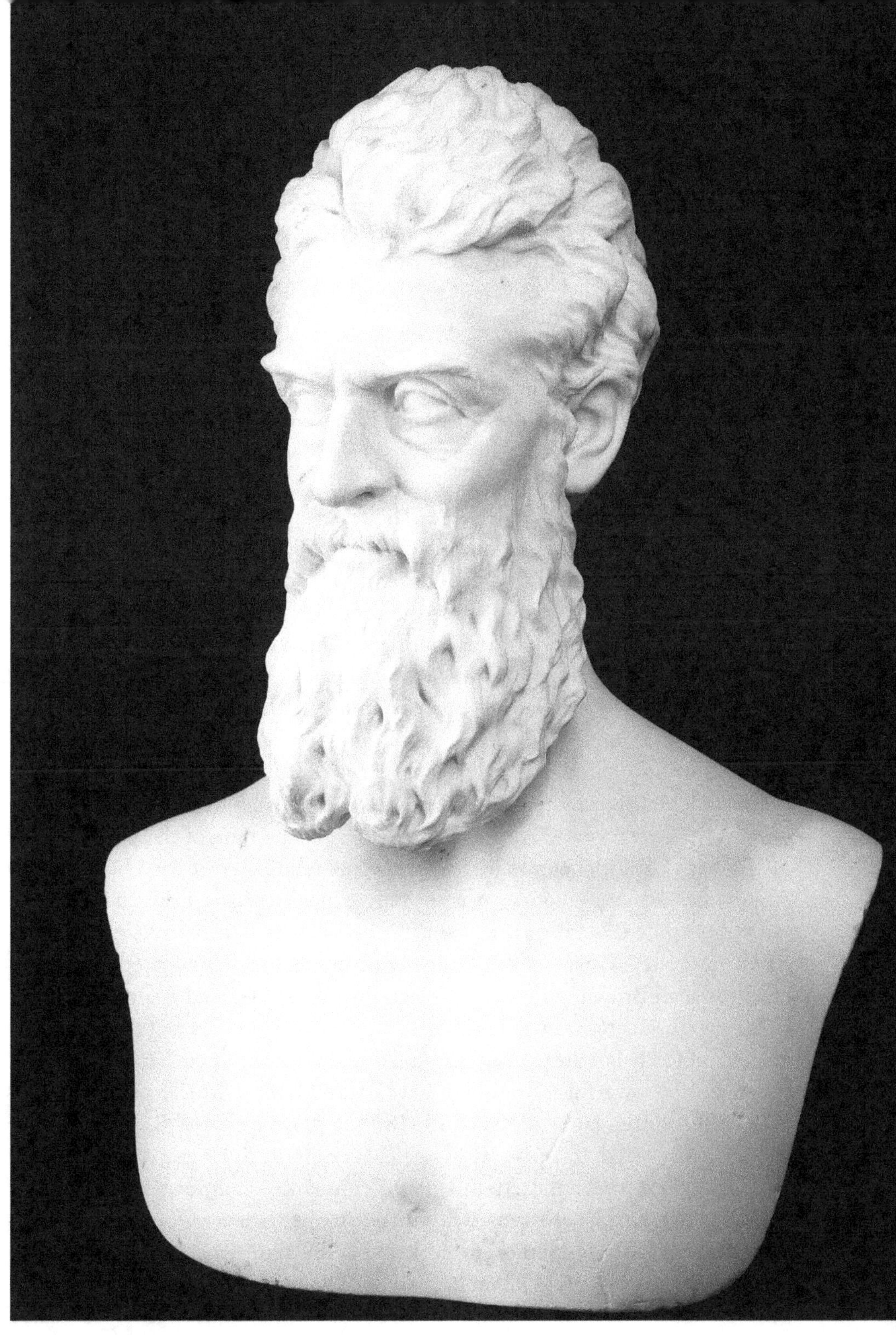

fig 18 *John Brown,* (bust) by Edward Augustus Brackett, 1860, marble, Tufts University permanent collection. Courtesy
of Tufts University.

As McDonald was to discover as she researched the history of this work, Brackett's John Brown was no ordinary sculptural commission. Unlike his busts of more conventional public figures, this one commemorates a reluctant subject whose impending execution would help ignite the Civil War. In order to fund this work, Brackett sought out Stearns, one of the men who had clandestinely sponsored Brown's disastrous raid on the armory at Harper's Ferry. To obtain the necessary drawings and measurements, he had to get himself smuggled into Brown's jail cell at a moment of extreme tension between North and South. As we shall see, this enterprise involved considerable risk to all involved. The bust itself is one of Brackett's finest creations. It presents Brown, not as a convicted criminal or broken failure, but as a fearless crusader touched by a kind of divine madness.

Brackett had undertaken the work in hopes of spreading Brown's abolitionist message, and prior to its entombment in the Tufts storeroom, the bust had served that purpose well. In his biography of John Brown, historian David Reynolds recounts the important role played by this sculpture in Brown's posthumous transformation from murderous fanatic to abolitionist martyr.[145] On January 1, 1863, the bust was the centerpiece of an Emancipation Day celebration hosted by George Stearns and attended by such luminaries as philosopher Ralph Waldo Emerson, abolitionists Wendell Phillips and William Lloyd Garrison, Louisa May Alcott of *Little Women* fame and her father, Transcendentalist preacher Amos Bronson Alcott, and Julia Ward Howe whose immortal *Battle Hymn of the Republic,* written to the tune of the popular song *John Brown's Body,* encapsulated the militant religiosity of the Union cause. Also in attendance, of course, was the heroic bust's creator, Edward Brackett.

As Reynolds describes the scene, "The bust, which many compared to Michelangelo's Moses, was an idealized rendering. It invested the stern, hatchet-faced Brown with a calm Jovian dignity. It gleamed against the black walnut wainscoting on the landing of the Stearns's' curved staircase as the hushed crowd below heard Emerson read his "Boston Hymn" and Julia Ward Howe gave a powerful recitation of her "Battle Hymn of the Republic."[146]

Several months later, on May 28, 1863, a plaster cast of Brackett's John Brown reappeared at a pivotal historical moment, during a parade for the sendoff of 54th Massachusetts Infantry Regiment, the nation's second unit of Black troops. Led by Boston abolitionist Colonel Robert Gould Shaw, their valor and exploits are memorialized in the 1989 film *Glory.* As the regiment marched out of Boston, William Lloyd Garrison was seen standing on Wendell Phillips' balcony resting his hand on the bust in what might be interpreted as a gesture of benediction for the departing soldiers. The bust's reach was extended through various copies in different materials. A bronze version was sent in 1860 to President Guillaume Fabre Nicolas Geffrard of Haiti, which had held a state funeral for Brown. A plaster cast was displayed at Boston's Faneuil Hall, the anti-slavery office in Boston and the Boston Athenaeum. The marble bust served as the basis for widely distributed medallion copies by Edmonia Lewis, Brackett's student and the first African American sculptor to gain recognition in Europe. The bust's admirers included Harriett Tubman, woman's rights activist Lydia Maria Child, Victor Hugo and Booker T. Washington.

The marble bust remained in Mary Stearns' possession until her death in 1902. After that, the entire estate was willed to Tufts, whereupon Brackett's masterpiece dropped out of sight, save for occasional references in letters and documents. Eventually it disappeared altogether until McDonald's discovery in 2015.

The reappearance of Brackett's masterpiece in the 21st century coincides with renewed attention to the kinds of issues that brought it into being. The role of slavery in American history, the halting progress toward emancipation, the human cost of the Civil War and the still unresolved state of race relations in the United States have brought new attention to figures like Lincoln, John Brown, Harriett Tubman and Frederick Douglass and to commemorative statues honoring key figures on both sides of the conflict. The story of Brackett's bust of John Brown is inextricably tied to the story of the abolitionist movement and its role in pushing America toward the end of slavery. As a result, it provides an opportunity to re-examine the forces that continue to shape the meaning of America in the 21ˢᵗ century.

Rising Tensions

In 1859, the year that Brackett created the bust, the nation was in turmoil. Only 71 years after the ratification of the U.S. Constitution, the compromises that had made the Union possible were tearing the nation apart. It was becoming impossible to escape the contradictions between the exalted statement in the Declaration of Independence that "All men are created equal" and the stipulation in the Constitution that those "bound to service" (a euphemism for slaves) were to be counted as three-fifths of a human being. Many of the founding fathers, including the author of those stirring words in the Declaration, were slaveholders, and the Constitution represented a deft effort to reconcile the divergent interests of the slaveholding South and the at least nominally free North. Throughout the 19th century, repeated concessions to the slave holding states were moving the country farther and farther away from the hopes, expressed by John Adams and others, that the South's "peculiar institution" would wither away on its own.

In the mid 19th century, a series of legislative and judicial decisions exacerbated the situation. Among the most onerous was the passage in 1850 of the Fugitive Slave Act. Under this law, federal agents were empowered to disregard state laws protecting their Black population and to forcibly return runaway slaves to their owners. In Massachusetts, where Abolitionist sentiment ran high, this abrogation of local law became a moral issue, and angry crowds faced off against bounty hunters and federal authorities in an increasingly unsuccessful effort to prevent the return of fugitives. Monetary incentives to slave hunters meant that even free Blacks were in danger of being kidnapped and shipped South to slavery. In several high profile cases, anti-slavery Bostonians stormed jails and exchanged fire with federal marshals after judges mandated the return of escaped slaves to certain torture and possible death. By privileging property rights over human rights the Fugitive Slave Act stoked antagonisms between reformers seeking to shelter escaped slaves and the police directed to enforce the Act.

Meanwhile, pro and anti slavery forces out West were engaged in what historian Andrew Delbanco has termed "the war before the war."[147] The Missouri Compromise of 1820 was a carefully calibrated effort to maintain the balance of power between slave and free States by drawing a line across the new western territories and banning slavery above the 36°30 parallel. The Kansas Nebraska Act of 1854 negated that compromise, instead leaving decisions about slavery in new territories to popular vote. This unleashed a series of violent skirmishes as pro and anti slavery forces attempted to keep the new State of Kansas, and its two U.S. Senators, in their camp. This ushered in an era known as "Bloody Kansas" marked by guerrilla warfare between proponents of slavery and members of the newly formed Free Soil Party who were determined to prevent the extension of slavery to the western territories. Then in 1857, with *Dred Scott vs Sanford*, the Supreme Court issued one of the most notorious legal decisions in the nation's history. Asked to rule on whether Congress had the authority to restrict slavery in any territories acquired after the nation's creation, the Court went further, declaring that no person of African descent, free or slave, could ever be a citizen of the United States.

By 1859 it was impossible to remain neutral on the subject of slavery. The country was beginning to splinter along lines that are still visible today. Liberal Boston, the largest city in the first state to abolish slavery, was a stronghold of abolitionism. But among White Bostonians opposed to slavery, there were many shades of opinion. Should the goal be simply to maintain the current balance of power in Congress, allowing slavery to exist where it was already established while preventing its spread elsewhere? Or should it be abolished altogether? Should the freed slaves be returned to Africa or allowed to become full citizens? Was it more important to abolish slavery or to hold the fracturing Union together? At the same time, a growing community of free Blacks were increasingly vocal in their calls not only to end slavery but to provide African Americans with the same rights enjoyed by the white citizenry.

And even in Boston, despite its reputation as a hotbed of anti-slavery activity, abolitionist sympathies were not universal. While Massachusetts has long prided itself as the first state to outlaw slavery, this victory was hard won. The 17th century Massachusetts Bay Colony had been a theocracy organized around the principle of self-rule. Lacking resources for the kind of high value products that would sustain trade with European markets, the colonists turned to the Caribbean where their timber, fish and produce found a ready market among the plantation owners of Barbados. They were able to exchange these for West Indian sugar that could in turn be traded in Europe for manufactured goods. Thus, while not itself a slave based economy, the colony was deeply enmeshed in the Atlantic slave trade.

Thanks to a vigorous local abolitionist movement, post-revolutionary Massachusetts abolished slavery in 1781. However, the state was part of a larger Union half of whose members were slave-holding states. In 1787 Massachusetts ratified a U.S. Constitution that protected slavery in the so-called Cotton states. Meanwhile Massachusetts' economy in the post war years remained linked to slavery, as it became a hub for factories that transformed Southern cotton into cloth. So while Massachusetts no longer permitted slavery within it's borders, it had not resolved the question of the morality and legality of slavery elsewhere.

By the time of Brackett's arrival in 1841, Boston was badly divided between those whose economic interests and employment depended on the cotton trade and increasingly vocal abolitionists who coalesced around such groups as the Transcendentalists, the Quakers, the Massachusetts Anti Slavery Society and the free Black community. Edward Brackett found himself in the middle of this struggle. As a Quaker he was naturally drawn to the Abolitionist cause. We have noted his exposure to the anti-abolitionist riots during his time in Cincinnati. There is no paper trail that documents his evolution into an ardent abolitionist but it is clear from a survey of his portrait subjects, acquaintances and circle of friends that his anti-slavery sentiments were reinforced by personal experiences and social ties.

Brackett's Tremont studio was a short walk from Faneuil Hall, the center of Boston's abolitionist activity. A meeting house with a storied history, the Hall was built by Peter Faneuil, a wealthy colonial era merchant and slave trader who probably used slave labor in its construction. He donated the building to the city of Boston shortly before his death in 1742. Rising above its blemished beginning, the Hall became a fulcrum of Boston's raucous political culture. During the buildup to the Revolutionary War Faneuil Hall became known as the Cradle of Liberty as rebels like Samuel Adams and John Adams protested the imposition of the Stamp Act and the Boston Massacre and incited the revolt that ultimately became the Boston Tea Party. Abolitionists were happy to trade on this reputation when they adopted the Hall as their preferred meeting place. Galvanizing events like the arrests of fugitive slaves and the passage of pro-slavery federal legislation brought huge crowds to the hall.

We can imagine Brackett among the rowdy throngs attending rallies in which Frederick Douglass decried the Fugitive Slave Act, William Lloyd Garrison denounced the pro-slavery bias of the U.S. Constitution and Wendell Phillips protested the arrest of escaped slave Anthony Burns. In fact, it seems likely that Brackett received the bulk of his education on the politics of the abolitionist movement at Faneuil Hall. And it may also be through these meetings that he met some of the figures who would become his patrons and portrait subjects. As in New York, Brackett threw his lot as an artist in with those of similar political and social sympathies. His busts from this era form almost a Who's Who of the Boston's White anti-slavery movement. These ties were to prove invaluable when he conceived his idea to create a bust of John Brown.

Brackett's abolitionist activities extended to Winchester, the town outside Boston where he had moved with his family in 1843. Ellen Knight, archivist for the Winchester Massachusetts Archival Center, has made an exhaustive study of the circumstances surrounding Brackett's John Brown bust. She reports, "Brackett's own anti-slavery sentiments were apparent in 1855, when he was one of three members of the new Winchester Republican Committee who drafted a set of resolutions sent to the state Republican convention. A portion read: "Resolved, That we, the citizens of Winchester, in view of the aggressions of slavery, especially the Nebraska outrage, with its assaults upon the elective franchise in Kansas, . . . will use all constitutional means to maintain the rights of freedom, and that we will, to the utmost, resist every aggression of the slave-power."[148]

This alarm over developments in Nebraska and Kansas spilled over to other members of the Brackett family. While Edward came east, his younger brother George had headed west to seek his fortune. On his way to California, George became involved with the Free Soil party at the height of the Bloody Kansas era. He stayed, and as we shall see, joined the fight to keep Kansas a free state.

Abolition's Sword and Trumpet

Brackett's portrait commissions underscore his political sympathies. Two of the artist's most influential patrons were among those celebrating his John Brown bust at the Emancipation Day party. William Lloyd Garrison and Wendell Phillips both bore physical scars for their fearless support of the abolitionist cause. Their activities during Brackett's early years in Boston provide a picture of the passions coursing through the city as the abolitionist fever mounted.

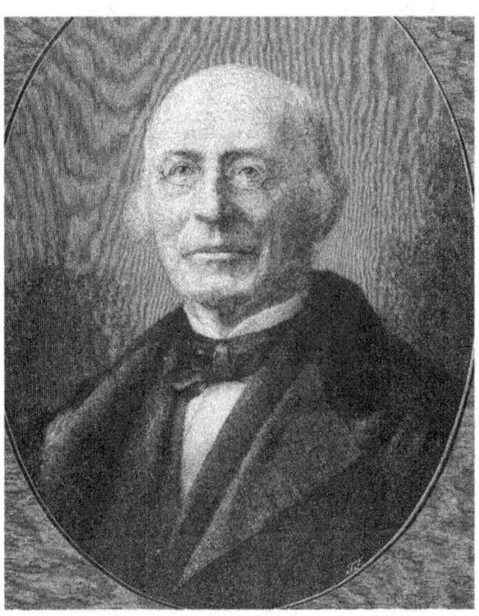

fig. 19 *William Lloyd Garrison*, unknown photographer, n.d.
Public Domain via Wikimedia Commons

Photographs of Garrison present a balding, bespectacled man who might seem more at home at a genteel tea party or library lecture than in the center of the raging battles of the Abolitionist movement. (fig 19) But Garrison's apparently mild mannered appearance masked a fearless firebrand. As the editor of the famous Abolitionist newspaper *The Liberator*, he is hailed as a key figure in the road to Emancipation. Consider, for instance, his call to arms in the first issue of *The Liberator*, published on January 1, 1831. "I will be as harsh as truth, and as uncompromising as justice. On this subject [abolition], I do not wish to think, or speak, or write, with moderation. No! no! Tell a man whose house in on fire to give a moderate alarm; tell him to moderately rescue his wife from the hand of the ravisher; tell the mother to gradually extricate her babe from the fire into which it has fallen; but urge me not to use moderation in a cause like the present. I am in earnest – I will not equivocate – I will not excuse – I will not retreat a single inch – AND I WILL BE HEARD."[149]

Brackett's bust has disappeared, so we don't know how he portrayed Garrison and whether the editor's combative character was reflected in his bust. But we do know that the sculptor impressed the newspaperman. We have noted Garrison's symbolic laying of his hand on Brackett's John Brown bust during the sendoff of the 54th Massachusetts Infantry Regiment. And, as we shall see, when Garrison was searching for a mentor for the aspiring African American sculptor Edmonia Lewis, the man he turned to was Edward Brackett.

While many of the leading figures in Boston's abolitionist movement came from privileged backgrounds, Garrison was a man of the people. He was the child of a British seaman who immigrated to the United States and then abandoned his family when his son was three years old. Garrison grew up amid poverty and spent his early years scrambling to help support his family. After working at a number of trades, at age thirteen he was fortuitously apprenticed to a newspaper publisher. Quickly working his way up from menial tasks, at twenty he was writing and managing the publication. Garrison spent his early twenties at various newspapers before hooking up with Benjamin Lundy, the editor of *Genius of Universal Emancipation*, a Baltimore based abolitionist weekly. Lundy was an advocate of gradual emancipation of the slaves, a position Garrison initially shared, but which he soon abandoned in favor of a more radical approach.

By 1831, Garrison had acquired the experience and resources to start his own newspaper in Boston (though it is reported that in the early years he and his co-publisher Isaac Knapp were reduced to sleeping on mattresses in a corner of the office.) As an abolitionist, Garrison held sharp views. In contrast to his mentor Lundy, he called for the immediate emancipation of the slaves. And unlike Lundy, he parted ways with the colonization movement that advocated the return of slaves to Africa. Garrison promoted the idea that the North should separate from the South and maintained that the Constitution of the United States was an immoral document because it sanctioned slavery. This would lead him, in 1854 to publicly burn a copy of the Constitution, denouncing it as "a covenant with death and an agreement with hell."[150] At the same time, he was an advocate of non-violent resistance, a stance that was not altered by his own treatment by pro-slavery mobs.

This treatment could be brutal. While still in Baltimore Garrison was convicted of libel for condemning a slaveholder from his hometown and asserting that slave traders should be sentenced to solitary confinement for life. He was thrown in jail and sentenced to six months. He was freed after seven weeks when a New York based abolitionist paid his fine, precipitating his departure for Boston. While he was somewhat more protected there, attacks on his life and liberty continued. The most egregious occurred in 1835; Garrison was assaulted during a speaking engagement at of the Boston Female Anti-Slavery Society and dragged through the streets by a crowd intent on tarring, feathering and lynching him. In this instance, he was only saved by the intervention of agents of the mayor who placed him for safekeeping in the city jail. Meanwhile, officials in Southern States continued to consider him a mortal enemy. He was indicted for "felonious acts" in North Carolina, while in South Carolina rewards were posted for the arrest of anyone caught distributing his paper. In 1831 the legislature of Georgia offered a $5000 reward for his arrest and conviction.

From an early base of support among mostly African American subscribers, *The Liberator* grew to become a leading abolitionist publication. Garrison promoted Frederick Douglass, the fugitive slave who went on to become the one of the most famous faces of the abolitionist movement. Garrison was also central to Abraham Lincoln's evolution on the slave question. After sharply criticizing the compromises made by the President to maintain the Union in the face of Southern intransigence, Garrison saw Lincoln eventually come around to his position on the imperative for emancipation.

Meanwhile, Garrison's position also evolved. One indication of this is his reaction to John Brown's raid on Harper's Ferry. Though he shared Brown's aims, Garrison was initially repulsed by the crusader's violent tactics. But by the time of Brown's execution Garrison had come to see these as a necessary evil. In a speech on the occasion of Brown's execution, Garrison declared, "Was John Brown justified in his attempt? Yes, if Washington was in his; if Warren and Hancock were in theirs. If men are justified in striking a blow for freedom, when the question is one of a threepenny tax on tea, then, I say, they are a thousand times more justified, when it is to save fathers, mothers, wives and children from the slave-coffle and the auction-block, and to restore them to their God- given rights ....."[151]

As the nation headed into war, Garrison evolved further, setting aside his pacifism to become a staunch supporter of Lincoln during the Civil War. Garrison continued to publish *The Liberator* through out the war, only ceasing in 1865 when the passage of the Thirteenth Amendment convinced him that his work was done.

Wendell Phillips, another of Brackett's subjects, was an attorney and orator who became an ardent abolitionist after he watching the angry mob drag Garrison through the streets of Boston. Phillips came to share Garrison's views on abolition, secession and the perfidy of the Constitution. He wrote frequently for *The Liberator*, was a regular speaker at Garrison's American Anti-Slavery

Society and joined the Boston Vigilance Committee, an organization that assisted fugitive slaves in avoiding slavecatchers. Unlike Garrison he was a blue blood, a Harvard graduate and son of the first mayor of Boston. In taking up the abolitionist cause, Phillips turned against his members of his class, some of whom he recognized in the mob that attacked Garrison.

If Garrison wielded his pen like a sword against the crime of slavery, Phillips was celebrated as "abolition's golden trumpet." Having studied rhetoric and oratory for four years at Harvard College, he emerged as a stirring speaker whose words could convert a hostile crowd. The first indication of this was his spontaneous speech at Faneuil Hall on December 8, 1837. A public meeting had been called to discuss the murder of E. P. Lovejoy, an abolitionist Illinois publisher shot by a proslavery mob that had stormed his office intent on destroying his press. After one of the speakers praised the rioters and compared them to the patriots who threw tea into Boston Harbor at the outset of the American Revolution, Phillips stood to refute this claim. He pointed out the fallacy of this comparison, noting that the tea party insurgents were rebelling against the imposition of illegal taxes, while Lovejoy was exercising his constitutionally protected freedom of the press. Then, he unfurled his rhetoric: "He (Lovejoy) took refuge under the banner of liberty, --amid its folds; and when he fell, its glorious stars and stripes, the emblem of free institutions, around which cluster so many heart-stirring memories, were blotted out in the martyr's blood. "

And, he called out Lovejoy's critics:

"But all you who believe, as I do, in the right and duty of magistrates to execute the laws, join with me and brand as base hypocrisy the conduct of those who assemble year after year on the 4th of July, to fight over the battles of the Revolution, and yet 'damn with faint praise,' or load with obloquy, the memory of this man, who shed his blood in defense of life, liberty and the freedom of the press!"

Finally he pointed where appeasement of the rioters could lead:

"Welcome the despotism of the Sultan, where one knows what he may publish and what he may not, rather than the tyranny of this many-headed monster, the mob, where we know not what we may do or say, till some fellow-citizen has tried it, and paid for the lesson with his life."[152]

The crowd, initially sympathetic to the pro-slavery argument, was cheering him on at the end.

Phillips threw himself into the abolitionist movement. He was also a lifelong champion of other oppressed and disenfranchised groups. He was a staunch supporter of women's rights and argued for citizenship for Native Americans. It may be in Phillips' capacity as abolitionist speaker at Faneuil Hall that Brackett first made his acquaintance. And no doubt Brackett was instrumental in bringing Phillips to Winchester. Ellen Knight reports that Phillips was one of the lecturers for the 1859-1860 season of the Winchester Literary Association, where he spoke on Toussaint L'Ouverture, hero of the Haitian Revolution.[153] Brackett's bust of Phillips has disappeared but the orator's admiration for Brackett is confirmed by the fact that he owned a plaster copy of the John Brown bust, given to him by Brackett's patroness Mary Stearns.

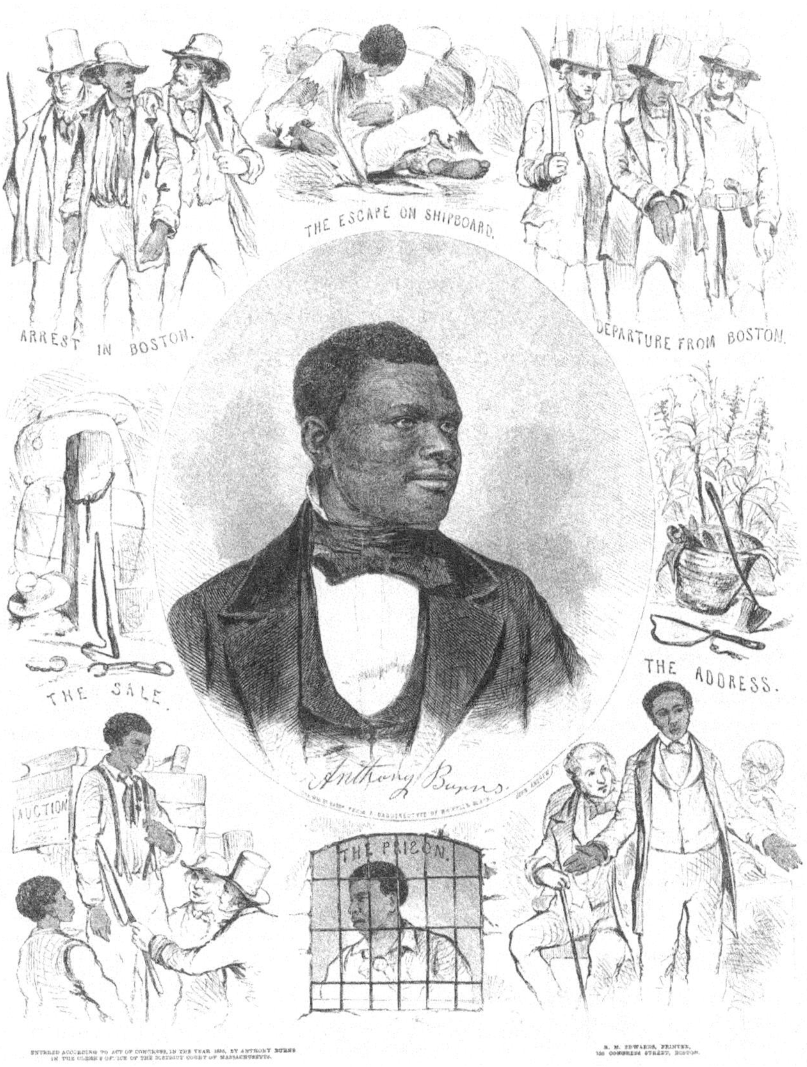

fig. 20 *Broadside illustrating key events in the enslavement, escape, arrest, return to slavery, and the later manumittence of Anthony Burns* by John Andrews, engraver, 1855, Printed In Boston by R.M. Edwards, printer, 129 Congress Street, 1855. Courtesy of PICRYL

The Anthony Burns Tragedy

In 1854, Phillips' activism embroiled him in one of the most galvanizing events of the antebellum era. (fig 20) The Anthony Burns case threw Phillips together with Richard Henry Dana Jr., Brackett's friend and mentor. Burns was a fugitive slave who had escaped from Virginia to Boston. There he got a job in a clothing store owned by a Baptist deacon. His brief taste of freedom ended on May 24, 1854 when he was arrested under the Fugitive Slave Act. As it happened, this was the same day that the U.S. Congress voted to negate the Missouri Compromise by passing the Kansas-Nebraska Act, thereby allowing new territories of the United States to institute slavery by popular vote.

This pair of outrages galvanized Boston's abolitionists who vowed to rescue Burns. Their sentiments were voiced by Phillips, who declared at an abolitionist rally in Faneuil Hall, "Nebraska! Why, it is knocking a man down; but, on the heel of that, claiming a fugitive slave is like spitting in his face when you have got him down." Invoking the sovereignty of the people in the face of the law's moral failure, he roared, "The question, to-morrow, is, fellow-citizens, whether Virginia conquers Massachusetts. - If that man leaves the city of Boston, Massachusetts is a conquered State." And he urged the crowd to action: See to it, fellow — citizens, that in the streets of Boston, you ratify the verdict of Faneuil Hall to-night, that Anthony Burns has no master but God!"[154] In fact, Burns' supporters didn't wait that long. Midway through this meeting, a posse amassed to storm the courthouse where Burns was being held. Rescuers breached the door with a battering ram and in the ensuing melee a guard was killed. After a furious hand-to-hand battle, the rioters were repulsed.

With Burns now under heavy guard, it was clear that any rescue would have to take place in the legal arena. Richard Dana, along with Robert Morris, one of the first Black lawyers in the United States, volunteered to defend Burns in the Federal court where his fate would be decided. Knowing that an argument based on the constitutionality of the law would fail, Dana crafted a defense based both on higher law and on muddying the identification of Burns as a runaway slave. He called witnesses who testified that they had seen the man on the dock in Boston before the date that Burns was alleged to have escaped. He also invoked the spirit of liberty, arguing in a four and a half hour speech, "If [you decide] against him, a free man is made a slave forever. . . May your judgment be for liberty and not slavery." And he warned of the accused's fate if he were returned to Virginia: "He would never see the Virginia sun. He would be sold at the first block, to perish after a few years of service on the cotton fields or sugar fields of Louisiana or Arkansas."[155]

Dana's eloquence was in vain. The judge ruled that the Fugitive Slave Act required the return of Burns to slavery. But the case had electrified the city of Boston. A crowd of 50,000, Brackett doubtless among them, lined streets draped in mourning as 2000 federal troops, local police and hired guards escorted Burns to the boat that would return him to Virginia. As one observer reported, "We went to bed one night old-fashioned, conservative, Compromise Union Whigs and waked up stark mad Abolitionists."[156]

Burns' fate was equivocal – upon his return he was chained to a shack for four months, after which a group of Boston abolitionists purchased his freedom. He enrolled in Oberlin College, where he became a minister and anti-slavery speaker, only to die eight years later of tuberculosis brought on by his mistreatment. Nor did Dana escape unscathed. He was assaulted on his way home from arguing the case by a pro-slavery mob and nearly killed.

Careening toward War

While we don't have Brackett's busts of Garrison, Phillips or Dana, we do have his portrait of Charles Sumner.(fig 21) That bust dates from 1855, a year after the Anthony Burns case and the year Brackett sponsored Winchester's anti-slavery resolution. The bust presents Sumner as a solemn man with the patrician air of a Roman Senator. He is swathed in the folds of a classical robe and his head tilts slightly up as if gazing into a troubled future. In fact Sumner was a pugnacious Massachusetts Senator who would pay dearly for his abolitionist sentiments a year after he was sculpted by Brackett.

Sumner is best remembered today for the brutal beating he received from a fellow legislator on the floor of the Senate following his scathing attack on slavery and its enablers. His anti-slavery credentials dated back to his childhood. His abolitionist father, Charles Pinckney Sumner, was a struggling lawyer who shocked 19th-century Boston by opposing anti-miscegenation laws. After graduating from Harvard Law School, the younger Sumner traveled in Europe, a trip that confirmed his own views about the innate equality of Blacks and Whites. He returned to Boston to practice law and from 1845 on he took on cases that challenged the legality of segregation. By the time he was elected to Congress in 1851 as a representative of the Free Soil Democrats, he was a furious opponent of the Fugitive Slave Act.

The caning that almost ended his life followed his impassioned denunciation of the Kansas Nebraska Act in a speech he titled "The Crime Against Kansas." Using the colorful language typical of antebellum rhetoric, he described the Act's intentions in sexual terms: "Not in any common lust for power did this

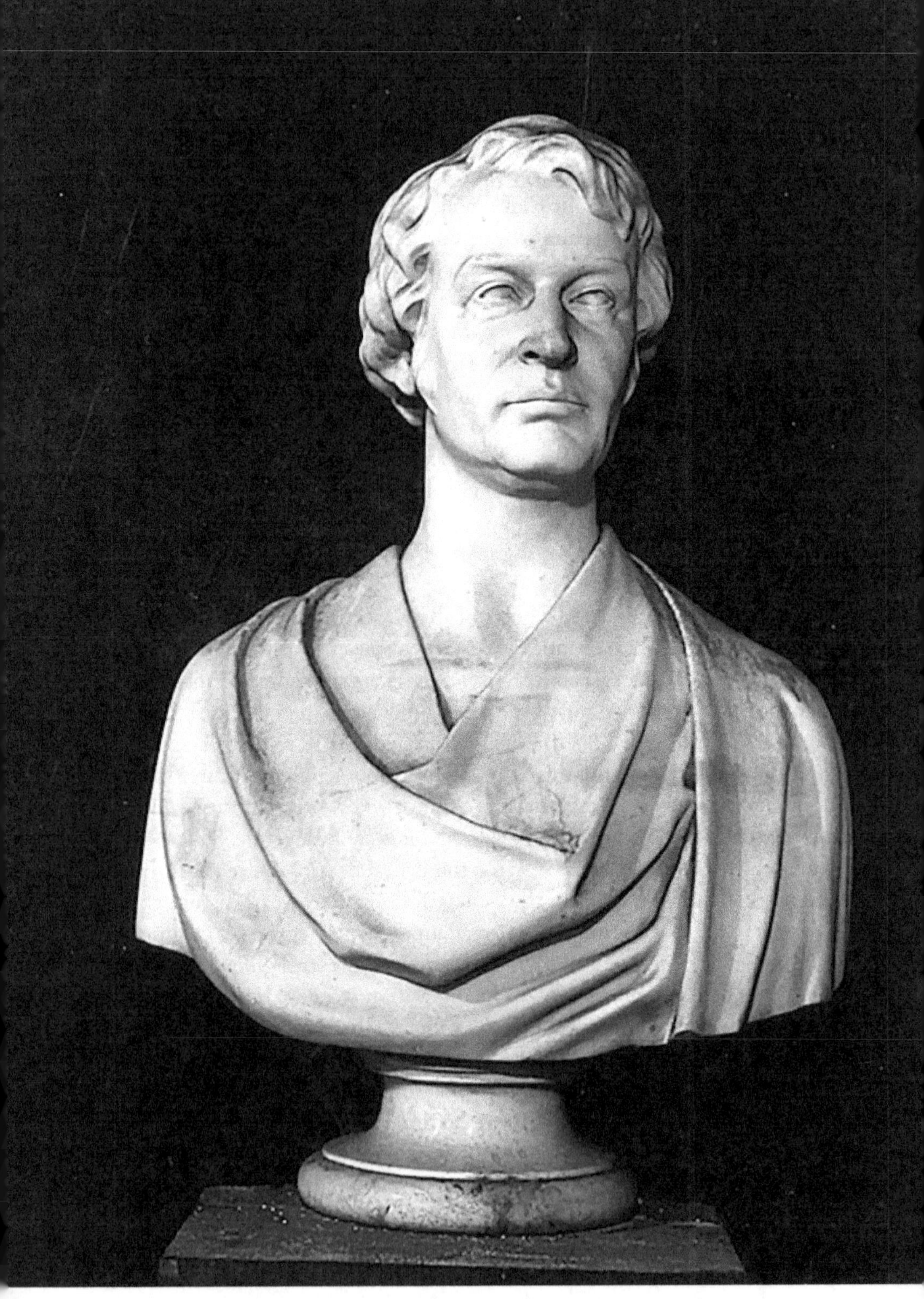

fig. 21 *Charles Sumner* by Edward Augustus Brackett, ca. 1858, marble, Harvard University Portrait Collection, Cambridge, Massachusetts object # S13. Courtesy of President and Fellows of Harvard College.

uncommon tragedy have its origin. It is the rape of a virgin Territory, compelling it to the hateful embrace of slavery; and it may be clearly traced to a depraved desire for a new Slave State, hideous offspring of such a crime, in the hope of adding to the power of slavery in the National Government."[157]

He extended the salacious metaphor in a description of Senator Andrew Butler of South Carolina, one of the authors of the Kansas Nebraska Act, declaring: "The senator from South Carolina has read many books of chivalry, and believes himself a chivalrous knight with sentiments of honor and courage. Of course he has chosen a mistress to whom he has made his vows, and who, though ugly to others, is always lovely to him; though polluted in the sight of the world, is chaste in his sight—I mean the harlot, slavery."[158]

Several days later, as Sumner sat at his desk on the Senate floor, Butler's cousin, Preston Brooks, himself a Congressman from South Carolina, crept up from behind to avenge his kinsman's honor. Brooks proceeded to beat Sumner senseless with a gold tipped walking cane, not even stopping when the cane broke in two. Sumner was so badly injured that he was not able to return to Congress for two and a half years. Reactions to the beating reflected the ever-growing divide between North and South. Southerners praised the assault and sent Brooks dozens of new canes, while in the North, the act was denounced as an extension of the brutality with which slaveholders treated their slaves.

Meanwhile, violence was ricocheting across the country. On May 21, 1856, the day after Sumner's speech, Lawrence Kansas exploded as a mob of 800 slavery supporters from around the territory gathered in preparation for an attack on the town. Thanks to the Kansas-Nebraska Act, the territory of Kansas was the focus of intense efforts by both pro and anti-slavery advocates, each endeavoring to bring the state into the Union on their side. Border Ruffians, coming over the border from the slave state of Missouri faced off against Free Staters who were determined to keep Kansas free of slavery. Lawrence became a target because it was an epicenter of Free State activity, having been settled just a few years earlier by anti-slavery activists from Massachusetts. At the time of the attack, the town had already been the site of various skirmishes, including the non-fatal shooting of a pro slavery sheriff as he attempted to arrest Free State settlers. In retaliation, the pro-slavers were determined to teach the town a lesson. With a cannon absconded from the town, they attempted to bring down the Free State Hotel which served as a way station for anti-slavery immigrants to Kansas. Failing to destroy the building by cannon fire, they burned it to the ground while also laying waste to the offices of the two abolitionist newspapers. Then they looted the now nearly deserted town whose residents had fled prior to the assault.

The attack produced only one casualty, a pro-slaver hit by debris from the falling hotel. However, the repercussions were enormous. The Sack of Lawrence, as it came to be called, was the opening salvo in a guerrilla war between pro and anti slavery forces that turned Kansas into the key battleground of the fight over the future of slavery in the United States.

Brother George Joins the Fight

One of the witnesses of the Sack of Lawrence was George Coleman Brackett, Edward Brackett's younger brother. George was on his way to California to take part in the Gold Rush and happened to be in Lawrence when the mob ransacked the city. In his 1886 testimony to the Kansas State Historical Society, George recalled his powerful reaction to the attack.[159] He and a friend immediately turned around and headed back to their home in Iowa to enlist volunteers to protect the Free State legislature in Topeka, Kansas. They had gotten as far as Leavenworth, Kansas and were boarding a steamer for St Louis when they were approached by a government attaché aware of their sympathies. He asked them to assist in a mysterious business that would take place the next day.

George agreed, and describes how he and his friend observed the steamer make an unexplained stop just below Kansas City. There the boat took on a small amount of wood and a disheveled tramp apparently employed as the wood-chopper. Later that evening, in the midst of an intense storm, the tramp appeared at their cabin door. He was revealed to be Andrew H. Reeder, the federally appointed Governor of the Kansas Territory. As a Free State advocate, Reeder was on the run from Border Ruffians who had already hounded him from office with the threat of an indictment for treason. Reeder changed his clothes in Brackett's cabin, and then George and his friend slipped off the boat with him. The trio made their way through the storm lashed countryside to the banks of the Mississippi River. George recounts, "I locked arms with the Governor, (remarking, 'Let the blind lead the blind;' that I hoped there was no ditch ahead into which we should fall,) because he held the umbrella and I had none." Narrowly escaping a landslide, they made it to the swollen river by sunrise. Hailing a ferryboat, they crossed over into the free state of Illinois, upon which the Governor remarked, "For the first time since leaving Lawrence, I feel easy and safe." Reeder would go on to proselytize and fund raise for the Free State cause. After his brush with history, George returned to Kansas. He spent the next four decades there, first as a lawyer and then as a horticulturist. He is remembered today as the founder of the state's pioneer nurseries.

Enter John Brown

This pair of outrages - the caning of Sumner and the Sack of Lawrence - had far reaching consequences. Among them were the transformation of John Brown from a rabble rousing abolitionist into a militant outlaw. Brown was enraged by these two events and took revenge in a bloody raid that still divides those who otherwise endorse his cause. Taking inspiration from the biblical verse urging "eye for an eye", on May 25, 1856, he and his sons conducted a midnight raid on the pro-slavery town of Pottawatomie Creek, Kansas. They pulled five men whom Brown deemed enemies of abolition from their cabins and marched them into the woods where they were hacked to death. Brown's biographer David Reynolds, argues that the Pottawatomie Creek massacre was a response, not just to recent events, but to a Southern culture of violence and lawlessness that Northerners had hitherto failed to adequately challenge. Reynolds maintains, "It was John Brown who, more than anyone else, 'brought Southern tactics to the Northern side,' as a contemporary journalist put it."[160] Brown changed the equation, revealing that abolitionists could be as vicious and murderous as their foes.

From this point on, Brown was a fugitive, sheltered and assisted by abolitionists who hailed him as a hero and hunted by Kansas officials and Border Ruffians who saw him as a murderer, traitor and terrorist. Boston abolitionists were mixed in their response to Brown's tactics. Many, like Emerson and his fellow Transcendentalists, continued to preach a gospel of non-violence. But as violence escalated, others became more sympathetic to Brown's militant approach.

For the next two years, Brown made periodic trips east, seeking arms, manpower and financial support for a proposed raid on the federal armory at Harper's Ferry, Virginia. Brown saw this as a prelude to a vast slave uprising that he believed would end slavery in America. He attempted to gain support from leading Black abolitionists. Frederick Douglass was apprised of Brown's plan early on, but ultimately refused to participate, arguing that the scheme was suicidal madness. Harriett Tubman was more receptive and worked with Brown to raise money to recruit free Blacks in Canada. But though she was very supportive of Brown, both before and after the raid, she did not, as he had hoped, join him in the action itself. However, Brown received a sympathetic hearing from some of Boston's leading White abolitionists. Among these were a group that would come to be designated the Secret Six and whose financial support ultimately enabled the raid.

The Secret Six were Theodore Parker and Thomas Wentworth Higginson, both ministers, Samuel Gridley Howe, a physician whose wife Julia Ward would later write *The Battle Hymn of the Republic*, Franklin Benjamin Sanborn, a writer and schoolmaster, Gerrit Smith, a social reformer and politician and George Luther Stearns, a wealthy industrialist who, with his wife Mary, would fund Brackett's bust.

Of the group, the wealthiest were Smith and Stearns. Raised in the anti-slavery Universalist Church, Stearns had made his fortune as a lead pipe manufacturer. He was pulled into the abolitionist cause through his connections to the Transcendentalist circle of Emerson and Thoreau and from his concern for the Free State issue. As the chairman of the Massachusetts State Kansas Aid Committee, Stearns got to know John Brown and became one of his major financial supporters. Stearns' ardent support of the anti-slavery movement is captured in an account by Henry Ingersoll Bowditch, a physician and fellow abolitionist who was a close friend of the family. He reports, "His [Stearns] magnificent house, large and airy, often hid the flying fugitive slave. The man-hunter found no quarters there, but his panting victim was fed and clothed and concealed until a fit time came for him to run to Canada. John Brown went there as one always welcome, always honored and helped with funds, without stint and without special inquiries as to the object he had in view. "[161] So when Brown came seeking funds for his assault on Harper's Ferry, he received a sympathetic hearing. In the end, Stearns would contribute $1200 as well as fifteen boxes of firearms toward the raid, though without insisting on knowing specific details of the plan.

It was during one of Brown's fundraising sorties to Boston that Edward Brackett encountered the now notorious abolitionist on the street. There are several accounts of this event – Bowditch places it in 1857, and notes that Brackett was "had been attracted by the dignity of [Brown's] mien."[162] Other more reliable reports place the encounter in June of 1859, just four months before Brown's ill-fated raid. A lively narrative appears in a letter written by abolitionist and woman's rights activist Lydia Maria Child for the *New York Tribune* in 1860. Child, who was also Mary Stearns' aunt, recalled "It is fortunate that he [Brackett} chanced to meet John Brown in the streets of Boston several months before his brave bearing at Harper's Ferry had made him world famous. The expression of the face and the carriage of the head attracted his artistic eye. He said to himself, 'There's a head for a sculptor.' He looked after him earnestly, and went back in order to pass him again. Upon inquiring who it was, he was told, 'That is old John Brown of Kansas.' The strong impression then made on his mind had much to do with his subsequent desire of going to Virginia for the purpose of modeling his head." [163]

If accurate, this encounter would have coincided with Brown's last trip to Boston. An account published in 1872 by Franklin Sanborn, another member of the Secret Six, outlines Brown's movements at this time. "Before leaving Boston for the last time, Wednesday, June 1, 1859, the sum of $2,000, which had been promised him at the Revere House meeting a year before, was made up and placed to his credit . . . John Brown also spoke at one of the Boston Anniversary meetings in Tremont Temple, the last week in this same May, and was present on Saturday, May 28th, at the weekly dinner of the "Bird Club," which then met at the Parker House."[164]

In his narrative, Sanborn describes the visual impression that Brown conveyed during the buildup to the raid. He reports that the once clean-shaven Brown started wearing what would become his trademark beard in 1858 in an effort to evade recognition. But clearly, this did not make him invisible. Sanborn recalls, "Brown's hotel, during his last visit to Boston, was the United States House. He was attended, generally, in his movements about the city and its neighborhood, by a faithful henchman, Jerry Anderson, a youth from Indiana who was shot at Harper's Ferry. Both were in rustic dress, but Brown, from his marked aspect and his flowing gray beard (which he first began to wear in Kansas in the summer of 1858), attracted much attention in the streets. He has been described by Judge Hoar (who had seen him in Concord, and perhaps had contributed to his fund from the same motives as Governor Andrew), in one of these street rambles, as calmly walking up Court Street in the midst of the hurrying throng, with his jack-knife in one hand and an apple in the other, which he was peeling and eating, quite unconscious of observation, while his young henchman, less accustomed to cities, walked a little behind him, gazing up at the signs and windows. Another remembers him plodding his way to the Providence Railroad Station, burdened with a heavy carpet-bag, and still escorted by his body-guard."[165]

This would be the John Brown who Brackett encountered on the streets of Boston. Despite the urgency of his cause, Brown still had time for portrait sittings, indicating the importance attached even then to the creation of iconic images to (as we might say today) brand popular movements. Sanborn continues: "In course of his stay in Boston he spent an evening at the house of a gentleman where William Hunt, the painter,[166] was also a guest, and an appointment was made with Brown that he should give Hunt a sitting for his portrait. It is unfortunate that this sitting never took place, for his portrait by Hunt would now be the best representation of him in his last year. Brackett the sculptor, whose fine bust of him has already been mentioned, also met him at this time; but the studies and measurements for his bust were made in a brief visit to Brown in his cell at Charlestown in the following November. Brown sat for his photograph to a Boston artist named Heywood, and it is from this picture, a half-length standing figure, with the hands behind the back, and the face turned a little aside from a front view, that all the common portraits of him are taken. It was used by Brackett in modeling his bust, in which, however, the features are somewhat idealized. "[167] (fig 22)

After his departure from Boston, Brown would go on to perform his ill-fated raid, which ended in the death of seven people, the failure of the surrounding slaves to rise up and Brown's capture and imprisonment. Brown's arrest galvanized the abolitionist movement. Brown's biographer David Reynolds argues that his post-arrest demeanor transformed Brown in the popular mind from a criminal madman into an abolitionist hero. He cites in particular the stirring speech that Brown gave at his sentencing in which the condemned man declared "I believe that to have interfered as I have done, as I have always freely admitted that I have done, in behalf of [God's] despised poor, I did no wrong, but right. Now if it is deemed necessary that I should forfeit my life for the furtherance of the ends of justice, and mingle my blood further with the blood of millions in this slave country whose rights are disregarded by wicked, cruel, and unjust enactments, I say, let it be done."[168]

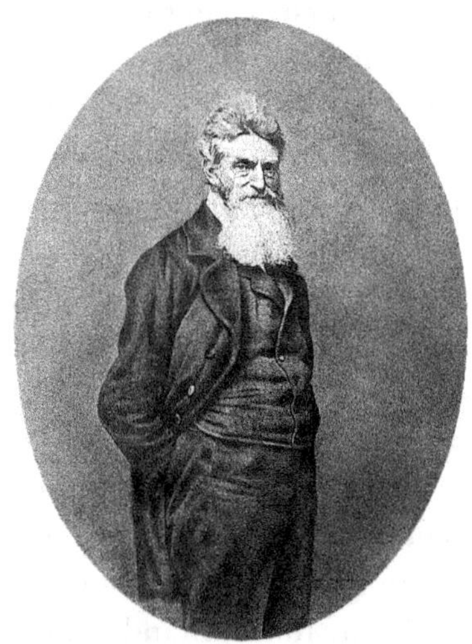

fig. 22 *John Brown*, reproduction of daguerreotype attributed to Martin M. Lawrence, 1859, Library of Congress Prints and Photographs Division Washington, D.C. 20540 USA. Courtesy of PICRYL.

Brackett's Perilous Project

Back in Boston, the Secret Six were in a state of extreme agitation. Howe, Sanborn and Stearns briefly left the country for Canada, while Higginson and Parker plotted to rescue Brown from prison. It was in this atmosphere that Brackett hatched his plan to memorialize Brown. Over the subsequent years, Brackett published several accounts of his trip, each offering details of different aspects of his trip. One, from the *Topeka Daily Capital*, appeared on Nov 14, 1889. Another is a narrative given by Brackett about a year before his death to Katherine Mayo, who published it in *The Evening Post* of November 13, 1909. We have as well a contemporaneous report on his visit by a correspondent who was in Charleston reporting on Brown's trial. These appeared in the *New York Daily Tribune*, spread over several editions in November 1859.[169] Splicing them together, we get a full picture of Brackett's exploit. In the *Topeka Daily Capital*, Brackett recalls,

"I could hardly sleep or eat, so absorbing was the desire that took possession of my mind. I had no money to make the journey to Virginia, and I finally went, in turn, to Dr. Howe and Wendell Phillips, requesting a loan for the purpose. Neither of them considered a marble bust of Brown really important, with so many other things to be thought of. But I said there is one man who if he cannot help me will listen, and perhaps give me furtherance."

That man was George Stearns – who did indeed express support and promised to consult with his wife Mary, an equally committed abolitionist. In the *Evening Post* account, Brackett reports,

Next day, Sunday afternoon, Mr. Stearns drove out to my house in Winchester. "Will you really go to Charlestown?" he asked me. "If so, I can find the money for you. How much do you require?"

"I scarcely know."

"Well, I am authorized by a lady," Stearns went on, "to give you this," and he placed in my hand $120 in gold coin." (The lady, of course, was his wife Mary.)

Brackett describes his trip down to Harper's Ferry where he arrived late in the evening. *There I went to the hotel, an old-fashioned country tavern. I walked up to the register, by the door, and signed myself, "E. A. Brackett, Boston," and at that time and place a man might quite as well have booked from Hell.*

Brushing aside the suspicious glances and verbal challenges from some of the inn's inhabitants, he set off the next day for Charleston, where Brown was being held awaiting execution. There the first person he encountered was Edward Howard House, a reporter for the *New York Tribune* who was there surreptitiously. Brackett reports: *Under cover of bona-fide credentials from a Boston pro-slavery paper, House was supplying the* Tribune, *as opportunity offered, with those long, picturesque, and stingingly ironical letters so bitterly resented in the South. As yet he was personally unsuspected, but the hunt was keen, and glad though he was to see a friend, House was on tenterhooks in this moment of recognition. So we made a feint of scraping acquaintance, for future use.*

House's reports were indeed full of wicked spleen. Take for instance, his description of the local press: *They are all thoroughly sound, and conducted on a simple principle of unsparing severity toward foes and dove-like gentleness toward friends. They unite the extremes of bitter and sweet. For all who come with credentials of adherence to the Pro-Slavery faith, they have words of sweetest welcome. For unreliable strangers, they have chilling admonitions, and for visitors who make no secret of their want of political sympathy with the prevailing creed, they have fierce ebullitions of rage.*

This fury, he makes clear, was turning the town into a powder keg. He admonishes his Northern readers, *You at a distance, can hardly form an impression of the rage for vengeance which is felt by the citizens of this place. When Brown was in court, on trial, there were always faces burning with hatred hanging over him, fiercely watching every movement that he made. In the event of an attempt at rescue, which has been the great fear all along, and to prevent which all these extraordinary military precautions are still kept up, the jailers have been instructed to shoot him and his companions instantly. The populace are resolute in their determination that their victims shall never be taken from them, and it does not seem that this determination is to be shaken by any expedient.*

Brackett and House both describe the difficulties the sculptor faced in his efforts to get into the jail to see Brown. Brackett carried letters of introduction to Virginia Senator James Murray Mason and Andrew Hunter, Brown's prosecuting attorney, both of whom received him cordially but as Brackett notes, seemed determined to thwart his mission *not by a direct denial, but by procrastination.* When Brackett pressed them, he reports that one of them *handed me a letter, written by a Democratic office-holder in my town of Winchester, which read, in effect: "Look out for Bracket. He is an Abolitionist and a spy."*[170]

House has great fun with the run-around Brackett received from Virginia officials. He says, *The jailor referred him to the Judge, and the Judge referred him back to the jailor. The jailor spoke of the sheriff's power to admit visitors within the jail, and the sheriff preferred to leave those matters to the Judge. The Judge again said that Brown had passed from his control, and that he did not consider himself bound to act in the matter. The Judge, however, was willing if the jailor was and the jailor was willing if the Judge was. Between them all, the sculptor's opportunities seemed to be growing fainter and fainter, until it was suggested that if he would wait a day or two, he could have every facility, but that the renewal of the excitement, caused by the Boston lawyer's extraordinary course, rendered it impossible to comply at present with his wish.*

The excitement House describes was palpable. In *The Evening Post*, Brackett recalls, *The scenes in the streets, at this time while the trials progressed, were indescribably crowded, excited, confused. During the early morning hours a constant stream of old wagons meandered in from all distances and directions through the countryside. As each arrived the driver would tie his horse to the fence with a bit of rope or "tow-strong," adding his outfit to the long row of ramshackle vehicles and harnesses rigged together with odds and ends of parti-colored this or that. Then the new arrival would proceed to the hotel bar, drink down a glass of raw whiskey, rub his forearm across his mouth, and amble over to the court house. In the afternoon, the stream ebbed.*

"Comin' in to-morrow?" one retreating figure would ask of another. "No—reckon I won't come in again till the hangin'."

The hotel man sided with nobody. He kept his hotel.

In this atmosphere, Brackett was seen as a highly suspect character. House notes, *The jailor moreover informed Mr. Brackett that his mission in town was well known, and that there was an immense opposition to it, some hundreds of people having called on him and insisted, with all the arguments they could bring, that no such thing should be permitted. . . Mr. Brackett will be obliged to return without accomplishing his object, for it is wholly impossible to satisfy the jealous Virginians that there is not in his visit here a great deal more than meets the eye. He has been told that he is 'a marked man,' and must bear the penalty.*

Brackett's *Evening Post* account continues: *At last, in despair of effecting my mission through diplomacy, I began to think of means more dark. But Capt. Avis, Brown's kind, but invulnerable, jailor, stood in my way. To attempt anything with his knowledge and without express official permission would be worse than useless. The assistant jailor, however, presented a different front. According to a story told me later, this man had known Brown in Kansas; but whatever the cause, he was willing to connive in my scheme to the extent of his power. Nevertheless he was greatly perturbed by the fear of discovery and made me promise never to tell the tale, should anything be effected through his agency, during his life-time. . .*

Finally, the opportunity arrived. The trial of Shields Green, one of Brown's negro raiders, came on, and Capt. Avis was obliged to conduct the prisoners from the jail to the court house. In anticipation of this movement, I had prepared a conventional drawing of a head. Taking the drawing and my measuring instruments and accompanied by Mr. Griswold [Brown's attorney], I went to Brown's cell. Mr. Griswold entered and explained to Brown my purpose.

Brown, who had no personal vanity, who felt that his work was done, and that his personality would soon cease to be of any moment whatever, was not interested. But when Griswold said, "It is at the desire of your Boston friends that Mr. Bracket comes." The old man at once acquiesced.

Now came our consideration of the underjailer's fears. For his sake I must be able to swear, if questioned, that I had never entered his prisoner's cell. So I stood on the threshold, sketch in hand, almost near enough to Brown to touch him, while Griswold, with my instruments and by my minute directions, made each measurement. These I noted down in their several places on my sketch, photographing the subject on my brain the while.

However, before that happy outcome, Brackett had to convince Brown of the seriousness of his purpose. He had been warned by Mrs. Stearns that Brown would initially refuse his request. In the *Topeka Daily Capital* he elaborates on the difficulty he faced in persuading Brown to assist him. *Through the open door I saw the object of my pilgrimage quietly reading but heavily loaded with chains. He was sitting in a chair, with both hands chained and his feet chained to the floor. Only those who saw in that miserable prison can have any adequate conception of the moral grandeur of his presence! Everybody and everything was dwarfed in comparison. He looked up from his book, when addressed by his counsel, and listened attentively to the request conveyed from me. Impressive as the scene was, I could not restrain a smile when his reply repeated the very words of Mrs. Stearns – "Nonsense! All nonsense! Better give the money to the poor!" When Mr. Griswold said he must remember that he was becoming famous and that posterity would like to see how he looked, the prophecy was again fulfilled and the response came even more emphatic, "No consequence to posterity how I looked! Give the money to the poor!" For some time Mr. Griswold labored to change his purpose, but finally turned to me (still standing outside the door) and said, "It is no use, he will not yield one jot. I am sorry for your disappointment, but it is useless arguing further." The moment then had come for the last resort. "Please say to him that I have come at the express wish and pecuniary expense of Mrs. Stearns, and that she will be deeply disappointed if I return without the measurements for a bust." I watched his face eagerly while Mr. Griswold repeated to him these words, on which hung all my hopes. As he listened I could see signs of interest, mingled with surprise, in his face; then a grave thoughtfulness. Presently his hands dropped at his sides, and he seemed lost in thought. Then lifting his head and straitening himself up, he said, with emotion: "Anything Mr. or Mrs. Stearns desires. Take the measurements."*

Returning to the *Evening Post* account, Brackett presents his trip's intriguing coda:

Meantime, during all these days, young House had been busily writing his reports, full of malice and laughter, for the Tribune. Still masked by his Democratic credentials, he associated Greeley with the Charlestonians and gleaned what news he wished without let or hindrance. But as the irritation aroused by his letters grew, so sharpened the search for the author. Therefore, it became increasingly necessary to observe all strategy in conveying the manuscripts to the destination. As I was packing my bag to leave, House appeared at my chamber door with a grave request to be allowed to make my toilet. Producing his copy, written on dozens of sheets of thin foolscap, he wound it around and around my calves and thighs, finally gingerly helping me into my trousers. In that costume, I reached New York, went at once to the Tribune office, and to Horace Greeley in person.

When Mr. Greeley heard that I came fresh from Charlestown, he was of course much interested, and wished to settle down for a talk.

"With much pleasure," said I: "but I am pretty heavily clad. Will you excuse me if I undress a little in your office?"

Scarcely concealing his surprise, Mr. Greeley consented. I took off my trousers forthwith, and sheet by sheet disrobed myself of a whole week's correspondence.

Greeley laughed aloud.

In what was probably the report that Brackett delivered to Greeley, House informs his readers of Brackett's ultimate success. He reports, *The adventure of Mr. Brackett, the sculptor, of which I have before informed you, had the oddest possible termination. It is a fact that, after all the watchfulness of jailors, all the interference of citizens, all the discouragements of Judge and Sheriff, all the refusals to which he was subjected, all the public determination that he should have what he wanted, he went away some time yesterday with the desired plans and measurements in his pocket.* Probably to veil the role played by the assistant jailor, House reports that Brackett got his measurements from a third party. He concludes, *The most amusing part of it to me is, that, now that the sculptor has gone away there is a considerable revulsion of feeling, and many persons express sorrow at his disappointment, which they think he ought not to have been made to suffer. To meet this, it is asserted that the authorities were really willing to admit Mr. Brackett, and that nothing but the positive and imperative refusal of Brown to see him, deterred them. To hear this, knowing that Brown did with perfect readiness afford opportunities of procuring the requisite measurements, and that he himself asked for Mr. Brackett in vain, does not add to one's confidence in Virginia veracity.*

John Brown was hanged on December 2, 1859, sixteen months before the outbreak of the Civil War. He had prophetically written in his final note: "The crimes of this guilty land will never be purged away but with blood."

A Sublime Portrait

By this time Brackett was back home, working on his bust. In her letter to the *New York Tribune*, Lydia Maria Child gives a picture of his state of mind. "When the artist returned, his soul was so completely absorbed in his work, that John Brown was continually before him, in the dreams of the night and the mental visions of the day. He read attentively all his writings and sayings, in order to become thoroughly imbued with his character. With such concentration of thought, perhaps it is not extraordinary that he should have produced an excellent likeness."[171]

Modeling the head first in clay, Brackett then made a plaster cast. He presented it to Mary Stearns who was so pleased she immediately ordered a marble copy. In a 1889 letter to Bowditch, she recalled, "Brackett has caught the expression which was stamped into my memory on that first interview and renewed and strengthened by every subsequent one: a moral grandeur which culminated in that miserable prison at Charlestown. On his return Brackett said to me, 'Mrs. Stearns, you have never seen John Brown. You can have no idea how he dwarfed everybody in Virginia; with what sublimity he sat in a dingy room, chained with ox chains to the floor!!!' That look must make the informing life of the statue."[172]

Mary Stearns commissioned a number of plaster copies to be distributed to friends of abolition as well as a bronze version that went to the President of Haiti who was holding a state funeral for Brown. Other recipients included the French poet and novelist Victor Hugo, the Kansas Historical Society, Booker T. Washington, Franklin Sanborn and Wendell Phillips.[173] The marble version remained in Mary Stearns possession and Bowditch reports, "Seldom, if ever, did Mr. Phillips enter the hall without standing before it, always newly impressed with the moral sublimity, it is so superbly represented, and sometimes adding in my ear, with characteristic pleasantry, "I wish mine were as good as this."[174]

Admirers included Charles Sumner, who declared "There is nothing the sun shines upon so like Michael Angelo's 'Moses' [175] and James Jackson Jarves, the dyspeptic art critic who concluded an essay otherwise eviscerating the American art scene with this praise of Brackett's John Brown: "Exhibiting with Olympian breadth of sentiment the intense, moral heroism of the reformer, it is an American type of a Jove, one of those rare surprises in art, irrespective of technical finish or perfection in modeling, which shows in what high degree the artist was impressed by the soul of his sitter."[176] Sanborn reports that when Harriett Tubman encountered it, "The sight of it, which was new to her, threw her into a sort of ecstasy of sorrow and admiration," and that when Brown's widow encountered it when it was on display at the Boston Atheneaum, she broke into tears. [177]

It is easy to understand the success of Brackett's bust. As Sanborn mentions, Brackett relied in part on a daguerreotype taken by Boston photographer John B. Heywood in May 1859 during his last trip to Boston. (In fact, House, the *Tribune* reporter, reports that Brackett tried to bring another photographer into the jail cell to get a last likeness but was stymied by jail officials.) One can see both similarities and the differences between the daguerreotype and sculpture. Heywood's image presents a half-length, three quarter view of Brown in the rumpled suit that he would be wearing when captured in Harper's Ferry. He slouches slightly and his hands are tucked into his pockets as he stares at the viewer with a steady appraising expression. Both daguerreotype and sculpture capture the full beard Brown had grown as a disguise during his travels out west and both present the fiercely furrowed brow and deep set eyes of a man of singular purpose. But, as in his death mask of Washington Allston, Brackett gives Brown the other worldly gaze of a man who is looking beyond us into the future and he eliminates all details of clothing in order to remove his subject from prosaic realities of daily life.

In his *Evening Post* account Brackett reveals that these were conscious decisions, made to suggest a distinction between Brown the man and Brown the symbol. He says, *The bust as you see it, is a little poetized. A man who paints a picture of a great man and puts no greatness into it, saying that he sees none, errs both in perception and in art. In this case the idealization is elusive—not to be located in any one feature. But it exists, and purposely, the more truthfully to express the character of the subject. Yet John Brown was not himself a great man, but rather a forerunner of great things. He was a blind instrument, blindly cutting the way to the death of thousands and the birth of a new age.*[178]

War!

And indeed, events were compounding. Brown's execution was the harbinger of the coming apocalypse. In 1860 Abraham Lincoln won the Republican nomination on the third ballot. He went on to win the Presidency with only 39% of the vote in a four-man race and without a single vote from ten of the fifteen slave states. Death threats forced the new President to travel to his inauguration incognito. Six weeks after Lincoln's election South Carolina took the lead in seceding from the Union, followed shortly thereafter by six more states who together declared themselves The Confederate States of America. In a final resolution of the Kansas/Nebraska fight, Kansas was admitted to the Union as a free state on January 29, 1861, with a vote made possible by the departure of a group of Southern Senators.

On April 12, 1861, little more than a month after Lincoln's inauguration, Southern forces fired upon Fort Sumter in South Carolina. The war had officially begun. The Civil War would last until May 9, 1865 and would take the lives of between 620,000 and 750,000 soldiers along with an undetermined number of civilians. It was and remains America's bloodiest conflict.

Though he had by now reached the venerable age of 41 and was the father of three children with another on the way, Brackett joined the war effort. From Dec 4, 1861 to March 6, 1862 he served as the First Lieutenant and Battalion Quartermaster for the 1st Massachusetts Cavalry. In the capacity he was responsible for gathering supplies and equipping the regiment prior to its reassignment down south. When the 1st Massachusetts Cavalry was moved to South Carolina, Brackett resigned his commission to stay behind in Winchester. For the remainder of the war, Brackett continued his association with the abolitionist movement and with his abolitionist friends. One consequential outcome of this was his contribution to the career of Edmonia Lewis, the first female American sculptor of color to achieve international renown.

Mentoring Edmonia Lewis

Lewis is a fascinating character. (fig 23) Many of the basic facts about her biography are unclear, in part because she became very skilled at crafting her own image. Throughout her life she gave numerous interviews in which her story would shift depending on her reading of her audience. Especially fuzzy are details surrounding her childhood and the origins of her art career. She was born near Albany, New York either in 1842 or 1844 to a free Black father and a part Chippewa mother, both of whom died when she was quite young. She was taken in by her mother's family and was given the name "Wildfire." Lewis would later paint a romantic picture of a wild and liberated childhood, saying, "Until I was twelve years old, I led this wandering life, fishing, swimming, and making moccasins."[179] Though she often later liked to characterize herself as an uneducated naïf, in fact she received a good education at an abolitionist school in New York. Then she enrolled in Oberlin College in Ohio courtesy of her half brother Samuel who had made a fortune in the California gold rush. At Oberlin, Lewis became embroiled in scandal. Again, stories are conflicting. Lewis was accused of poisoning two fellow classmates, both of whom recovered. As the accusations spread throughout the community, she was set upon by a mob and almost killed. She stood trial for the crime but was acquitted for lack of evidence. In what today looks like trumped up charges motivated by racism, she was later accused of stealing art materials and abetting a burglary and was barred from graduation.

After her unhappy sojourn in Ohio, Lewis moved back East. She later liked to describe the life-changing story of her encounter with a sculpture of Benjamin Franklin in Boston. She recounts being overwhelmed and, not knowing the

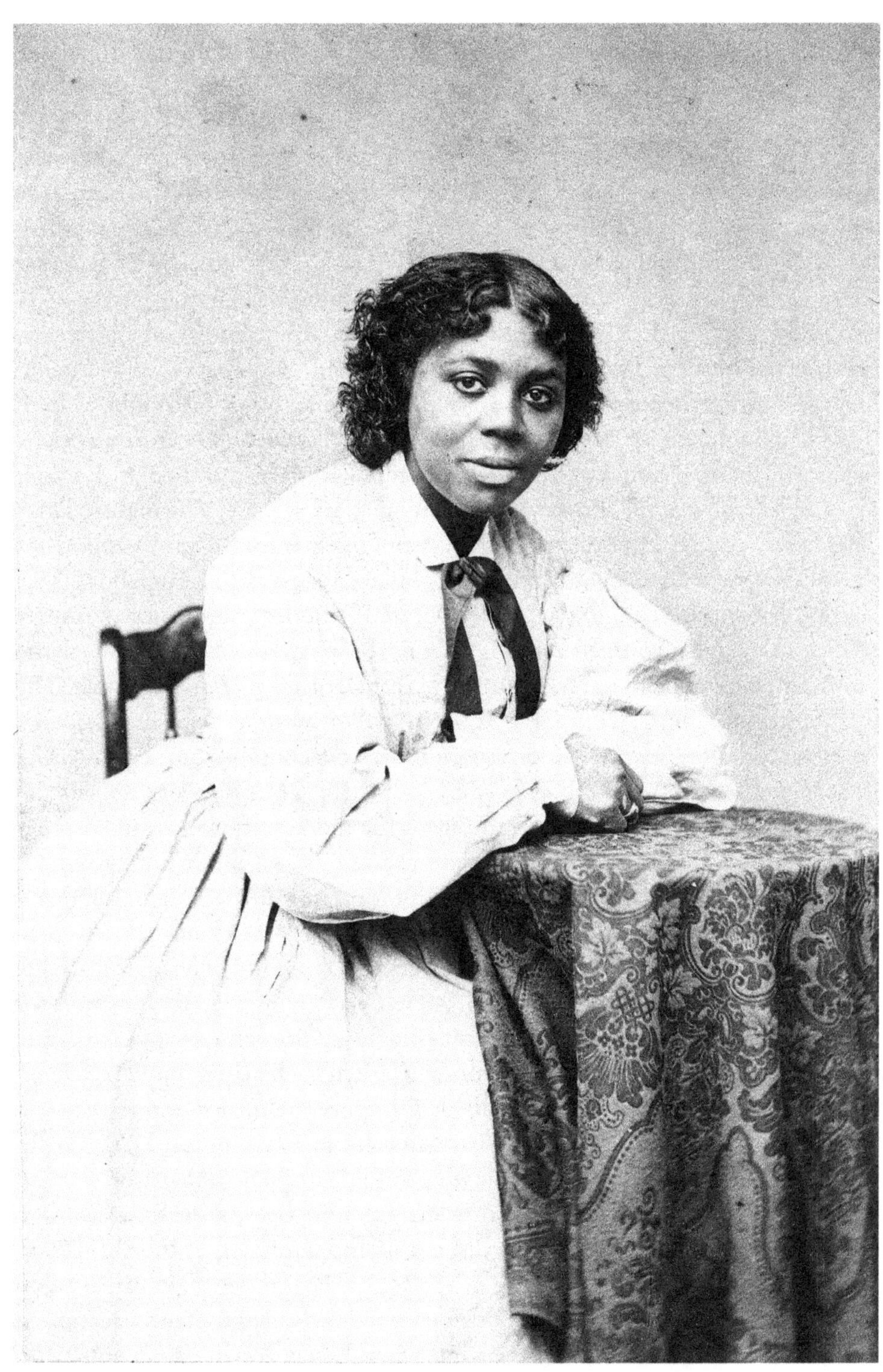

fig. 23 *Edmonia Lewis visiting card*, photo by Augustus Marshall, 1870, Collection of the National Museum of African American History and Culture. Courtesy of the Smithsonian Museum.

word for sculpture, declaring, 'Oh, how I would love to make a man in stone!'[180] This naivete was certainly feigned as she had been studying art and working from casts of classical sculptures at Oberlin.

What is undisputed is that Lewis eventually made her way to Italy where she was part of what Henry James termed "that strange sisterhood of American 'lady sculptors' who at one time settled upon the seven hills in a white, marmorean flock."[181] During her years in Rome, Lewis was celebrated by critics and collectors on both sides of the Atlantic and her studio was a gathering place for luminaries passing through the city on the Grand Tour. She gained attention both for her busts of figures like Abraham Lincoln, William Lloyd Garrison, Henry Wadsworth Longfellow, Frederick Douglass, Ulysses S. Grant and John Brown, and for various "ideal" works that explore Native American and African American themes. Some of these relate directly to slavery and emancipation. *Forever Free* (now at the Howard University Gallery of Art, Washington, D.C) depicts an African-American man and woman emerging from the bonds of slavery. Several sculptures are drawn from Henry Wadsworth Longfellow's epic poem *The Song of Hiawatha* which celebrated America's indigeneous history prior to European contact. Among these are *The Arrow Maker* (now at the Smithsonian American Art Museum) and the *Marriage of Hiawatha* (owned by the Stark Museum of Art in Orange, Texas). As a result of her acclaim, Lewis was awarded a number of important and lucrative commissions, culminating in her much celebrated *The Death of Cleopatra*. (fig 24) This work depicts the legendary queen seated in a royal throne at the moment of her death with her head flung back as the poison from the venomous asp enters her system. It created a sensation at the Centennial Exhibition in Philadelphia in 1876 and was subsequently shipped to Chicago for the 1878 World's Fair.

However by 1890 Lewis career was in free-fall, a casualty of changing artistic tastes. The neo-classicism she had mastered was giving way to a fashion for Romanticism inspired by Rodin. Even her famous Cleopatra disappeared, only to be recovered in 1988 when art historian Marilyn Richardson found it covered in house paint in a storage room outside Chicago.[182] Cleaned and repaired, it is now ensconced in the Smithsonian Museum in Washington D.C. Lewis' place and date of death were unknown until 2011 when Richardson located her unmarked grave and found records documenting Lewis' death in London on September 17, 1907 of Bright's disease, an inflammation of the kidneys.[183]

Edward Brackett enters this story in 1862 at the beginning of her career when Lewis, fresh from Ohio, arrived in Boston armed with a letter of introduction to William Lloyd Garrison. In an 1873 interview, Lewis described her entry into the Boston art world: " [Garrison] gave me an introduction to Mr. Brackett,

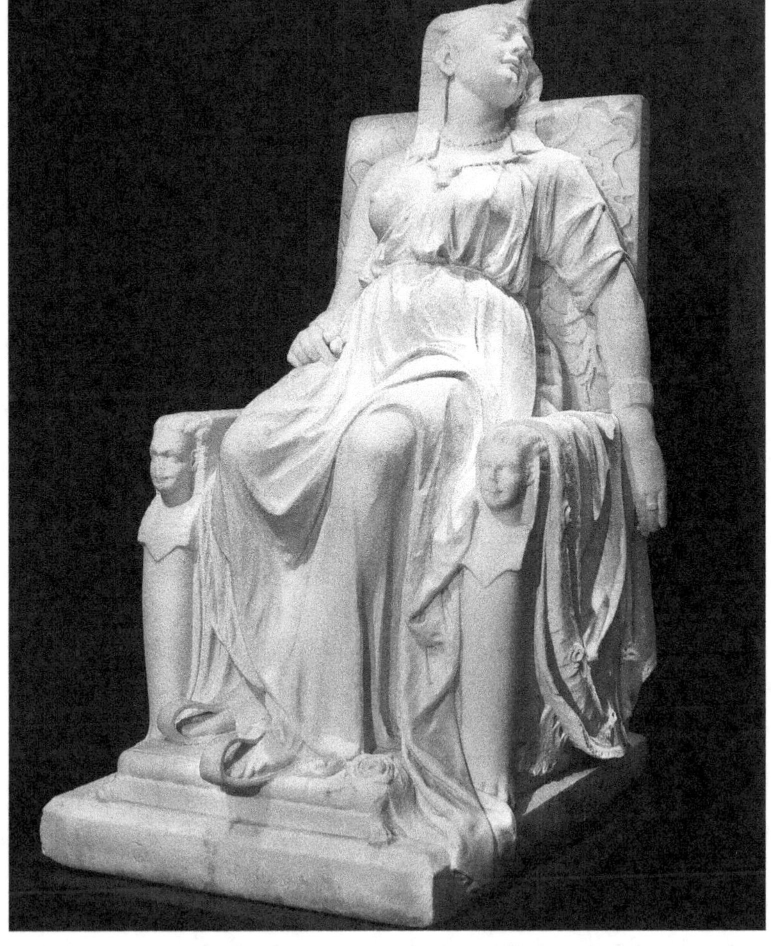

fig. 24 *Death of Cleopatra* by Edmonia Lewis, 1876, marble, Smithsonian Art Museum. Courtesy of Creative Commons.

an artist, and he gave me a lump of clay and a little baby's foot. He asked me to work at it. I asked if I might stay there, and he said 'No.' I went to my little room and made a foot out of the clay as well as I could. I took it to Mr. Brackett, and every time I did so he broke it up, until three weeks had passed. He then seemed really pleased with my work, and gave me a lady's hand to do. I worked on the lady's hand, and got on nicely. Then I worked on a medallion."[184]

The medallion was of John Brown, based on Brackett's bust and crafted with the artist's sanction. Already exhibiting the savvy marketing flair that would bring her success in Italy, Lewis then sold copies of this medallion at anti-slavery meetings. Seeking more buyers, she placed an ad in Garrison's *The Liberator* that read as follows:

MEDALLION OF JOHN BROWN – the subscriber invites the attention of her friends and the public to a number of Medallions of John Brown, just completed by her and which may be seen at rooms No. 89, Studio Building, Tremont Street. M.

Lewis followed this up with a bust of Robert Gould Shaw, the fallen leader of the all-Black 54th Massachusetts regiment. Copies sold briskly to abolitionist admirers of the Boston hero. And she began accepting orders. In the interview above, she continues, "Dr. Bowdrege [Henry I Bowditch], of Boston, gave me an order to make a medallion of his father, who was an old navigator. He gave me twenty-five dollars for it. It was my first order. Then I made a bust of Voltaire. About that time I got a studio. And called myself an artist, although my friends laughed at me for it."[186]

These friends included a number of Boston's leading female abolitionists. They encouraged her and worked to find her patrons while privately revealing a discomfort with her drive and manners. This double standard, various contemporary commentators charge, reveals an underlying strain of paternalism that verged on racism in the thinking of White abolitionists. One of Lewis' biographers, Charmaine Nelson, remarks, "Although patrons and mentors such as Lydia Maria Child and a fellow artist such as Anne Whitney may have expressed pain and regret about doing so, they diminished, belittled, or chastised Lewis, often relying on commonly held Black or Native stereotypes, in letters written directly to the sculptor or to other acquaintances or family." [187]

By 1866, through sales of medallions, the Shaw bust and other commissions, Lewis had put together enough money to make the pilgrimage to Italy. She would later complain about her reception in Boston, telling an interviewer in 1878, "I was practically driven to Rome in order to obtain the opportunities for art culture and to find a social atmosphere where I was not constantly reminded of my color. The land of liberty had no room for a colored sculptor."[188]

Brackett's mentoring of Lewis was relatively short-lived. The Brown medallion went on sale in January 1864 and by that August, according to one of Lewis' abolitionist friends, he had "given her up." [189] The reason for the break is not provided, so we can only speculate. Did Brackett belatedly feel affronted that Lewis was using copies of his John Brown to advance her career? Did he believe, as Lydia Maria Child maintained, that Lewis was jumping the gun and putting her ambition ahead of her training? Was he jealous of the fact that this young woman was going to make the voyage to Rome that he had never been able to manage?

Reflecting the malleability of Lewis's self-presentations, by 1878 Brackett disappears altogether from Lewis' accounts of her early history. This is evident in newspaper reports and in a speech given by Henry Highland Garnet, pastor of New York's Shiloh Presbyterian Church during a dedication of Lewis' bust of John Brown. As the first Black Presbyterian Church in America, Shiloh had been an important stop on the Underground Railroad. With Lewis beaming in the audience, Garnet extolled her virtues and retold the story of her arrival in Boston where now it was William Lloyd Garrison, not Brackett, for whom she proved her mettle by modeling a baby's foot out of a lump of clay.[190]

If Lewis' relationship with Brackett ended badly, she nevertheless learned much from him. Along with hands-on lessons in modeling, she also absorbed Brackett's strategy for getting on in the art world. Lewis' biographer Kirsten Buick suggests that she gleaned from Brackett that an artist's potential for fame rested on the recognizability and renown of the subjects he or she chose to depict. [191] This is clearly reflected in her early decision to sculpt Robert Gould Shaw and John Brown, both viewed as martyrs to the cause by abolitionists. In Italy, she achieved considerable success with the bust of John Brown celebrated by Henry Highland Garnet above. While news reports of the time suggest that she created it from photographs, Lewis' sculpture bears a remarkable resemblance to the famous bust sculpted years earlier by her mentor. One might also see Brackett's influence in her *Death of Cleopatra*, which like his *Shipwrecked Mother and Child*, presented the figure as a corpse that some critics found jarringly realistic.

War's End

In 1863, Brackett created one last Civil War related bust. His sculpture of General Benjamin Franklin Butler is now in the National Portrait Gallery of the Smithsonian Institution. (fig 25) Butler holds an equivocal place in abolitionist history. Born in New Hampshire and raised in Massachusetts, Butler was a staunch Democrat who supported Jefferson Davis in the 1860 Democratic National Convention. Though he was not an abolitionist, he was a Unionist. After a career as a lawyer and political operative in Massachusetts, he joined the Union Army where he gained an unsavory reputation for abrasive tactics and self-dealing. He acquired the nickname "Spoons" for his theft of silverware from Southern homes during his military campaign. He was also dubbed "Beast Butler" during his tenure as commander of Union occupation forces in New Orleans. There he gained notoriety for his "Woman's Order" which declared that any woman who showed disrespect for the occupying Union soldiers would be treated as "a woman of the town plying her avocation" (in other words a prostitute.) He was known for his shameless self-promotion, opportunism and general tactical incompetence.

Such negatives are counterbalanced by Butler's role in moving the Union toward emancipation. In the early stages of the war, Lincoln's focus on saving

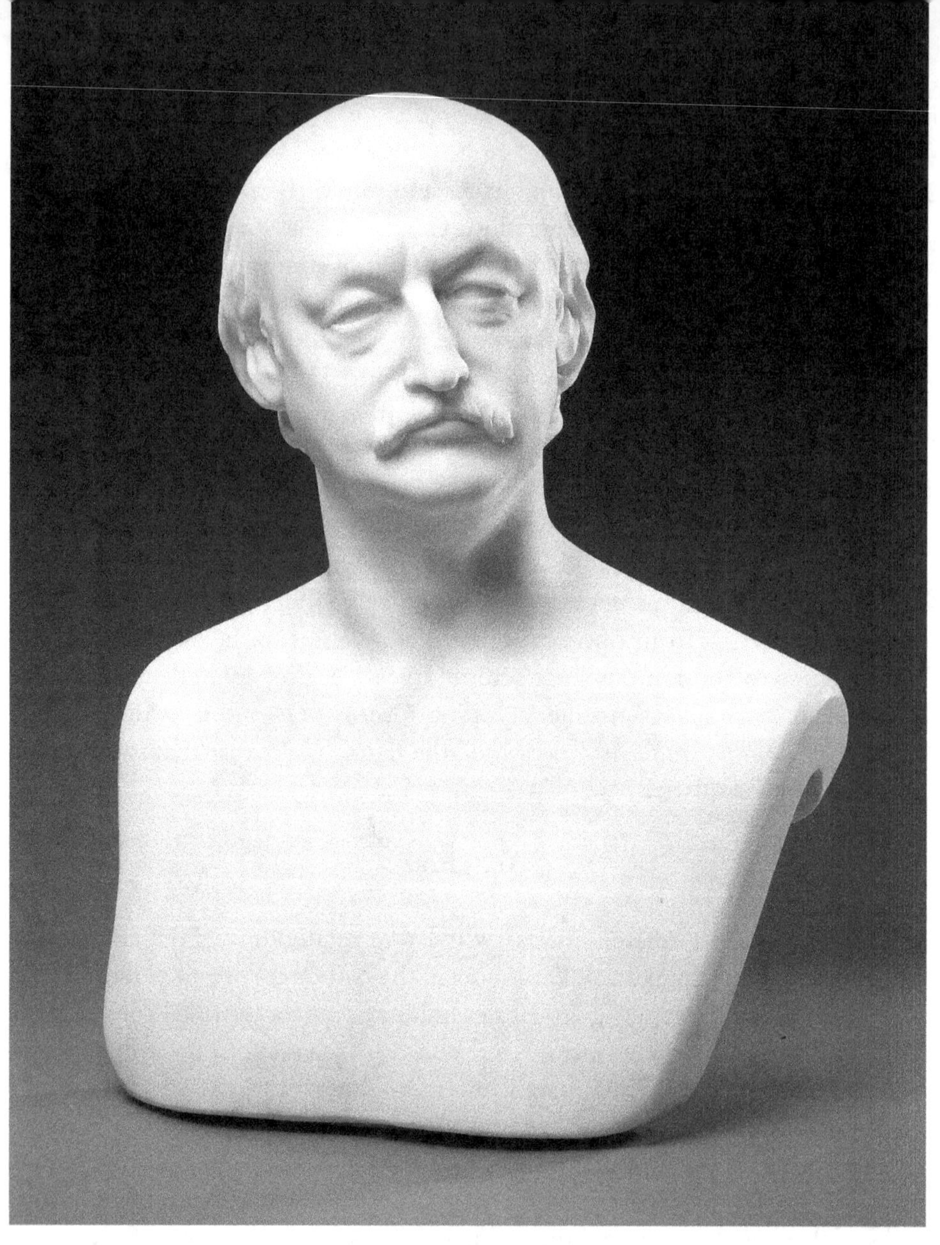

fig. 25 *Benjamin F. Butler* by Edward Augustus Brackett, marble, 1863, National Portrait Gallery. Courtesy of the Smithsonian Institution.

the Union yielded a promise that the Union army would honor the Fugitive Slave Act and protect the human property of enslavers in states that had not seceded. In a widely publicized and very controversial incident, the commanding officer at Fort Pickens in Pensacola, Florida ordered the return of a group of fugitives who had daringly escaped their masters through miles of swampland. Abolitionists were outraged, and some, like Lydia Maria Child, expressed a wish for sufficient Union defeats to convince the free states to support emancipation.

Three months later, in May 1861, Butler faced a similar situation when three fugitives arrived at his command post in Fort Monroe, Virginia. The situation was somewhat clearer, as by now Virginia has seceded. But even more decisive for Butler was the fact that these men told him that their master, a Confederate colonel, planned to send them to South Carolina to build fortifications for the Confederate war effort. Seeking a justification for defying the Fugitive Slave Act, he ingeniously decided to declare the fugitives "contraband," meaning they were goods illegally smuggled across enemy lines which need not be returned to their owners. When word of this designation spread, thousands of other fugitives made their way to this and other "contraband camps" situated near Union encampments located in the occupied South. These camps became stations for recruiting Black men of military age into the Union Army.

Brackett's bust of Butler captures his pugnacious character. In his representation, Butler's head tilts slightly as he gazes out of heavy lidded eyes with a crafty, calculating expression. Photos of Butler reveal that Brackett somewhat idealized his portly subject who nevertheless wears an air of gruff irritability. But however dour this representation appears to modern eyes, Butler was pleased with the bust, and in a letter to his wife wrote, "Do you want to see me? Do the next best thing. Send down to Brackett and get the marble bust which he has done. Get up a handsome pedestal for it – he has been paid for it."[192]

In 1865 the war ended, slavery was abolished by the Thirteenth Amendment to the Constitution, Lincoln was assassinated and Reconstruction began. Though history has demonstrated how incomplete the nation's journey toward racial equality has been, there was a sense among some weary abolitionists that their task was done. Notably, William Lloyd Garrison closed his abolitionist newspaper in December of that year. But in fact the trauma brought on by the Civil War was not so easily healed. The task of mourning fueled a rise of interest in the Spiritualist movement, which promised that the dead were still conscious and accessible. Such beliefs offered solace to many of the Radical Republicans who had struggled so profoundly for the end of slavery, Edward Brackett among them.

Chapter 4
MATERIALIZED APPARITIONS

In 1908, Edward Brackett put out an engaging little compilation of his writings on his experiences with spiritualism. Titled *Materialized Apparitions: If Not Beings from Another Life, What Are They*, it relayed his encounters with beings "from the other side" as well as his theories and speculations about them. The excerpt below captures the spirit of this text and foregrounds one of his repeated visitors:

"What claimed to be my niece came to me in a very beautiful illuminated dress. I asked her to appear to me at the next séance dressed in the same way. I took a friend with me to that séance, expecting to astonish him with the wonderful illumination. But, instead of keeping her promise, she came out in a dark dress, such as I had never seen her wear. As my friend had gone up to the cabinet with me, I was greatly disappointed in the way she came, and said, 'Bertha, why do you come in this dress?' Placing her right elbow in the palm of her left hand and her index finger on her lip, in a bashful, coquettish way, she said, 'I'm in mourning.' I said, 'For what?' She replied, 'I expect I have lost my friend.' I said to my companion, 'This is something new; I don't understand it.' While we were both looking at her, instantly the dark dress disappeared, and she stood before us radiant in her beautiful garments. With a girlish laugh she threw her arms around my neck, kissed me and said, 'It is all right now, uncle.' The disappearance of the dark dress was quite as marvellous to my friend as the illumination."[193]

Materialized Apparitions recounts Brackett's evolution from spiritualist skeptic to believer. Key to his conversion were his repeated encounters with Bertha, a spirit who identified herself as the materialization of his departed niece. Brackett had never met the living Bertha, as her family lived hundreds of miles away and Bertha had died twenty years before at the age of four. But he was delighted to discover that the dead toddler had grown up into a charming young woman during her years in the spirit world.

Bertha was a frequent visitor to the over one hundred séances that Brackett attended in the mid 1880s. He reveled in her playful coquetry and intelligent conversation and recounts in *Materialized Apparitions* how she enjoyed playing little tricks while conjuring objects out of thin air. In the excerpt above, he uses this incident to illustrate his principle that spirits are most receptive to those who approach them with sympathy and love.

Bertha's appearances took place in private sessions in darkened rooms where small groups had gathered in the company of a professional medium. There were dozens of mediums in the Boston area, and Brackett sampled many of them, though he had certain favorites. Each medium had a distinctive style and particular technique for communicating with the dead. However there were certain constants. Séances generally took place in parlors that had been outfitted with black curtains. Often they featured "cabinets" like the one mentioned above. These were small rooms within the room where the medium would retire to contact her (mediums were usually female) "control". Control spirits served as a bridge between the visible and invisible worlds and invited other spirits to appear. In a single session as many as forty or fifty apparitions might present themselves, often materializing inside the cabinet but sometimes rising as from a mist on the floor, or suddenly emerging full blown alongside the chair of one of the séance's living participants. Once materialized, they took the form of flesh and blood humans, though often they glowed with an unearthly illumination.

Brackett's encounters with Bertha had a whiff of eroticism about them. The youthful spirit appeared in filmy dresses with arms bared so as to demonstrate that she had nothing concealed in her sleeves. Other visitors to these séances reported with amusement how the sexagenarian Brackett enjoyed taking Bertha's arm and parading around the séance room with her. However, as his wife and young daughter were also frequently in attendance, it seems clear that nothing untoward occurred between spirit and living human.

Like many of his contemporaries, Brackett came to spiritualism following the death of a loved one. His first wife Amanda died at age 51 in 1871 of causes that are not recorded and he penned a number of poems to her loving memory. In 1872 he remarried - his new wife Elizabeth was his niece by marriage and the daughter of Amanda's sister. The two explored spiritualism together, sometimes bringing their young daughter, also named Bertha, with them to séances. With his usual energy, Brackett threw himself into the study of spiritualist practices, recording his investigations and theories in *Materialized Apparitions*.

Brackett believed himself a hard-nosed observer and he reports how he carefully examined the rooms and cabinets in which the séances took place. He satisfied himself that there were no secret doors or hiding places for confederates and on occasion he accompanied the medium into the cabinet to make sure she was not assuming the role of the embodied spirits. He believed the "perceptive faculties" he had developed as a sculptor and his "thorough abhorrence of fraud, whether in the séance-room or in the pulpit," put him in an ideal position to evaluate the validity of spirit manifestations. Once he had convinced himself of its validity, Brackett's belief in spiritualism was unwavering. He continued to believe and to defend the practice, even when, a decade later a young actress came forward and reported that she had posed as Bertha.

Spiritualist America

From the perspective of the 21ˢᵗ century, it is easy to mock Brackett's credulity. Today spiritualism is generally relegated to realm of crackpot theories, parlor tricks and spooky entertainments. But in the 19ᵗʰ century, it permeated all aspects of American life and was taken seriously by people in the highest reaches of government, science and the arts. Mary Todd Lincoln held séances in the White House and reported visitations from her departed son Willie. Thomas Edison worked on a "spirit phone" that would let the living communicate with the dead. Cornelius Vanderbilt, richest man in America, ascribed his business success to advice from market savvy spirits.

There are many reasons for spiritualism's hold on 19ᵗʰ century America. Certainly a major factor was a pervasive sense of mortality emerging from the deadliest of all American wars. The Civil War had cost the lives of an estimated 2% of the population. The death toll is estimated at between 600,000 and 700,000.   Nor was the war itself the only cause of death during the period. Added to the direct death toll were epidemics of deadly diseases like cholera, smallpox, malaria, and yellow fever. These were exacerbated by the unsanitary conditions of army camps, polluted waterways, unburied bodies of animals and soldiers and the dislocation of large numbers of former slaves. Meanwhile rates of maternal death in childbirth remained high throughout the 1860s – estimated at 500 to 1,000 maternal deaths for every 100,000 births. Thirty percent of children born in the post war years did not reach the age of five. Surrounded by so much death, it is not surprising that the living sought solace in the idea that their departed loved ones remained nearby and accessible. Spiritualism had already taken hold in the antebellum years. But interest exploded in the years after the war. By 1880 there were an estimated eight million spiritualists in America and Europe.

Changing attitudes toward faith nourished the movement. Spiritualism exists on a continuum between religion and science. It posits the existence of a spirit world but does not explicitly require a belief in God. And it conceives of an intangible realm that is subject to the tools of empirical research. It is no coincidence that spiritualism emerged at a time of astonishing scientific discoveries and new technologies based on the existence invisible forces – among them electricity, electromagnetism, radioactivity, the telegraph, and the x-ray. In this context, the existence of a spirit world that might be accessed through what was sometimes dubbed the "spiritual telegraph" did not seem far-fetched. Many of the same experimental methods applied to prove now accepted phenomena were also used to demonstrate the persistence of life beyond death.

The slippery nature of spiritualism's identity may explain its appeal to a world whose certainties had become unsettled. Spiritualism played into an increasing discomfort with the hellfire and brimstone pronouncements of Calvinist versions of Christianity. Instead it took its place alongside credos like Quakerism, Universalism and Unitarianism that replaced Calvinist convictions of human depravity with a belief in humanity's essential decency. Instead of hell, spiritualists looked forward to an afterlife of continued spiritual growth in which they could remain connected with their living loved ones. As we shall see, spiritualism became deeply entwined with many of the most progressive social reform movements of the day. Abolitionists, advocates of women's and children's rights and Temperance crusaders counted numerous spiritualists among their ranks.

The Birth of a Movement

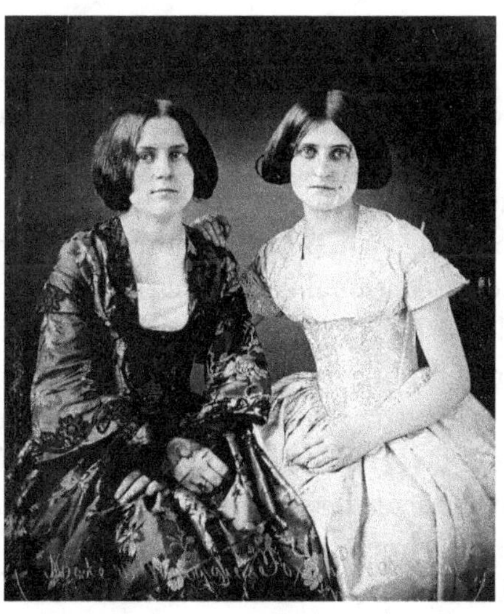

fig. 26 *Kate and Maggie Fox, Spirit Mediums from Rochester* by Thomas Martin Easterly, 1852. Public domain, via Wikimedia Commons.

Many histories of the spiritualist movement date its inception to the night of March 31, 1848 when two young girls living in upstate New York startled their parents with demonstrations of unexplainable raps apparently emanating from the walls and furniture of their old farmhouse. These initially were linked to a murdered peddler supposedly buried within the house, but before long the Fox sisters Maggie and Kate were participating in spirit communications throughout the state. (fig 26) Their much older sister Leah, joined them, setting herself up as a medium and eventually becoming their manager. Initially contact with the other side was cumbersome, with the spirits only able to answer yes or no questions. But soon the technique was refined, as spirits were introduced to recitations of the alphabet that allowed them to rap out words and whole sentences.

The story of the Fox Sisters has become legendary – as their fame grew, so did the emergence of other mediums and other means of communicating with the dead. Over time, spiritualist practices evolved from the simple rapping of the Fox sisters to include table tilting, automatic writing, trance lectures in which ordinary people (usually women) spoke with great erudition under the influence of spirits and séances which took place in darkened rooms or involved cabinets in which mediums ensconced themselves while spirits materialized in solid human forms. Photography became a vital spiritualist tool, recording the production of ectoplasm from entranced mediums and the auras of spirits hovering over living subjects. Scientists bound, probed and interrogated mediums in efforts the separate fraudsters from genuine spirit channels. The creation in 1886 of the Ouija Board democratized spiritualism, providing a method by which anyone could contact spirits by placing fingers on a planchette, - a heart shaped, moveable piece of wood - and letting hidden energies spell out words. The Ouija Board was met with opposition both by religious authorities who deemed it demonic and by professional mediums whose livelihoods it threatened. Today it remains the most popular form of spirit communication.

The Fox sisters became national celebrities as they took their show on the road. They added flourishes like the communication of two simultaneous messages, the transcription of messages in reverse script and the use of blank cards upon which words seemed to spontaneously appear. By the late 1880s, however, the aura of the Fox girls had dimmed. Kate and Maggie had married, Maggie was widowed and had converted to Catholicism, and both had become heavy drinkers. They became estranged from Leah, whom they accused of exploiting them. In 1888 Maggie dealt a near mortal blow to the movement by recanting in public in exchange for a $1500 speaking fee. She declared that she and Kate had made the rapping sounds by manipulating their knuckles, joints and toes. She recanted her recantation a year later, but was never embraced again by the spiritualist movement. Within four years all three sisters were dead.

Antecedents

While the Fox sisters ignited the Spiritualist frenzy, the ground had been prepared by various developments over the previous century. In the 18th century the Swedish philosopher, scientist and mystic Emanuel Swedenborg gained widespread attention following his assertion of a tangible connection between the material and spirit worlds. Swedenborg's many writings comprise an effort to reform Christianity by reinterpreting the Bible under the aegis of what he suggested was Divine Revelation. He proposed an ecumenical theology, outlined correspondences between the spiritual and physical realms and reread the creation myth as a narrative of humanity's transition from the materialistic to the spiritual realm. In a foretaste of spiritualism, Swedenborg maintained that there are levels or planes of existence through which the spirits travel as they evolve toward perfection and that these spirits could serve as intermediaries between God and the living. By his death in 1772, Swedenborg had published more than 30 voluminous works which would go on to influence thinkers as diverse as Arthur Conan Doyle, Ralph Waldo Emerson, William Blake, Robert Frost, Jorge Luis Borges, Carl Jung, Immanuel Kant, Helen Keller, Joseph Smith, D. T. Suzuki, and W. B. Yeats.

Seventy-five years later, in 1845, the self described "Poughkeepsie Seer" Andrew Jackson Davis claimed that Swedenborg's spirit spoke to him during a series of mesmeric trances. Little remembered today, Davis was a major force in 19th century spiritualism. Prior to his emergence as one of the movement's prime movers, he worked as a young man as a shoemaker's apprentice and then spent several years working with a trance healer. He was largely uneducated and claimed to have read only one book by his sixteenth year. Nevertheless, after his visitation, the twenty one year old Davis dictated a volume that, according to Dr. George Bush, Professor of Hebrew at the University of New York, (and distant relative of the two President Bushes) dealt with "the profoundest questions of historical and Biblical archaeology, of mythology, of the origin and affinity of language, and the progress of civilization among the different nations of the globe. . ." Bush added that Davis's erudition and learning ". . . would do honor to any scholar of the age, even if in reaching them he had the advantage of access to all the libraries of Christendom."[194]

Davis' tome was titled *The Principles of Nature, Her Divine Revelations, and a Voice to Mankind.* It was published in 1847, one year before the Fox sisters reported their mysterious rappings. In the book Davis predicted the coming of spiritualism (as he would later predict such developments as the automobile, the typewriter, and the airplane,) noting: "It is a truth that spirits commune with one another while one is in the body and the other in the higher spheres . . . and this truth will ere long present itself in the form of a living demonstration."[195] And indeed, he would later reveal that on the morning of March 31, 1848 - the day the Fox Sisters would unleash Spiritualism on the world - he wrote in his diary: "About daylight this morning a warm breathing passed over my face and I heard

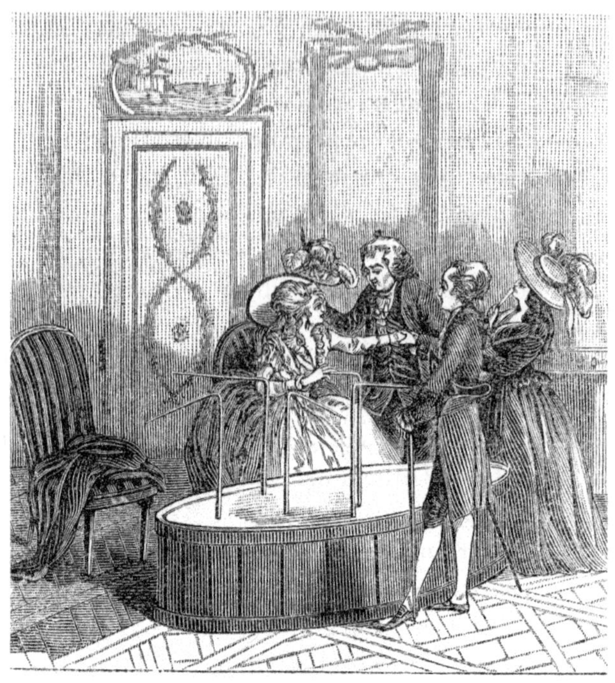

fig. 27 *Le Baquet de Mesmer*, depiction of Franz Anton Mesmer's "baquet", a
large wooden tub filled with "magnetized water," engraving, n.d.
Courtesy of Wellcome images, London.

a voice, tender and strong, saying: 'Brother, the good work has begun—behold
a living demonstration is born.'"[196]

Davis would become one of the most important theorists of Spiritualism.
He provided a philosophical link between spiritualist manifestations that were
many people's introduction to the movement and a philosophy that advocated
social reform, an embrace of natural harmony and an anti-Calvinist vision of
the divine order.

An equally important forerunner was Franz Anton Mesmer, a Viennese
born physician and healer who made his reputation in pre-revolutionary Paris.
While Swedenborg's philosophy was steeped in a belief in God, Mesmer was
a materialist. He suggested that illness was caused by an imbalance of natural
forces within the body. His theory of "animal magnetism" was in keeping with
late 18th century scientists' fascination with invisible forces. He maintained
that an invisible magnetic fluid circulates through human body and can be
manipulated to cure the body or influence the mind. Two centuries before the
hot tub became a Los Angeles staple, he developed a group cure that involved
a tub containing magnetized water. (fig 27) Participants sat around the outside

of the tub and unblocked the flow of magnetic fluid in their bodies by pressing iron rods emerging from the tub against the afflicted body part. Many of them fell into trances or convulsions from which they emerged reportedly cured.

On the eve of the French Revolution, a Royal commission investigated the efficacy of Mesmer's treatments and concluded that mesmeric fluid did not exist. A broken Mesmer died in exile in 1815. However, his theory gained new life in the 19th century when it became associated with the promotion of spiritual rather than physical health. As such it lost its connection with conventional medicine and became associated with occultism, exorcism and alternative therapies. Today mesmerism is recognized as a precursor to hypnotism but in the mid 19th century its trance states were believed to unlock access to the spirit world.

Brackett Chimes In

Edward Brackett was one of many whose path to spiritualism was paved by studies of Swedenborg and Mesmer. He opens *Materialized Apparitions* with a tribute to Swedenborg and to the philosopher's belief that spirits advance to higher states of existence through the cultivation of feelings of love and affection. Brackett also describes how his initial interest in mesmerism, sparked by lectures on the subject that he attended in New York in 1840, blossomed into a late life involvement with spiritualist materializations. By the time he wrote *Materialized Apparitions* (excerpts appeared in the Spiritualist journal FACTS in 1885 and the whole was published in 1908), Brackett had put aside his sculptural career and was pouring his creative energies into writing. In poems, polemics and autobiographical ruminations he continued to explore questions raised by spiritualism, as well as his interest in what came to be known as "New Thought". Along with *Materialized Apparitions*, he also explored these ideas in a meandering text titled *The World We Live In*.

Meanwhile Brackett continued to write poetry, much of which related to his scientific and spiritual concerns. One long poem titled *Pseudo Science* offers a meditation, by turns humorous and philosophical, on his disagreements with the materialistic view of reality that he sees embodied in Darwin's theory of evolution. It expounds on his distaste for those who sought to apply the methods of objective science to spiritual phenomena and expresses his own confidence in the Divine Intelligence. Published as part of a collection in 1904, its playful tone is suggested by its opening verse: "The gods have ceased to play their pranks,/ But in their place the modern cranks/ Rush in to fill the vacant ranks."[197]

From today's perspective, much of what Brackett believed is wrong. He dismissed Darwin's theory of evolution and Pasteur's germ theory as pseudo science. He was highly skeptical of psychological theories of the unconscious. On the other hand, recent developments in science have undermined the strict objectivity once attributed to the scientific method. They have also tempered once firm divisions between mind and matter, "natural" and artificial intelligence and life and non-life. Seen in this light, Brackett's skepticism suggests alternate paths to understanding the interrelationship of material and immaterial realities. His lively writings offer a window into the worldview of a curious and well-read 19th century amateur. They are worth reading, not for any contribution to the standard narrative of modern science, but because Brackett wrestled with the kind of questions that continue to bedevil us today. How does one resolve the conflict between faith and science? Is it really that easy, when one is confronted with emerging disciplines, to draw a firm line between science and "pseudo science"? How can we be sure that what we think we know is really true? Brackett's writings provide a way to understand from the inside how these kinds of dilemmas were experienced in late 19th century America. In the process they will help us understand the roots of our own vision of the world.

Brackett was predisposed to the new faith of spiritualism by both his philosophical predilections and his scientific interests. By adulthood he was no longer a practicing Quaker, but as we have already noted, his early immersion in that faith's open-mindedness had reinforced his political sympathies. We get a glimpse of Brackett's genial approach to religion from an anecdote recounted in the *Brackett Genealogy*. Its writer relates: "Brought up in strict Quaker faith, the habit of independent thought has made the dogmas of religion especially distasteful to him. The following story shows a line of reasoning of his. A good orthodox deacon passed his house daily in taking a cow to pasture, and many were the arguments they had on religion. One Sunday morning the deacon found him working in his garden and remonstrated. A few weeks later the deacon worked on Sunday to save his hay from spoiling. 'Why, deacon' said Mr. Brackett, 'are you working on Sunday?' The deacon answered, 'Yes. You see that thunderstorm coming. I shall lose my hay if I do not.' Mr. Brackett asked, 'How much is your hay worth?' 'Five dollars,' answered the deacon. 'Well, deacon,' said Mr. Brackett, 'I do not see much difference between us in our working on Sunday other than that I work on that day for my pleasure and you work for five dollars.'"[198]

Rethinking Death

Spiritualism provided independent thinkers like Brackett with a way to reconcile a belief in the spirit world with a rejection of the constricting doctrines and pessimistic theology of more established religions. In his writings, Brackett returns again and again to the failings of Christian doctrine, characterizing it as a collection of "unfortunate dogmas and speculations, the mummery of theatrical forms and ceremonies."[199] He condemns the implications of Christianity's focus on Christ's sacrifice, seeing it as contrary to his very American concept of human freedom. He says, "It seems strange that any one who understands human life, its individualities and its responsibilities, could have accepted any such idea. No one can assume the sins of another. Each one is responsible for his own errors. It is in vain that he pleads that some one else has paid the penalty."[200] But at the same time Brackett held firmly to what he referred to as "the pure teachings of Christianity" which he characterizes as its "wonderful embodiment of a pure democracy – the brotherhood of man, epitomized in the one sentence – 'that ye love one another.'" [201] Such sentiments, as we shall see, were part of a movement known as the New Thought.

Brackett's beliefs included an embrace of such practices as spiritualism, mesmerism and phrenology that were regarded with suspicion by conventional religious folk. In *Materialized Apparitions* he takes a jab at a neighbor, presumably the deacon mentioned above, for rejecting spiritualism while declaiming its consolations. He says, "My ministerial neighbor throws theological brickbats at me because I choose to study a subject which he has not the courage to face, and which, if not a reality, he lied about in his last funeral sermon, when he told the mourners that their 'dear friend is not dead, but still living and hovering around them.'"[202]

Aside from spiritualism, Brackett's closest religious affiliations were with the Universalists and the Unitarians. These two closely aligned sects would merge in 1961, but even in the mid 19th century they shared basic philosophical tenets. These included a rejection of Calvinist notions of predestination, hell, and a vengeful God in favor of a belief in the upward progress of mankind. On the issue of salvation, Universalists went even further than Unitarians. While Unitarians declared that all people can saved, Universalists believed all people will be saved. Both groups embraced what we would today characterize as progressive social positions on the rights of women, children and enslaved people. Both extolled the use of human reason in religious matters. And both were receptive to spiritualism and its preoccupation with human perfectibility and social reform.

Brackett's ties to Unitarianism are suggested by his family's choice of a Unitarian minister as speaker at his funeral. His sympathies for Universalism are indicated by the fact that he was commissioned by Boston's Universalist community to create the funerary monument for Hosea Ballou I, the clergyman and theological writer who was one of the founders of the American Universalist Church. Brackett spent four years on this large marble sculpture, completing it in 1859. (fig 28) His seven foot high figure of Ballou is draped in a robe and grasps a book in one hand. The great man's pose and expression express quiet resolution. He stands on a large pedestal that is plain but for large carved letters spelling out his last name. A guide to the cemetery published in 1864 explains that no other inscription was needed as "his epitaph is written in the hearts of those who loved him."[203]

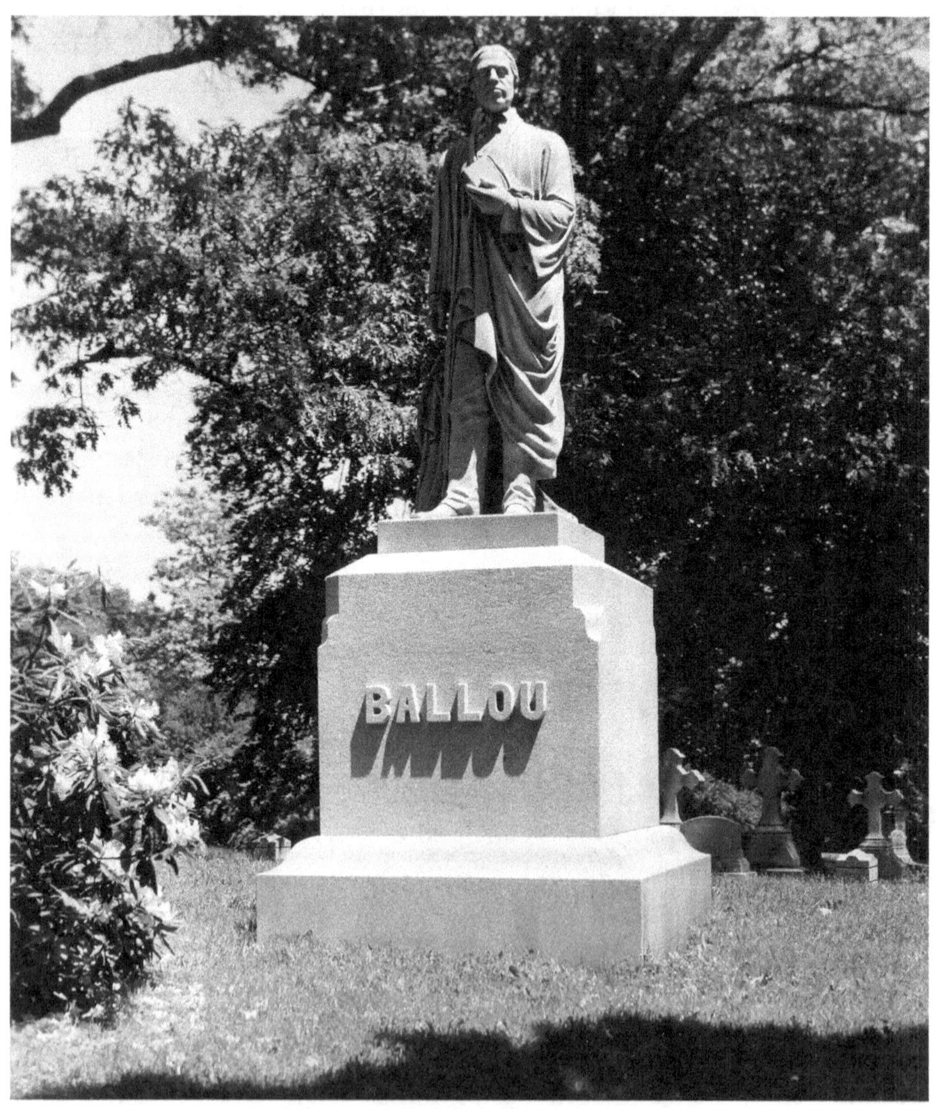

ig. 28 *Reverend Hosea Ballou*, by Edward Augustus Brackett, 1859, granite, Mt. Auburn Cemetery, Cambridge, Massachusetts. Courtesy of Mt. Auburn Cemetery.

This monumental figure towers over Boston's Auburn cemetery to this day. The absence of conventional motifs of mourning is striking. Surrounding monuments and tombs feature sorrowful angels, bereft survivors, recumbent representations of the dearly departed, crosses and urns. The Ballou monument, by contrast, presents its subject in the fullness of robust life. It offers a sculptural testament to the continuity of life after death. The monument also suggests the evolution of Brackett's ideas about death.

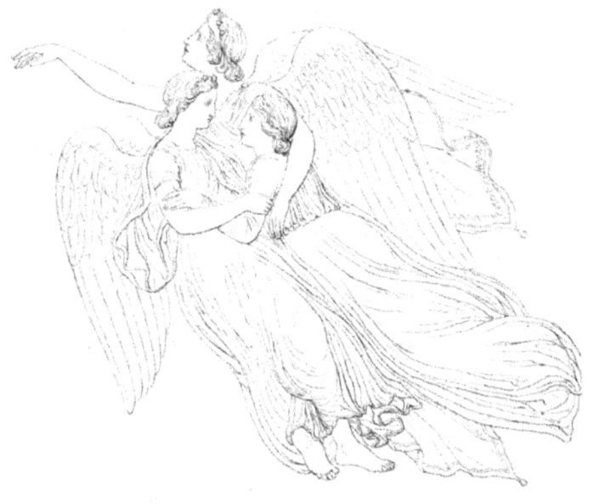

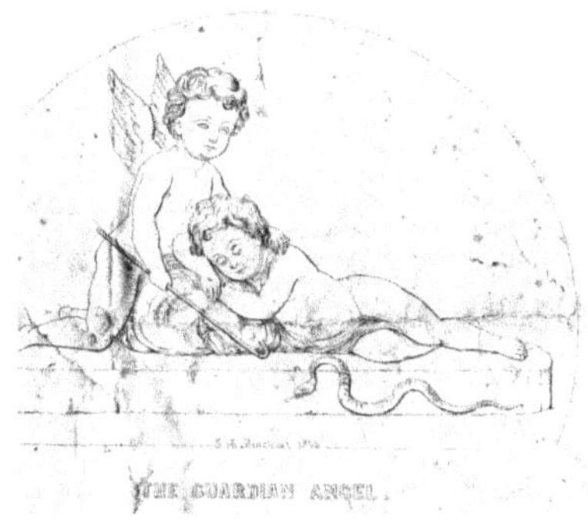

fig. 29 *The Ascension* by Edward Augustus Brackett, engraving, published in a folio of drawings, *Works*, 1844. Courtesy of the Winchester Massachusetts Archival Center.

fig. 30 *Guardian Angel* by Edward Augustus Brackett, engraving, published in a folio of drawings, *Works*, 1844. Courtesy of the Winchester Massachusetts Archival Center.

In 1844 he had published a folio of designs for funerary monuments that he offered for commission. (fig 29) (fig 30) Based on poems by contemporary poets, they deal in the more traditional tropes of death, sleep and memory: guardian angels, sleeping babies, grief stricken mourners, shooting stars and a young woman lifted to heaven by a pair of angels. They do not yet evoke the lively spirit world that Brackett would embrace as he delved more deeply into spiritualism.

But even in 1844, Brackett was advocating a humanistic approach to death. In a brochure accompanying the folio, he called for more sculpture in cemeteries, remarking, "The effect would be highly beneficial. [Cemeteries] would cease to be wholly the home of the dead, and would become silent, but powerful teachers of the immortality of virtue. Their faith would be strengthened, the spiritual would become more real, and our feelings would be less often chilled."[204] As an added benefit that he didn't find necessary to mention, this approach would also have increased business for sculptors like himself.

Whatever his relationship to Universalism and Unitarianism, however, it is clear that Brackett's heart belonged to spiritualism. It seems likely that its essential democracy appealed to him. Historian Ann Braude has made a study of spiritualism and the feminist movement and she asserts that the new religion represented "both rebellion against death and rebellion against authority."[205] She points out that spiritualism was informally organized with no single governing body. It had no hierarchy and was built around individual mediums who had the gift of clairvoyance, rather than on appointed leaders or learned theologians. Given that the vast majority of these mediums were female, it also provided an unprecedented path to professionalism for women, offering them the ability to make their own money and have public influence. As a result, Braude maintains, "Spiritualism became a major—if not *the* major—vehicle for the spread of women's rights ideas in mid-nineteenth-century America. . . . While not all feminists were Spiritualists, all Spiritualists advocated woman's rights."[206]

The convergence of spiritualism and feminism provided Brackett's *Shipwrecked Mother and Child* with a curious double life. As recounted in Chapter 2, Brackett's sculpture was inspired by a famous 1841 shipwreck. He exhibited a small plaster version in Philadelphia in April 1850 and finished the marble sculpture in January 1851. The completed work was displayed at the Wadsworth Athenaeum later that year. By this time the public was consumed by speculation surrounding Margaret Fuller's death by shipwreck on July 19, 1850.

The details of Fuller's tragedy made an indelible mark on the public consciousness. At the time of the wreck, the famed feminist writer was returning to New York after four years in Italy with her new husband and twenty month old baby. Fuller had made her name as the editor of Ralph Waldo Emerson's Transcendentalist journal *The Dial* and as the author of *Women of the Nineteenth Century,* a groundbreaking study that made the case for women's rights. She had spent her time in Italy issuing dispatches about political upheavals in the Italian states while writing a monumental history of the rise and fall of the 1849 Roman Republic. Her return was eagerly awaited by her friends and readers.

The boat bringing Fuller home was approaching Fire Island on the night of July 19 when a wild storm blew up. The ship ran aground on a sand bar fifty yards from the shore and most of the crew and passengers jumped off to swim ashore. Fuller, who couldn't swim, stayed on board with her husband and child. On the beach, scavengers gathered to cart away cargo that washed ashore but made no effort to summon help. As horrified survivors watched from the land, a giant wave washed the family overboard. Only the child's body was recovered. Also lost was Fuller's Italian manuscript.

While Fuller never explicitly embraced the spiritualist movement (the Fox sisters had burst on the scene just two years before her death while she was in Italy), her writings indicate a sympathy with spiritualist ideas. She had undergone mesmeric therapy for a painful shoulder and in a 1846 essay on Swedenborgianism had rather convolutedly remarked, "As to the power of holding intercourse with spirits enfranchised from our present sphere, we see no reason why it should not exist, and do see much reason why it should rarely be developed, but none why it should not sometimes." [207] Many of her friends agreed and in fact Horace Greeley, her editor at the New York Tribune made several attempts after her death to reach her spirit through mediums.

Following her death, Fuller's fame as a feminist grew, thanks to a posthumous compendium of her writings put together by her close friends Ralph Waldo Emerson, James Freeman Clarke, and William Henry Channing. Feminists in the spiritualist movement took to asking her through mediums to comment on changing notions of women's role and place in society. For fifty years after her death, Fuller (or rather her disembodied spirit) remained an active participant in discussions of the feminist movement.

Brackett's *Shipwrecked Mother and Child* comes into this story because the work came to be closely associated with Fuller's death. This sculpture of a dead mother cradling her dead child supported spiritualist ideas about the persistence of love beyond death, while also illustrating feminist conceptions of the Perfect Mother. It played as well into narratives about Fuller's refusal to abandon husband and child in the face of imminent death, and to suggestions that she went to her death willingly so that they could all be together on "the other side." As a result many contemporary accounts of the sculpture identified it as a portrait of Fuller. The idea that Brackett's work was inspired by Fuller's death continues to pervade mentions of the sculpture to this day.

Feminists were not the only social reformers attracted to spiritualism. Progressives of all stripes were drawn to its agenda of individualism and human perfectibility. Many of Brackett's abolitionist friends were also spiritualists. William Lloyd Garrison, for one, was deeply involved with the spiritualist movement. So was Brackett's patron, George Luther Stearns as well as Thomas Wentworth Higginson and Gerrit Smith, other members of the Secret Six. Prominent Black leaders, such as Frederick Douglass, Sojourner Truth and Harriet Tubman regularly attended spiritualist meetings and conventions. Abraham Lincoln did not share his wife's avid spiritualist views, but he was open to the movement, especially as it supported his agenda. In fact, his biographer

David Reynolds describes how a medium named Nettie Colburn delivered a lecture to Lincoln on need to free the slaves while in a trance state.[208]

While John Brown himself was a staunch Calvinist and given to delivering fiery sermons on the nature of evil to his sons and followers, his posthumous life was permeated by spiritualism. During the Civil War, Union soldiers marched to battle singing a spiritualism inspired anthem: "John Brown's body lies a-moldering in the grave/ But his soul goes marching on…"

Spiritualism also found a home in the art world. Sculptors like Hiram Powers and Harriett Hosmer (one of Henry James' "marmorean flock" in Rome) were both deeply influenced by spiritualism. Powers came under the sway of Swedenborg as a young man and hosted Swedenborgian services and séances in his studio in Florence. In describing the ambition behind his idealized marble figures, he used a spiritualist metaphor: "the merest film separates our eyes from a view of . . . [the spirit] world." Harriett Hosmer reported visitations from spirits from childhood on. She embraced spiritualism in earnest after being exposed to it by an anatomy teacher who was also a medium. Her beliefs made their way into a number of her sculptures, among them *Hesper*, the personification of the evening star that dies at first light, only to be reborn as the morning star and other figures like Medusa, Daphne and Puck who exist between two states of being.

Hosmer's interest in spiritualism also underlay a quixotic effort to create a perpetual motion machine powered by magnets, a project that consumed much of her energy late in life. Her biographer, Kate Culkin, sees a connection between this pursuit and her embrace of spiritualism. Culkin remarks "Significantly, arguments for and against spiritualism broke down along lines similar to those about perpetual motion."[209] Both processes involve a defiance of the principle of conservation of energy, instead suggesting that the existence of an excess energy that flows beyond mechanical or spiritual bounds. Thus, the creation of a successful perpetual motion machine would bolster claims of a scientific basis for spiritualism. Hosmer felt so strongly about this that she declared, "I would rather have my fame rest upon the discovery of perpetual motion than upon my achievement in art."[210]

Art historian Charles Colbert has made an extended study of the links between neoclassical art and spiritualism. He sees the generalizing idealism practiced by artists like Powers and Hosmer as an effort to express the unique traits of a subject that were not extinguished at death. He notes that spiritualists were apt to compare the improved appearance of materialized spirits to the marble perfection of statuary. And he suggests that the penchant for portrait busts in the 19th century went beyond pure egotism and represented the patron's desire to commune with his or her descendants from the spirit world. [211]

Colbert has considered the case of art critic James Jackson Jarves in depth, and reinterprets his aesthetic theory in light of his spiritualist beliefs. Jarves hoped to elevate the taste of America's patron class by persuading them to cultivate an interest in Medieval and Renaissance art. He believed this would develop the mental faculties associated with beauty which they could then carry with them into the next life. Hence, as Colbert points out, Jarves provided a spiritual justification for the rapacious collecting habits of the robber barons. He also posited a line of artistic inspiration that was literally passed on from dead spirits to living masters. And he suggested that the emerging science of connoisseurship, whereby experts determined the authorship of Old Master artworks, involved not just careful comparisons of style and materials, but also an actual communion with the spirit of the dead artist. This insight allows us to see Jarves' praise of Brackett's John Brown in a new light. When Jarves remarks on "what high degree the artist was impressed by the soul of his sitter,"[212] it would seem he was not speaking metaphorically.

The Popular Embrace of Phrenology

Jarves was also an aficionado of phrenology, the popular science that connected bumps on the skull to specific mental traits. Like spiritualism and mesmerism, phrenology was wildly popular in the 19th century. While all three disciplines are generally discredited today, they were once seen as the cutting edge of knowledge. All three would-be sciences challenged prevailing notions of the mind as a non-material substance inserted into the body by the Creator at birth and removed at death. Instead, they emphasized the unbreakable connection between the spirit or mind and the physical body. By linking mental and spiritual realities, they made the invisible visible - spiritualism through ectoplasm, spirit writing and materialized apparitions, mesmerism through cures effected by the redirection of mesmeric fluid through the body and phrenology through the use of skull maps that allowed skilled practitioners to read an individual's character. The three practices were also connected by an optimistic vision of human potential. Control of these invisible forces could allow for spiritual growth and self-improvement. This was a far cry from Calvinist notions of predestination, Original Sin and mankind's inherent depravity.

Phrenology was the brainchild of Viennese physician Franz Joseph Gall who was driven from his native country in 1802 for promoting heretical ideas. His theory would find a receptive home in United States in early 1900s. There, its combination of scientific analysis and optimistic psychology made it the perfect study for a people who, in de Tocqueville's words, "conclude that everything in the world may be explained, and that nothing in it transcends the limits of the understanding."[213]

Phrenological charts divided the brain into dozens of discrete "organs" each corresponding to a particular character trait. (fig 31) There were, for instance, organs whose manifestations on the skull revealed the subject's degree of Benevolence, Secretiveness, Avarice, Artistry, Humor, Conscientiousness and Combativeness. While some phrenologists did private consultations, others turned their "science" into a road show and used it to detect audience members' virtue or hypocrisy and predict future behaviors.

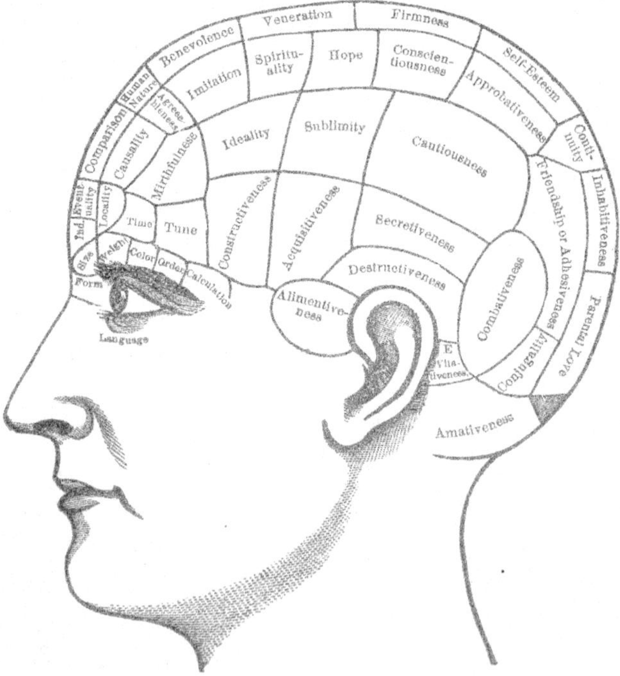

fig. 31 *Phrenological head*, 1882, from *Forty years in phrenology*, Nelson Sizer, Wellcome Library, London, Courtesy of Creative Commons.

Today phrenology is universally regarded as a pseudo science. However, while doctors no longer feel patients skulls for tell tale character bumps, aspects of phrenological theory have proved surprisingly prescient. Contemporary neuroscience links certain aptitudes to specific parts of the brain and suggests that behavior and physiological characteristics of the brain may mutually influence each other. Cognitive psychology also rests on the understanding that the mind is composed of independent faculties, now conceived as networks rather than organs, and reveals that complex mental functions like reading can be broken down into separate components. So, if phrenology's bumps have been discredited, there has been a validation of its larger conception of the mind as a collection of faculties that can be linked to physical sites in the brain.

19th century artists, in particular, were entranced by phrenology. Art became a way to analyze the character of figures from the past. A phrenological study of Michelangelo's self-portraits determined that he had a "Bilious and Nervous temperament," and a distorted degree of "Combativeness, Self-Esteem, and Firmness." Phrenological analysis of portraits of George Washington revealed his qualities of "Secretiveness, Firmness, and Caution." Artists also used Phrenology in their own works. Hiram Powers arranged the bumps on the forehead of his Greek Slave, for instance, to express the spirituality of her mind. Thomas Crawford endowed his sculpture of Beethoven with a ridged forehead, thereby explaining the master's musical success by way of his possession of the phrenological organ of Tune. [214]

All this casts new light on Brackett's insistence on undertaking the dangerous trip to West Virginia to get John Brown's measurements. The photograph of Brown which was one of his sources would not have provided the necessary phrenological information. While Brackett did not discuss phrenology directly in his writings, he traveled in a milieu that was very phrenologically oriented. Many of his friends, subjects and patrons were deeply impressed by the new science. An early patron in New York was James Stanley Grimes, a leader of the Western Phrenological Society who wrote extensively on phrenology, mesmerism and physiology. Other friends and acquaintances who literally had their heads examined included William Cullen Bryant, Horace Greeley, Richard Henry Dana, Walt Whitman and even John Brown himself, whose son John Brown Jr. was for a time an apprentice at a phrenology office.

The Crow's Nest

An even stronger link between Brackett and phrenology is found in his architectural project, which came to be dubbed the Crow's Nest. In 1850

Brackett undertook to build a house on his land in Winchester. He followed a set of plans for the creation of Octagonal shaped houses set out in a how-to book by Orson Fowler titled *A Home for All*.[215] In this building project, Brackett was participating in a trend that saw a thousand such homes constructed across the country in the 1850s. Houses made to Fowler's plans were sparely ornamented, relatively inexpensive to execute and made better use of space than the conventional rectangle, all reasons for their popularity. Fowler's octagonal plans could be adapted by the builders or homeowners to suit individual needs. Because they radiated from a central hall, Octagon Houses used less heat and had better air circulation. Their eight sides permitted more windows and hence more light. In their flexibility and cost effectiveness, these buildings anticipated both the modular homes popularized by Buckminster Fuller and Frank Lloyd Wright's proto-suburban Usonian House.

But for Fowler the promotion of the Octagon House was part of a larger agenda. Fowler came to his interest in home design following a hugely successful career as the foremost popularizer of phrenology in the United States. He had been converted to phrenology as a student when he and his fellow classmate Henry Ward Beecher (the future minister, abolitionist and brother of author Harriet Beecher Stowe) heard a lecture on the new science in Boston.

Fowler's writings on phrenology made him a celebrity, as did his "Phrenological Cabinet" a medical office and public display of hundreds of real and replica skulls that gave P. T. Barnum's traveling sideshow a run for its money. While the theory of phrenology flirted with such unsavory ideas as eugenics and racial determinism, Fowler himself was an avid social reformer. He published abolitionist writings in his American Phrenological Journal and was a crusader for women's and children's rights. He was a vegetarian, a health advocate and the author of a controversial sex manual that promoted female sexual satisfaction. This latter, published in 1870, would ultimately be his undoing. Accusations of obscenity and immorality - it was charged that he had "debauched the minds of young females, and sown the seeds of a prostitution of the sexes under the guise of education" [216] - shattered his reputation, leaving him to die in obscurity in 1887.

But in the 1850s when he was distributing *A Home for All*, Fowler was riding high. The first edition of the book, published in 1848 contained long disquisitions on phrenology and lifestyle choices that were shortened in later editions. It also espouses the vital connection between phrenology and the arts, for as Fowler remarks, "In a few years every artist must be a Phrenologist, or be out of employ."[217] Historian Charles Colbert has analyzed Fowler's Octagon plans in relation to his phrenological theories and suggests that his house designs correspond to his model of the human brain. References abound in his *Phrenological Journal* to the building as a metaphor for the human brain – the cranium is compared to a castle of many rooms, each devoted to a specific function and the human brain is described as a three-story house with a skylight.[218] Fowler's Octagon House plan is conceived along these lines with the more material and physical functions (among them heating, storage and food production) relegated to the basement and lower floors and such spiritual/cultural/intellectual activities as entertainment, gymnastics and sleep ensconced in the upper floors.

Fowler put these principles into play in his own home, a sixty-room mansion he erected on a one hundred and thirty acre lot in Fishkill, New York at the height of his fame. (fig 32) It rose four massive stories, each wrapped with a veranda, and the whole was topped by an octagonal cupola. The main floor of this monumental building contained a parlor, a sitting room, a dining room and an amusement room, while the upper floors held numerous bedrooms, each with its own dressing room, along with a children's playroom, a gymnasium and a room for visiting clergymen. It also featured the latest in domestic technology. Features included central heating, pipes and heaters for hot and cold running water, indoor flush toilets, a roof cistern to collect rain water, natural gas lighting, a water filtration system, and a gravity-fed water system. The house was completed in 1853 and immediately became a local attraction.

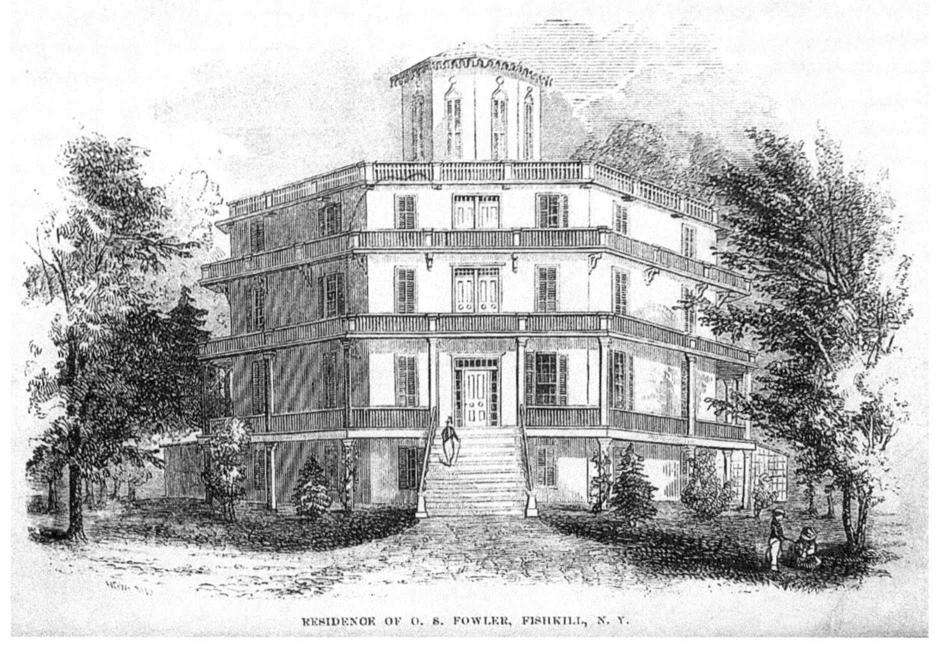

fig. 32 *Fowler Octagonal Mansion in Fishkill, N. Y*, lithograph, 1854, published in O. S. Fowler, *A Home for All*, NY: Fowler and Wells Publisher. Courtesy of Creative Commons.

Sadly, its glory days were very brief. Economic upheavals in the lead-up to the Civil War reduced Fowler's fortune. After renting it as a boarding house for several years, he was forced to sell his dream house, which had now been dubbed Fowler's Folly by local residents. The house went through thirty owners in a little more than a decade. After a leaking cesspool poisoned several of its last inhabitants, it was dynamited as a derelict by the city of Fishkill in 1897.

Fortunately, Brackett's less grandiose Crow's Nest had a happier fate. Today it is a private residence and is listed on the National Register of Historic Houses. The current owners have removed some of the egregious additions made over the years and have brought it back to the state of elegant simplicity reflected in photographs from Brackett's time. (fig 33)

Despite their numerous mutual acquaintances, it's not clear whether Brackett knew Fowler personally. There is some conjecture that Brackett could have provided Fowler with model busts for his Phrenological museum during his time in New York. Brackett's wife Amanda Folger Brackett and Lydia Folger Fowler, Orson Fowler's sister in law, were distant cousins and their families both hailed originally from Nantucket so they may have known each other. But all such links are speculative.

What is not in dispute is that Brackett used the first edition of Fowler's *A House for All* as the basis for the design of his Octagon House. The better selling second edition of the book curtailed the phrenological discussions and advocated

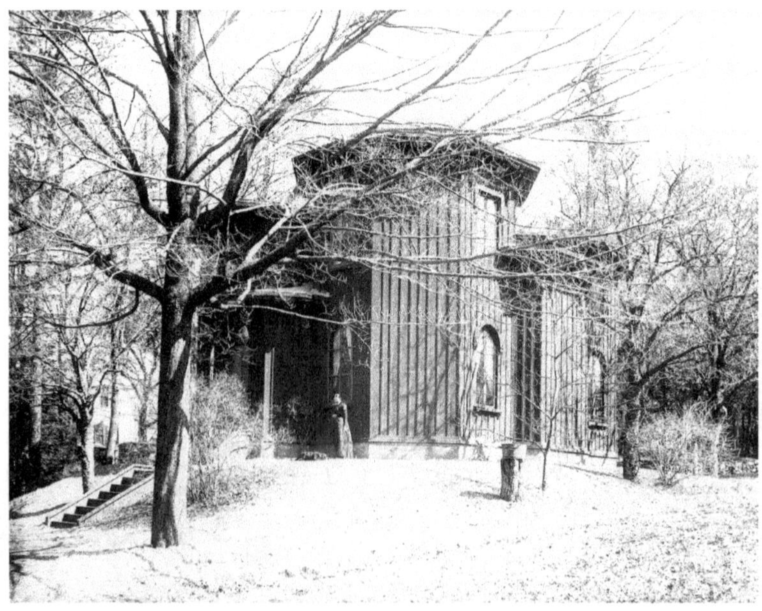

fig. 33 *Edward A. Brackett Octogon House,* undated photograph. Courtesy of the Winchester Massachusetts Archival Center.

concrete as a building material. The 1848 edition used by Brackett explained how to construct an Octagon House using a lattice-like wood construction in which boards are stacked horizontally to form walls. Brackett used this technique to create a design that appears unique in the annals of Octagon house lore. While the exteriors of most Octagon houses, including Fowler's Folly, are composed of a single octagon, Brackett joined together five room sized octagons, each of a different height. Thus instead of presenting a simple massive structure, the Crow's Nest has a much more complex and picturesque profile, with towers abutting each other and topped by individual roofs. Ultimately Brackett's design suggests a castle whose central two story octagon rises like a battlement over the stepped components below. The house sits on a hill which today overlooks the well tended town of Winchester, Massachusetts. Here Fowler may be invoked: "Men with the eagle form of nose and physiognomy . . . will build on high ground, where they can have a commanding prospect."[219]

Brackett certainly enjoyed the practical advantages of Fowler's prototype. But it is tantalizing to imagine that he may have designed his Octagon House with his own phrenological characteristics in mind. It also seems possible that he may have chosen the octagonal form because it suited his spiritualist inclinations. Octagon Houses were considered conducive to spirit activity because there were no dark corners in which evil entities could lurk. There are numerous accounts of spiritualists building Octagon houses and holding séances in them.

Brackett Discovers the Seance

At the time that Brackett was building his Octagon House, he had already begun his explorations of mesmerism and spiritualism. In *Materialized Apparitions* he dates his first glimmerings of interest to 1840 when he attended a lecture in New York by Robert Collyer, an English physician who was spreading the gospel of mesmerism across the country. Collyer maintained that mesmerized individuals could converse with departed spirits. Brackett reports that initially he believed that Collyer "was a humbug, and Mesmerism a fraud. "[220] However, at the urging of a friend he agreed to attempt some experiments and quickly found himself enthralled. He and his friends began to meet weekly to continue their study, presumably casting various subjects into trance states. Brackett continued his investigations following his move to Boston a year later, where he found a fellow explorer in Dr. William F. Channing, an electrical engineer whose claim to fame is the invention of the fire alarm.

Brackett reports "From the intensity of my nature and a daring due to ignorance, I carried these experiments, probably, further than any one else. Several times I pushed my subjects where neither pulse or breath was discernable, require all my exertions and presence of mind to restore them to their normal state." He continues, "It was during these experiments that I discovered the close relation between mesmeric sleep and what we call death, and to me it gave unmistakable evidence of another life. My subsequent long investigation of what is called mediumship, which is only a form of mesmerism, in no wise changed the conclusions I had reached."[221]

Brackett describes the same trajectory from skepticism to conviction when he began to explore the world of séances. He describes his first séance in detail, but doesn't report the exact date. However it appears to have taken place in the early 1880s. That leaves a long gap between Brackett's early mesmeric experiences in the 1840s and his intense study of séances chronicled in *Materialized Apparitions*. Why the long interregnum?

A number of explanations suggest themselves. Marriage, children, the effort to establish an art career, Brackett's immersion in horticulture and animal husbandry and the building of the Octagon House all no doubt placed his occult studies on the back burner. So did external events. The abolitionist movement, the Civil War and the upheavals of Reconstruction all were remaking the world. In addition, in the interim between his engagement with metaphysical concerns, the object of his study was also changing. Mesmerism evolved into spiritualism, and manifestations of the spirit world progressed from the rappings of the Fox Sisters and public demonstrations by trance lecturers to a postwar norm of séances in intimate domestic settings.

Amanda's death in 1871 would have refocused Brackett on the possibility of life after death, and indeed he takes up this subject in a number of undated poems. Among the most touching is one titled *Always Present*:

"All around us forms are drifting,
Floating, gliding, always near;
Though our eyes may never see them
Still we know that they are here.
Often in my quiet study,
When the lamp is burning low,
There is one who sits beside me,
Parted from me long ago.
Not more certain flows life's current,
Or the things I touch and see,
Than the glory of her presence
With the love she brings to me."[222]

However it was another fifteen years after Amanda's death before Brackett attended a séance. Why wait so long? In fact, Brackett was a late-comer to séance spiritualism. By the early 1880s, the séance had exploded as a popular pastime, with dozens of mediums in every city hawking their talents in spiritualist publications. Charges of fraud were rampant and the popular media were full of dramatic accounts of the exposure of prominent mediums. By the time Brackett turned his attention to these practices, séances conducted by professional mediums in private homes had become a major form of domestic entertainment. Mediums were paid by the assembled seekers, and tended to be blatantly self-promotional. Ads in spiritualist publications announce in bold letters such services as "Platform Test Séances", "Full Form Materializations", "Magnetic Healing", "Written Communications with Spirit Friends on paper and handkerchiefs" and "Spirit Photography." The commercial imperative to produce a good show every time led even supposedly legitimate mediums to employ tricks and subterfuge. This made it difficult to distinguish between fake and real spirit appearances.

As a result of this frenzy, scientists were beginning to make systematic investigations into the techniques and claims of individual practitioners. The Society for Psychical Research, which still exists, was founded in Britain in 1882 by a group of psychologists, scientists and other scholars for purpose of exploring various paranormal activities. Its early members included psychologist William James and psychical researcher Richard Hodgson with both of whom Brackett would ultimately spar. The Seybert Commission, composed of faculty members at the University of Pennsylvania, spent the years 1884–1887 investigating the practices of respected spiritualist mediums. Both these bodies ending up debunking the vast majority of the situations they investigated. But as William James pointed out, the pervasiveness of false manifestations didn't negate the possibility of real ones. He famously remarked, "If you wish to upset the law that all crows are black, you mustn't seek to show that no crows are; it is enough if you prove one single crow to be white."[223]

Brackett began with similar intentions. Once again, as he had in his initial encounter with mesmerism, Brackett cast himself in the role of impartial investigator who could sift through conflicting claims. In *Materialized Apparitions*, he noted, "I felt, whether right or wrong, that my experience in Mesmerism, and the long training of my perceptive faculties as a sculptor, which enabled me to detect the slightest differences between objects, was as good a preparation as one could have for studying this class of phenomena."[224] Further, he opined, "Materialization was either a great truth or a stupendous humbug. Thousands of intelligent persons believed in it, on what appeared to me uncertain evidence. Was it not a disgrace to science that this had been allowed to go on so long without any honest attempt to investigate it? If I could only get the inside track, how easy it would be to expose it!"[225] But from this skeptical starting point, he quickly emerged as an impassioned defender of séance spiritualism as it faced a growing catalogue of fraud allegations.

Materialized Apparitions is divided into two parts. The first is an account of Brackett's experiences at various séances with different mediums and the second presents his efforts to theorize the phenomena of materialization and to rebut its debunkers. Thus, in part one, we are thrust into the world of séance spiritualism. Although the effects produced in séances varied from medium to medium, Brackett focused on materializations, which he described as "the alleged production of visible and tangible apparitions out of seeming nothingness."[226] The most dramatic of these were full body figures – or forms – as Brackett referred to them. Séance participants were also treated to other effects. Many of these suggest the sleight of hand associated with magic shows, which were an equally popular form of entertainment at the time. Brackett describes skeins of luminous cloth materializing and dematerializing before his eyes, flowers apparently plucked out of thin air, figures emerging in a blast of light or sinking into the floor. These marvels all took place in the shadows because the spirits required dim light in order to show themselves.

In keeping with his role as self appointed researcher, Brackett took it upon himself to examine the cabinets to which mediums retired in order to conjure the spirits, going so far in several cases to present drawings of the room. These he believed proved that there was no place for confederates to conceal themselves or for materializing objects to be stashed. He measured the heights of mediums and the heights of the materializing figures to demonstrate that the medium could not be impersonating the spirits. He sat in various parts of the séance room where he believed he would be able to detect any movement by confederates slipping in and out of hidden doors to pose as spirits.

Brackett admits that some manifestations were clearly deceptive, as when a medium whom he did not usually frequent brought forth a false version of Bertha. He notes, "In following the rôle of strict investigation, and in honestly relating what has come to me at these séances, I am forced to state that the form that appeared on this occasion was not Bertha, and that there was, as subsequent events proved, an attempt to deceive me."[227] However, rather than accuse the medium, he chose to blame the spirits themselves, remarking "Mrs. Sawyer is a gentlewoman and a strong medium, but she is surrounded by a coarse magnetism, the baleful influence of which she seems powerless to resist."[228]

In the end, however, he decided to set aside his skepticism as he determined that the more accepting one was of these "forms", the more rewarding would be the encounter. "Science may wrangle over the supposed movements of molecules and atoms, and the correlation of forces; may dissect the bird to find its song; but love alone shall set the boundaries of knowledge," he wrote. "The key that unlocks the glories of another life is pure affection, simple and confiding as that which prompts the child to throw its arms around its mother's neck."[229]

This observation leads into the second part of *Materialized Apparitions*, which Brackett titled *Opinions and Theories*. Here Brackett sifts through a variety of observations. He has harsh words for the scientists and religious authorities of his day. He charges that the former are overly materialistic: "Walking with faces toward the ground, they refuse to look up, or admit the existence of anything beyond 'matter,' denying the possibility of spirit, and claiming that the earth contains within itself the 'promise and potency' of everything that is or has been."[230] Religious authorities, meanwhile, ignore Christianity's deep connection to spirit manifestations: ". . . the idea of another life, imperfectly outlined in the Bible, was taken from a religion founded upon occult manifestations; . . . He whom he calls Lord and Master not only taught healing by laying on of hands, but exemplified Materialization in the transfiguration on the Mount, and in his bodily appearance to his disciples, after his death, in a room with closed doors. . . "[231]

The text presents Brackett's explanation for what he has observed. Here he follows the convoluted accounts common among séance spiritualists who maintained that materializations were created out of a secondary kind of matter emanating from the entranced medium's body. According to this theory, the spirits use this to form the bodies seen by séance participants. Sometimes spirits resemble their source material - the medium's body. But if they are strong enough they can break free and can assume other forms. Are these forms actually the spirits of the departed loved ones? Though Brackett generally seems to believe so, he leaves open the possibility that they are not. He remarks, "I do not care to discuss the question as to who or what Bertha is; I know she is not the medium, nor a confederate, and that her materialization of objects is genuine. In my long and delightful association with her, extending over more than two years, I have never been able to detect the slightest thing that would lead me to doubt that she is what she claims to be."[232]

One key aspect to Brackett's theory is the power of love. He suggests that the spirits respond to affection and acceptance and recoil from hostility. This is why the hard-nosed scientific investigators consistently failed to find convincing evidence of spirit life. It also explains the instances of fraud — Brackett maintains that spirits are swayed by the atmosphere in the séance room and that better spirits emerge through better, less mercenary, mediums.

Brackett concludes *Materialized Apparitions* with an expression of faith: "All along the pathway of my investigations glow a thousand things never to be forgotten. Who shall say the gates are not ajar, and that our loved but not lost ones are not passing to and fro? Poor in spirit and weak in affection must they be who can meet these beings as I have met them, and not feel that there comes, from the association with them, a richer and fuller life."[233]

Brackett, William James and Mrs. Ross

In the course of the hundred plus séances that he attended as part of his investigations, Brackett occasionally found himself in the company of skeptics. This drew him into a notable controversy that underscored the sharp divisions between true believers like himself and the investigators who were attempting to establish a scientific basis for spiritualism. On several occasions he attended séances in the company of psychologist William James. As part of his work with the Society for Psychical Research, James was investigating the practices of mediums. He was on the lookout for fraud, but was also hoping to find his White Crow – that rare individual who really was in contact with spirits from the other side. James and members of the Society transformed the domestic setting of the séance into a kind of laboratory. They concocted various tests to uncover tricks and detect genuine spirit activity. By modern standards some of their methods, which included trussing mediums, subjecting them to strip searches and hitching them up to radiometers, electroscopes, and dynamometers to detect possible mesmeric energies, might seem to verge on S & M.

On December 27 and 28, 1886 Brackett and James attended a pair of séances that were presided over by the medium Mrs. Hannah V.Ross, a well known fixture on the séance circuit. Ross worked with a "control", a Native American spirit named Bright Star, who served as the channel for dozens of other spirits. James had heard enough about Ross to believe that she might be the genuine article. The first séance was arranged by his fellow scientist Alfred Russel Wallace, the second by Dr. James Robinson Nichols, a physician, chemist and writer of popular scientific essays.

Wallace is a particularly fascinating figure on the spiritualist circuit. He was a co-discoverer of the theory of evolution, independently coming to the idea of natural selection simultaneously with Charles Darwin, and it is often argued that his current obscurity stems from his embrace of spiritualism. Despite his groundbreaking scientific work, he refused to see the theory of evolution as a refutation of religion. He maintained that there were limits to an evolutionary theory that focused only on the physical body. Instead, he maintained, there also had to be a Divine Intelligence that directed humanity's spiritual evolution. Séances, he believed, were a tool by which this higher power might be detected. This was a conviction that he shared with Edward Brackett, with whom he was acquainted and for whom he expressed admiration on several occasions. Though he is little more than a footnote today, in the 1880s Wallace was a well-known and highly respected scientist. His involvement with these séances likely reassured investigators like James of its potential legitimacy.

In a letter to James regarding the December 27 séance, Wallace set out the conditions for the event. He suggested a party of 10 or 12 observers and noted that while Mrs. Ross had agreed to let séance participants search the room for hidden openings, she would not submit to an intrusive search of her person. In an aside that suggests his respect for our subject's investigatory skills, Wallace adds, "If you can get *Mr. Brackett* to join us it would be an advantage."[234]

The conditions having been met, the séance commenced at Mrs. Ross' home. According to Wallace, eight or nine figures emerged from behind the curtain, one of them being Brackett's niece Bertha. A reporter for the spiritualist publication *Banner of Light* was also in attendance. He described the impression Bertha made on the assembled group "Mr. Brackett's niece Bertha, came; she was quite strong, and passed around the room, vivaciously greeting all in her characteristically pleasant way. Mr. B said, 'You are not quite as tall as you are at some other séances.' She replied, "I come here just as I am in spirit-life; in my feelings and actions I am, and always expect to be, a child.'" The report continues, "The appearance of Bertha attracted much attention. She is a most singular embodiment of youthful beauty and child-like affection."[235]

In his own report, Wallace confirmed Bertha's presence remarking, "Mr. Brackett has often seen her develop gradually from a cloudy mass, and almost instantly vanish away." [236] Wallace also encountered spirits of individuals known to him. He reported, "One was a beautifully draped female figure, who took my hand, looked at me smilingly, and on my appearing doubtful, said in a whisper that she had often met me at Miss Kate Cook's séances in London. She then let me feel her ears, as I had done before to prove she was not the medium. I then saw that she closely resembled the figure with whom I had often talked and joked at Signor Randi's, a fact known to no one in America. The other figure was an old gentleman with white hair and beard, and in evening-dress. He took my hand, bowed, and looked pleased, as one meeting an old friend. . . . at length I recognized the likeness to a photograph I had of my cousin Algernon Wilson, whom I had not seen since we were children, but had long corresponded with him, as he was an enthusiastic entomologist, living in Adelaide, where he had died not long before. . . . These two recognitions were to me very striking, because they were both so private and personal to myself, and could not possibly have been known to the medium or even to any of my friends present"[237]

James, however, took a more jaundiced view of the proceedings. In an account written several months later he revealed his disillusionment with Mrs. Ross. First, he described how Wallace, who had been seated in a position from which to detect any comings and goings of confederates, was pulled away by a spirit, who then covered the doorway with her robe, making such exposure impossible. Even more damningly, James noticed that the drapery of one of the female forms who emerged from the cabinet was caught up above her knees, and that she appeared to be wearing the same black trousers as the male spirit who had just exited the room.

The next day, James, Brackett and Wallace attended a second séance with Mrs. Ross organized by Nichols. This time, James described a form purporting to be the spirit of a child and suggested it resembled a dummy. He remarked that when he asked to touch its hand, he felt "four adult finger tips, held together and surrounded by a sort of 'mit' drawn down to the knuckles." [238] Thus James concluded, "The facts I have underscored, added together, were sufficient to convince me personally that whether mediumship was or was not an element of Mrs. Ross's performance, roguery certainly was, and I resolved not to waste any more time upon performances given at her own house. Good carpentry can make a secret door in any wall."[239]

James' letter was published in the *Banner of Light*. His missive came in the wake of a notorious and much publicized raid on Mrs. Ross conducted by a group of anti-spiritualists vigilantes on January 31, 1887. A *New York Times* report on this melee described a scene that devolved from decorum to chaos. After sitting quietly through the beginning of the séance, the twelve spies disrupted the proceedings at a prearranged signal. One pulled the gauzy covering from the face of the spirit with whom he had been conversing, while another struck matches to illuminate the interior of the cabinet. Another pulled aside the curtain and landed a blow on the medium's Native American "control" who was threatening him with a raised chair. Yet others grabbed Mrs. Ross and her husband, who was in the process of pulling a revolver. The Times reported that the raiders found four boys and a little girl who had posed as spirits inside the cabinet along with an "ingenious mechanical contrivance" that opened a hidden door. The report continued, "Mr. and Mrs. Ross made no attempt at explanation, but refunded the money paid by each person who had witnessed the séance."[240]

While James did not attend the raid, he acknowledged that it confirmed his own suspicions about Mrs. Ross. In his letter to the *Banner of Light*, he remarked dryly "I learn that now, many days after the capture of her confederates by Mr. Braman and his friends, she invites a more rigid scrutiny still of the cupboard and wall and shows an affidavit from her landlord that the house is what it was before her lease. I do not learn, however, that spirits still continue to emerge from the cabinet many at a time, with the sliding doors closed as they used to do before the catastrophe; nor do I see why a secret opening through a wall may not be unmade in forty-eight hours by the same skill which made it."[241]

Brackett and Wallace rejected these accusations and together conducted an investigation of the Ross séance room, concluding that there were no secret passages. In a response to James in the *Banner of Light*, Wallace disputed James' descriptions of the December séances. He argued that in fact confederates could not have gotten by him where he was seated and that the wall where James imagined an opening was papered and plastered and inspected by the participants prior to the séance. He also pointed out that the raiders had failed to collect the names and identities of Mrs. Ross's alleged confederates, making their report impossible to confirm. He concluded, "It is by such thoughtless statements as these that most of the accusations against mediums are supported; but when they are made by an investigator, who claims to be both unprejudiced and scientific, they should be either upheld by an appeal to facts or unreservedly withdrawn."[242]

Brackett expressed his outrage in more colorful terms. James, he argued in his response in the *Banner of Light*, "appears to be singularly unfit to investigate so delicate a subject, for both mediums and the so-called materialized forms show a decided aversion to him, and I understand that in the twenty-five or thirty séances which he has attended, not a single form has ever come to him personally, and whenever anyone has tried to bring them in contact with him, it has been with great difficulty that they could be induced to approach him."

After condemning James's ungentlemanly behavior toward Mrs. Ross who had fallen ill following her brutal treatment by the raiders, he charged, "With the advance of civilization there has come to the front a class of men known as specialists who cultivate a part of their intellect to the dwarfing of their other faculties. In many things they are the weakest of mortals; having no power to stand against public opinion, their knees knock together and they go down with the first adverse wind that blows."[243]

Such defenses did not shield Mrs. Ross from further indignities. She and her husband were raided again on April 14, 1887 and arrested for fraudulently obtaining money. Mr. Ross was subsequently brought to trial (Mrs. Ross was discharged because the law assumed that in such cases the wife was coerced into crime by her husband.) At this fraught moment, Brackett stepped forward in an attempt to vindicate the beleaguered medium. On May 17 he invited Mrs. Ross to preside over a séance to be held at the Crow's Nest. Removing her from her home was no doubt an effort to prove that no chicanery was involved. The event was written up for the spiritualist publication *FACTS* by Alonzo E. Newton, a well-known spiritualist writer and editor. [244]

According to Newton's report, a cabinet was constructed at Brackett's Octagon House by hanging curtains against a dead wall in the sitting room. While the men inspected the cabinet, the ladies in the party were invited to examine Mrs. Ross to ensure that she was not hiding any devices or costumes. In the séance that followed, Newton noted the arrival of twelve or more "forms" of various sizes and apparent ages, from children of four or five years to full-grown adults. He reported, "These, I think, were seen more or less distinctly by all present, and some were touched or handled by their friends, proving their tangibility. Moreover, several of them were able to speak, and thus tell their names or otherwise identify themselves to their friends, though countenances were hardly distinguishable. The medium being of a large frame, the contrast presented by smaller frames was easily noticeable. The medium's voice was repeatedly heard in the cabinet, while forms were out in the room, and in several instances two forms appeared at the same time."[245] Bertha appeared for Brackett and Newton was greeted by an old, long deceased friend who, he asserted, could not have been known to anyone there except for his wife.

Such proofs convinced Brackett and Newton of Mrs. Ross's authenticity. But the report was not enough to reverse the notoriety that now surrounded her. In the subsequent trial, Mr. Ross was acquitted on the grounds that the plaintiff had likely entered the séance expecting to be deceived. But the damage to the Rosses' reputations was done and they never regained their stature in the spiritualist community.

The Waning and Second Life of Spiritualism

But in any case, the spiritualist craze was already abating. Exposés and critical reports by scientific bodies like the Society of Psychical Research were taking their toll and by the 1890s retired mediums who had fallen on hard times became the recipients of charity. Brackett himself was to be the subject of an expose himself in 1892 with the publication of an article in the *Boston Herald* in which a young actress confessed that she had been hired by various mediums to act as Bertha. She described how she materialized by creeping behind the black curtain behind him and counting the chairs until she reached his place. She reported, "I came to him 'strong and lively,' in cabinet language, always calling him 'uncle,' and grasping him by the hand and leading him up to the cabinet for whisperings with the 'spirits,'"[246]

Despite all this, Brackett's faith in spiritualism remained unshaken. *Materialized Apparitions*, which brought together his various writings on the subject, continued to have fervent fans. One notable reader was Sir Arthur Conan Doyle who was first drawn to spiritualism in 1887 around the same time that he was inventing his famous detective. Doyle published copiously on the subject and believed that his explorations of spiritualism, rather than Sherlock Holmes' feats of ratiocination, would be his lasting legacy.

In Volume II of Doyle's monumental *The History of Spiritualism*, published in 1926, Doyle seconded Brackett's belief that unless spirits are approached in the spirit of love they will appear false and fraudulent. He averred, "Spiritual people, in whose presence the medium feels thoroughly happy, see by far the finest manifestations. Although spiritual phenomena are governed by fixed laws, those laws so work in practice that Spiritualism undoubtedly partakes much of the character of a special revelation to special people. Mr. E. A. Brackett, author of that remarkable book, 'Materialized Apparitions,' expresses the same truth in another way. His view will, of course, excite derision in so-called scientific circles, but it embodies a deep truth. It is the spirit of his words rather than their literal interpretation that he means to convey: The key that unlocks the glories of another life is pure affection, simple and confiding as that which prompts the child to throw its arms around its mother's neck."[247]

Materialized Apparitions remains in print. It is available on Project Gutenberg and in facsimile editions offered by Amazon and Google Books. And it lives on in the research of modern day spiritualists and believers, including, I discovered while researching Brackett, a book by the prolific psychic historian N. Riley Haegerty.[248]

From a 21st century perspective, it is hard to square the rationalizations of figures like Wallace, Doyle and Brackett with the overwhelming evidence of fraud and chicanery in the practice of 19th century mediums. Was it all merely wishful thinking? Is it evidence that delusions can invade even the finest minds? Or is it possible that these men were grasping at something that goes beyond physical explanation? Today spiritualism remains omnipresent in the sphere of popular entertainment. Countless films, television shows and novels envision a world awash with occult energies, afterlife narratives and spirit manifestations. This could be written off as a reaction to a world where magic and mysticism have been flattened by technology, or as a shot in the dark against forebodings of nuclear, climate or pandemic induced apocalypse. But one can also read this fascination as a manifestation of the time honored human desire to defy death.

Today this desire takes different forms – in place of rapping spirits and materialized apparitions we have scientific investigations into near death experiences, research on the potential of cryogenic preservation of life at the moment of death (a possibility being quietly explored by billionaires like Peter Theil, Jeff Bezos and Elon Musk) and speculations about the merger of human and digital intelligence. How quaint will such ideas appear a century from now?

Which leads to the other lesson we might carry from the 19th century's obsession with spiritualism. Despite the mythology of science's straightforward march toward truth, in fact the advance of knowledge is a circuitous and often sideways process. It should be humbling to our own notions of scientific certainty to recall the history of 19th century science. A science in formation can encompass many ideas later deemed erroneous. Meanwhile, its own errors can blind it to fruitful avenues of investigation that were prematurely shut off before their potential was realized.

As a citizen scientist and amateur investigator, Brackett was willing to plunge into the theoretical debates of his day. From the middle of the fray, he wrestled with the potential for knowledge to create a better world. He pursued proofs of spiritualism because he believed it provided the basis for a bracing new vision of morality. He maintained, "If what I have stated be true,—if the experience of others shall prove that I have not been deceived,—then the whole system of ethics must undergo a complete revolution. Man will no longer be regarded as an animal, confined to earth, but a direct emanation from a superior intelligence, holding in his nature a dual existence, connecting him at one and the same time with both the seen and unseen worlds."[249]

This hope sustained him throughout his life. It would manifest itself during the last chapter of his life as he transferred his considerable energies from the practice of art to the nascent field of environmental conservation. His last thirty-five years were dominated by twin concerns with the practical and philosophical aspects of science. His interest in biology, conservation, horticulture, and the scientific breeding of plants, fish and animals coexisted with a continuing concern with the apparent contradictions between faith and science and the larger implications of the remarkable scientific discoveries that were laying the basis for the world we know today.

Chapter 5
SCIENCE AND PSUEDO SCIENCE

In 1873 Brackett closed up his art studio in Boston. It was, according to one report, "one of the bitter trials of his life."[250] The closure of the studio represented the end of one chapter in Brackett's life. But it was also the beginning of another. In 1872, around the same time that he was bidding farewell to his art career, Brackett was appointed Chairman of the Massachusetts Fish and Game Commission, a position he would hold for the next twenty-seven years. This new direction did not come out of nowhere. Even during his long struggle to survive as a sculptor, Brackett had immersed himself in the selective breeding of fish, animals and plants. Various accounts have him running a winter greenhouse, keeping bees, cultivating a new variety of grapes and crossbreeding fish and pheasants. These were interests that ran in the family. His father had worked, apparently not very successfully, as a farmer for several years. His younger brother Gustavus Brackett became a celebrated horticultural expert and Chief of the Iowa Department of Agriculture's Pomology Division. Gustavus authored such still available books as *The Pear And How To Grow It* and *The Fig: Its History, Culture and Curing*. Meanwhile, Edward's Boston based brother Walter, with whom he remained very close, had graduated from a middling career as a portrait painter to become a celebrated painter of fish. (fig 34) In 1872 a quartet of Walter's fish paintings were exhibited at the Crystal Palace in London. In 1895 Walter would be given the honor of repainting the Sacred Cod, a carved-wood sculpture of an Atlantic codfish that celebrates the Massachusetts codfish industry. This nearly five-foot long effigy dates back to pre-Revolutionary days and still hangs suspended in the chamber of the Massachusetts House of Representatives.

Edward Brackett's own naturalist activities included experiments with methods of fish propagation. At one point he constructed a fish hatchery in an old freight car on his property, experimenting with the breeding of shad and salmon. This project brought him to the attention of the founding members of the newly created Massachusetts Commission on Inland Fisheries. This led to his appointment, first as a board member, then ultimately as Commission Chairman.

Finally, after years of financial precarity, Brackett had a secure salary, a respected place in the community and a new mission. He threw himself into his new assignment. He arrived at a time when conservationists were just awakening to the problems created by over-fishing and hunting, as well as threats to the Massachusetts ecosystem posed by loss of wildlife habitat.

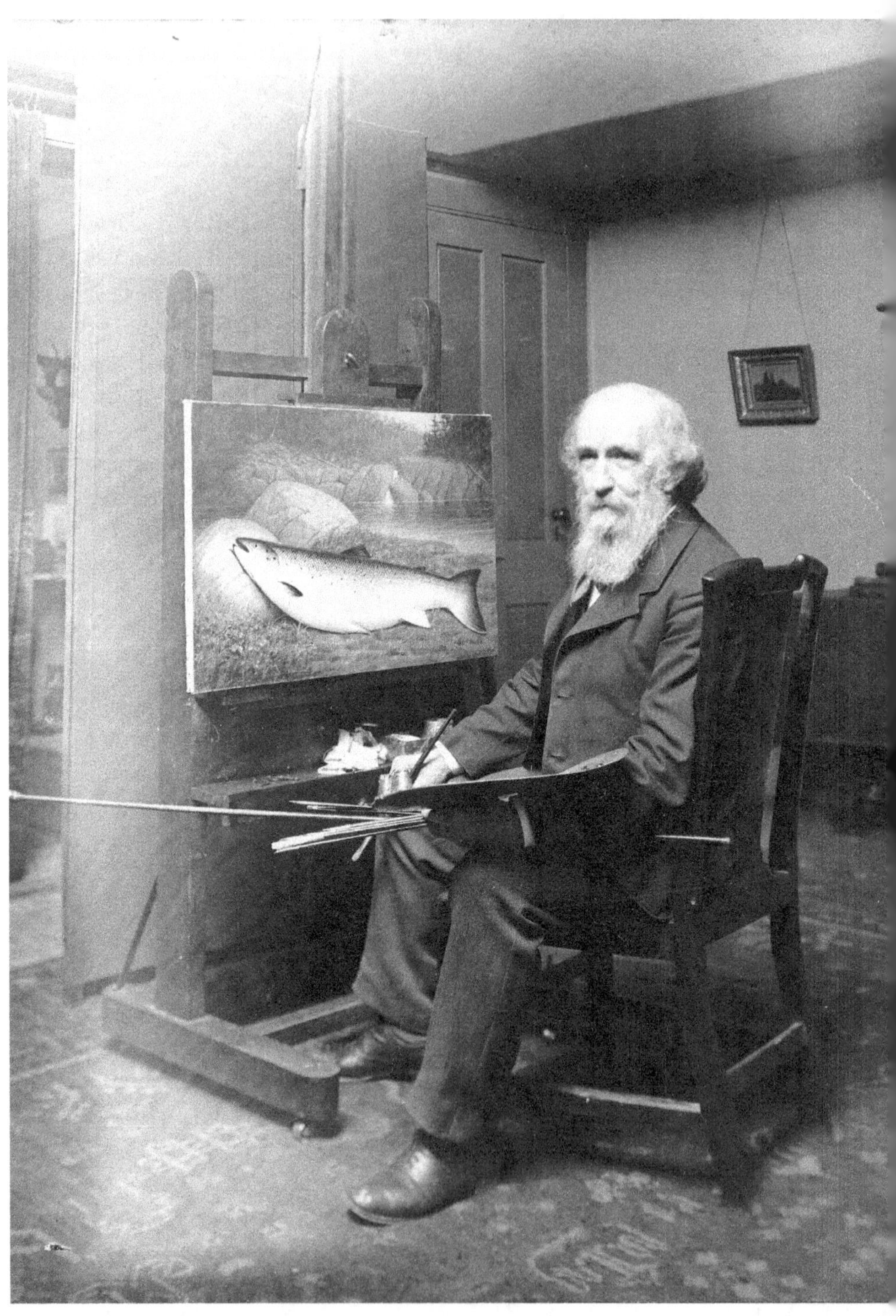

fig. 34 *Walter Brackett working in his studio in Boston, Massachusetts,* circa 1880, Photographic print, collections of Maine Historical Society. Courtesy of the Maine Memory Network via Maine Historical Society.

During his years as Wildlife Commissioner, Brackett immersed himself in these concerns. He transformed his makeshift fish hatchery into Massachusetts' first state hatchery, thereby providing a means to stock state rivers with game fish. He poured his creativity into ingenious inventions, improving hatching trays and devising fish ladders designed to facilitate the migration of fish over natural and artificial barriers. He also participated in a precedent setting lawsuit that ultimately went to the Supreme Court serving to establish the public's right to natural waterways.

A Scientific Gadfly

But while he embraced his new role, Brackett did not abandon his old interests. He continued to read widely and to explore the latest scientific ideas and social debates. The published writings from his later years reflect a desire to reconcile his mystical and spiritual interests with the new scientific discoveries that were upending his countrymen's sense of the world. He most directly addressed these issues in three late works. One is a rambling set of essays titled *The World We Live In* that presents a peculiar mix of eastern mysticism, scientific theory, traces of Wordsworthian Romanticism, and a stinging critique of established religion and science. The other two are long poems that present humorous rebuttals to two of his bête noires – the materialist basis of 19th century science and the misguided investigations into spiritualism by the American Society for Psychical Research.

I started writing this book in 2020, the first terrible year of the Covid pandemic. In Brackett's poem *Pseudo Science*, published in 1904, I encountered a passage that seemed uncannily relevant to our 21st century situation:

"No matter where,
They all are there,
The million germs that fill the air,

And through our life they warp and weave
A deadly blight in air we breathe,
And poison all our dreams of bliss
With thirty microbes in a kiss.

Worse than any Spanish blister
Is the kissing of a sister;
Never touch your father or your mother,

Never come too near your lover;
Ten feet from him take your stand,

You may drop upon your knees,
Throw him kisses if you please,
But never dare you touch his hand;"[251]

This actually offers a pretty fair description of life in the pre-vaccine phase of Covid. In fact however, Brackett is presenting a satirical take on Dr. Louis Pasteur's then newly ascendant germ theory of disease. He uses his wry wit to express his skepticism about the idea that unseen microbes passing between individuals are the cause of infectious disease. While the theory is settled science today, in the late 19th century it was competing with other explanations, among them that epidemics were caused by poor sanitation and miasma, or bad air, emanating from rotting organic matter.

Pseudo Science, like Brackett's other long poem *The Voyagers*, is heavily footnoted, revealing his close attention to the scientific debates swirling around these issues. In the passage above, for instance, he offers these notes:

"Note 4: 'Thirty microbes in a kiss.' A German Scientist has found that there are no less than thirty different kinds of microbes in the average human mouth.

"Note 5: 'Never dare you touch his hand' M. Crouzel, a French chemist, has discovered that there are 83,450,900 bacilli in the average hand, the shaking of which is a frightful source of spreading disease."

Brackett relegates germ theory and other prevailing ideas to the status of scientific fads supporting a purely mechanistic vision of nature. The poem suggests Brackett's complicated relationship with science. Its title *Pseudo Science* employs a term in common use today to describe theories that use apparently scientific methods to promote false or unproven beliefs. But in fact much of what Brackett is targeting as Pseudo Science - including the theory of evolution, germ theory and early theories of the subconscious self – are today commonly accepted while the ideas he espoused – among them spiritualism, intelligent design and New Thought, the 19th century precursor to the 20th century's New Age movement - are now considered misguided fallacies.

Rather than dismiss Brackett's opinions as sheer wrong-headedness, I propose instead to delve into the reasons for his beliefs and the larger cultural and scientific context in which these debates were taking place. Looked at in this way, his statements - some reasonable, some fanciful and misguided and some preposterous - offer insight into many of the controversies that roiled the 19th century. They become a fascinating lens through which to understand how a growing skepticism toward established religion butted up against discomfort with science's pure materialism, leading many of the period's leading thinkers to search for credible links between science and faith.

Evolutionary upheavals

The theory of evolution is a case in point. When this theory arrived in 1858 it further shredded the already frayed relationship between science and religion. By the mid 19th century the biblical creation story had been undermined by geological discoveries that set the age of the planet back many millennia from the 6000 years advocated by creationists. Instead of acts of God, geologists explained the topography of the earth by way of natural forces like earthquakes, volcanoes and other natural events. Meanwhile botanists and explorers were documenting the incredible diversity of plant and animal life across the globe, creating ever greater difficulties for theologians who continued to insist that boundaries between species were inviolable and that each had been created independently by God.

The theory of evolution pushed divine intervention even further out of the picture. Maintaining that different species evolved from common ancestors, it suggested that they take their present forms through adaptation to their environment by means of the process of natural selection. The theory describes how tiny variations make individuals more or less fit for survival and how over time more successful variations displace less successful ones. Chance and randomness displace God as the agent of species change.

Evolution was the simultaneous and independent creation of two men – Charles Darwin and Brackett's future associate, Alfred Russel Wallace whom we met in the last chapter. (fig 35) Both men based their ideas on extensive travel through the natural world with intense study of botanical specimens. Almost simultaneously, both came to nearly identical conclusions. Wallace was still in the field in the remote Indonesian island of Halmahera while Darwin was convalescing at his home in London when their findings were presented to the Linnean Society of London, igniting a furor that has not yet completely died down.

Initially Darwin and Wallace were hailed as co-discoverers and indeed they worked together to proselytize for their theory. Today of course Darwin is generally known as the father of the theory of evolution while Wallace has largely disappeared from the popular imagination. To understand why, we must look beyond the convergence in their thinking on evolution to understand the essential differences in their backgrounds, dispositions, philosophies and subsequent activities.

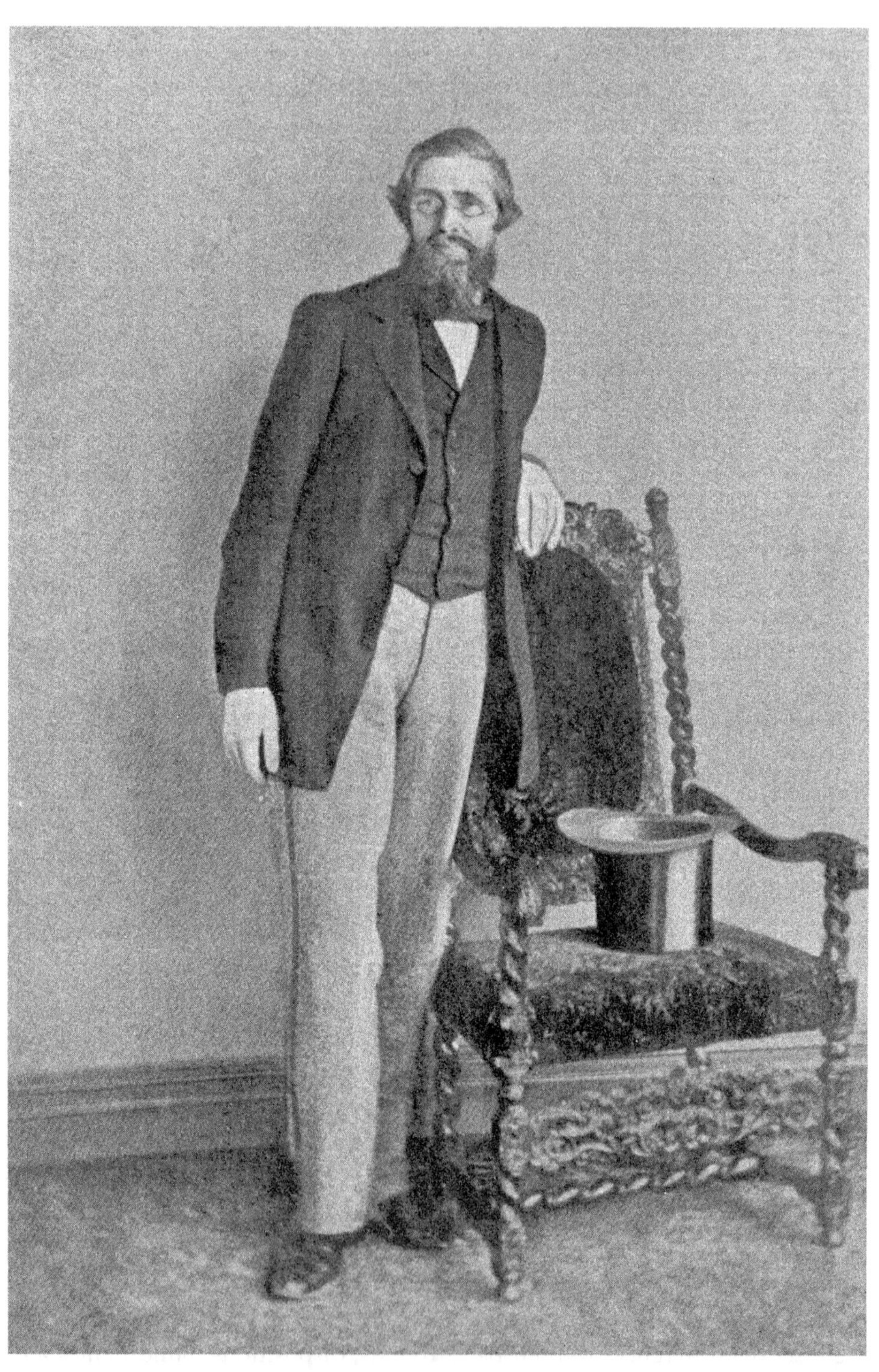

fig. 35 *Alfred Russel Wallace*, portrait published in *Alfred Russel Wallace: letters and reminiscences* by James Marchant, 1916. Wellcome Collection gallery. (L0025210) Courtesy of Creative Commons.

Darwin came from a privileged background, studied at the University of Edinburgh and Christ College, Cambridge and was able to undertake the travels that led to his discovery with funding from his father. The first book that he wrote from this material, *The Voyage of the Beagle*, became a best seller and gave him a prominent public profile.

The younger Wallace, by contrast, was self-educated and self-supporting. When he was a boy, family difficulties forced him to leave school and he began his career as an apprentice surveyor for his older brother. Leaving his native Wales for London, he was exposed to radical social ideas, leading to a lifelong sympathy for the travails of the working class. He also became fascinated with insects and after reading Darwin's *Voyage of the Beagle* and other books of natural science decided to explore the South American tropics. He planned to finance his trip with the sale of insect and animal specimens to collectors and museums back home. In this, the early days of modern botany, there was a thriving market for examples of new and unknown species. Unfortunately, all Wallace's specimens and most of his notes were destroyed in a fire on the ship during his return voyage. But the intrepid Wallace forged ahead, traveling again to the East Indies. It was there, while suffering from a fever, that he conceived of the basic outlines of the theory of natural selection as the answer to various scientific questions that had been bedeviling him. He wrote his ideas up and sent them to Darwin whom he had once met briefly in London.

Darwin immediately recognized that the younger man had succinctly outlined a theory that he had been mulling over for two decades. With Wallace still in the East Indies Darwin could have rushed his own work into print and taken full credit, but admirably he arranged instead for their ideas to be presented simultaneously to the scientific community. Upon his return the self-effacing Wallace was willing to let the older and more prominent Darwin take first billing. For years afterwards they worked together to promote the theory of evolution in the face of backlash from clergymen and more conservative scientists.

Their amicable relations were strained in 1869 when Wallace concluded a published review of a work by geologist Charles Lyell with the speculation that aspects of human development – especially with regard to language, consciousness and moral reasoning – cannot be explained by natural selection and point instead to the operations of an "Overruling Intelligence" guiding human beings toward spiritual perfection.[252] Darwin answered swiftly and in great distress: "I differ grievously from you and am very sorry for it; I can see no necessity for calling in an additional and proximate cause in regard to Man . . . I hope you have not too completely murdered your own and my child."[253]

In Wallace's view, there was no contradiction between an embrace of natural selection as the mechanism for the evolution of non-human species and a belief in humanity's unique status and special destiny. There has been a tendency to attribute this turn in his thinking to his embrace of spiritualism and its confidence that human spiritual development continues beyond the grave. As we have seen, he put these beliefs into practice when he joined with Brackett to defend the embattled medium Mrs. Ross. But Wallace's willingness to separate physical from mental and spiritual evolution was also a function of his humanism. His resistance to a purely materialistic vision of human consciousness was in keeping with a value system that rejected many of the complacent certainties of the era's intellectual class. The original Darwin/Wallace theory of evolution was intended simply as a scientific explanation for the diversity of species throughout the globe. However, it was easily adapted to validate existing social and economic arrangements. The phrase "survival of the fittest" has become identified with evolution theory. The term was actually coined by sociologist Herbert Spencer and only later taken up by Darwin as shorthand for the mechanism of natural selection. It has come to be associated a vision of life as a ceaseless and relentless battle for survival. Such ideas were easily adapted to support a rapacious, unregulated capitalism, an imperialist subjugation of "inferior races" and a class system that justified privilege as the reward for innately superior fitness.

Wallace resisted this justification of the status quo. He actively lobbied for land nationalization, argued for the education of women and resolutely rejected the eugenic program advocated by Francis Galton, Darwin's cousin. Galton sought to improve "human stock" by applying the principle of natural selection to human mating. Rather, Wallace declared: "Leave heredity alone until we have made the environment of every child from conception to death the best possible for its full and free development, and then we can begin to think about the influences of heredity, which may be small."[254]

Such convictions lay behind Wallace's campaign against the policy of mandatory smallpox vaccination. This is a resistance he shared with Brackett. Today we know that smallpox vaccination saved many lives and that vaccine hesitancy contributed to the huge death toll during the Covid pandemic. In the late 19th century, however, germ theory was new and the mechanisms underlying vaccination were unknown. In a 1907 news item in the *Boston Herald*, Brackett expresses skepticism toward the "Pasteur treatment", whereby individuals are inoculated against disease with a small amount of the infectious virus. He scoffs at the treatment provided to a group of people exposed to hydrophobia, the 19th century term for rabies, remarking, "I have always supposed that a disease must exist before it can be cured. But what of their future? They have gone home with their bodies *inoculated with the vile serum from a sick dog or a guinea pig* and so a new microbe has been introduced, a pugnacious fellow who is supposed to feed on hydrophobia germs. When they have been destroyed, *what will the serum germ do next?*"[255]

While Brackett dismissed vaccination as a logical absurdity, Wallace opposed it on two fronts. On scientific grounds, he doubted the statistics used to advocate for vaccination. But he also objected from a social perspective. He pointed out that mandatory vaccination was unequally applied to rich and poor, placing the onus on the individual rather than the social conditions that facilitated the spread of disease. He directed attention instead to the need for improvements in public sanitation, waste management, air and water purity and the crowded conditions of the urban poor. "Health," he remarked, "is the best resistant to disease, and not the artificial giving of a mild form of a disease in order to render the body immune to it for a season. Vaccination is not only condemned upon the statistics which are used to uphold it, but it is a false principle—unscientific, and therefore doomed to fail in the end."[256]

As Wallace's argument suggests, it would be a mistake to characterize today's embrace of ideas like germ theory and evolution simply as the triumph of science over ignorance. In the late 19th century, value free science was not the gold standard for truth that subsequently became. As we have seen in the last chapter the desire to reconcile science and faith engaged some of the era's finest minds. So did questions about the ethical dimensions of the search for knowledge, Mary Shelley's 1818 novel *Frankenstein* being just an early expression of this scepticism. Thus, while the rift between Darwin and Wallace on the subject of Divine Intelligence revealed a major fracture in their approach to evolution, the rift not complete. The two continued to correspond and explicate their theory even after Wallace's startling departure from evolutionary orthodoxy. As evidence of their continued mutual respect, Darwin was subsequently responsible for arranging a much needed subsidy for the financially struggling Wallace. It was only after Darwin's death that Wallace disappeared from the history of evolution. By the 1930s Darwin's *On the Origin of Species* was regarded as the Ur-text of evolution theory.

The professionalization of science contributed to Wallace's disappearance. Both he and Darwin had gained most of their practical scientific education in the field. But while Darwin was able to translate that upon his return into some strong institutional affiliations, Wallace remained an outsider. In the days when the study of disciplines like biology, chemistry and physics was moving from independent amateurs to trained scientists, Wallace's lack of educational qualifications made him suspect among those hoping to establish science as a respected profession. And it probably didn't help that Wallace channeled so much of his energy in his later years to unfashionable social causes and to ideas like spiritualism that were anathema to established scientists.

Wallace was not alone in resisting the march of professionalism and its dedication to scientific objectivity. In *The Reason for the Darkness of the Night*, John Tresch provides a startlingly revisionist biography of Edgar Allan Poe.[257] Tresch reveals Poe's keen interest in matters of science culminated in *Eureka*, a massive prose poem which outlines a theory of cosmology that Poe believed would be his most lasting legacy. The text, mostly ignored by other Poe scholars, suggests a vision of time and space that anticipates such current scientific ideas about spacetime and the Big Bang. It also contains elements that align with Brackett and Wallace's spiritual concerns, outlining, for instance, a future where "the sense of individual identity will be gradually merged in the general consciousness."[258] Tresch places Poe's interests in the context of his era's scientific turmoil, remarking, "Foreclosing the world's essential mystery, science was crystallizing a view of nature as a passive, lifeless storehouse of matter and facts to be observed, mastered and exploited to human's chosen ends." Tresch adds, in a look ahead to the implications of this idea in our own time, ". . . the stance of "neutrality" allowed science to be complicit in destructive and unjustifiable designs."[259]

Battling "Pseudo Science"

Wallace's views provide a context for Edward Brackett's ruminations on science and pseudo-science. There are strong parallels in their backgrounds, interests and beliefs. Given their acquaintance, mutual admiration and their joint efforts on behalf on the medium Mrs. Ross, Brackett would have been very aware of Wallace's ideas about spiritual evolution. His sympathies would have been further strengthened by the affinities between their circumstances. Like Wallace, Brackett was an autodidact from a humble background whose struggles had put him in sympathy with the down-trodden. Like Wallace he was unwilling to accept a purely materialist explanation of human existence. And like Wallace he was aware of the disdain with which members of the scientific establishment regarded non-degree holding interlopers into their discipline.

These sentiments bleed into his poem *Pseudo Science* as he picks apart what he sees as the flaws in the theory of evolution. Brackett's vision may also be conditioned by his artistic background – although he had left his sculpture career behind, he retained an artist's sensibility. His conviction that the cosmos has an aesthetic shape ran squarely against the Darwinian emphasis on the random nature of the variations that produce the process of natural selection.

Brackett begins his poem by satirizing the materialist bias of the purveyors of science:

"With their microbes and their matter,
How they grin, how they chatter.
Like cannibals around their fires,
They are eating up their sires."

He mocks the reduction of being to matter:

"In the microbe there must be
Everything that comes to thee . . .
In a little drop of slime
Lies the world we call sublime;
Lies the promise of a nation;
Lies the secret of Creation."

He then turns his attention to the theory of pre-natal influence. Here he is touching on an aspect of evolution theory that Darwin later discarded. This is the idea that it is possible for an organism to inherit physical characteristics acquired by its parents during their lifetime. In Darwin's time the mechanism by which variations were transmitted between generations was still unknown, making this speculation plausible. Today it is generally accepted that our genetic inheritance is determined by the interaction of maternal and paternal DNA. However, recent discoveries suggest that trauma, stress and various environmental conditions may in fact play some role in genetic inheritance, leading to a reassessment of the long standing rejection of the idea that acquired characteristics can be passed on from one generation to the next.

Brackett devotes considerable attention to lampooning this concept, perhaps because its determinism negates the role of divine guidance in human development. He satirizes the idea of pre-natal influence with the peculiar tale of a Black woman who is confined in an all white cell and gives birth to a White child. While the story's equation of Whiteness with beauty grates on the modern ear, it also suggests a social critique. Brackett seems to be pointing out the hypocrisy of defenders of the former slave states who ignore the obvious evidence of rape and miscegenation visible in the complexions of the formerly enslaved population. Instead he suggests that defenders of the Old South prefer more fanciful explanations for this mixed racial makeup:

"Not here alone these changes flow,
For in the sunny South, we know,
Where virtue waves her loving hand
O'er all the children of the land,
Such things can be. '
Tis only fright
That turns one half the negroes white."

His next target is the idea of the dual mind, which he attributes to a Dr. Hudson. This would be Thomson Jay Hudson, psychical researcher and author of books like *The Law of Mental Medicine* and *The Law of Psychic Phenomena*. Hudson posited the simultaneous existence of an "objective mind" and a "subjective mind," each capable, under certain conditions, of independent action. (Working along similar lines, Sigmund Freud would enumerate three minds: pre-conscious, conscious, and unconscious.) Hudson further maintained that the trances of spiritualist mediums were caused by contact, not with spirits of the dead, but with the subconscious of the medium or that of his or her subject.

Given his deep commitment to spiritualism, Brackett rejected this attempt to find a psychological explanation for the psychic phenomena he had witnessed. He dismisses as absurd the idea of a divided consciousness because it threatens the very idea of human identity and agency. He disparages the logical consequences of the idea in a footnote, suggesting that, if true, "The latter [the objective self] is governed entirely by suggestion and is totally devoid of moral responsibility. The atrophy of the objective self is the cause of all crime."

Brackett versified his speculations on this theory, suggesting how it would wreak havoc on interpersonal relationships:

"The dreams of love that once you knew
Have faded like the morning dew.
Sub - conscious self in Mary's life
Refuses now to be your wife,
And so you have domestic strife,
The certain trend the fruitful source
That paves the way to all divorce."

And surveying the poem's collection of "pseudo scientific" ideas, he muses:

"But greater still that lying elf
That Hudson calls sub-conscious self.
If what he says proves to be true
Then in yourself there dwelleth two:
How can you tell which one is you?"

The poem ends on a plaintive note with the image of a world whose glory and beauty have been diminished by the new materialist versions of science:

"Far away in Life's mid-ocean,
Where the waves have ceased their motion
And the stars have lost their light,
Neath the hopeless gloom of night,
Where no friendly hand is beckoning,
Where the pilot's lost his reckoning,
Freighted with its speculations, —
Dreary, gloomy speculations,
That have cursed the life of nations,
Drifts this scientific bark,
Crumbling, rotting, in the dark."

One feels here echoes of Matthew Arnold's great poem *Dover Beach* where the ebbing of the "Sea of Faith" leaves behind only "confused alarms of struggle and flight,/ Where ignorant armies clash by night." Like many of his contemporaries, Brackett felt unsettled by the implications of a universe governed solely by mechanistic rules. But he was not anti-science, as his work as a naturalist demonstrates. Like Wallace he was simply not willing to cede human consciousness to the operations of a set of random variations.

The Sorry Voyage of The American Society for Psychical Research

The image of a scientific bark floating adrift returns in Brackett's other long poem, *The Voyagers*.[260] This narrative reveals that the ultimate purpose of Brackett's scientific explorations was a defense of spiritualism. *The Voyagers* targets the American Society for Psychical Research. That organization, which we encountered in the last chapter, was founded in 1884 as an offshoot of the London based British Society for Psychical Research. Its mission was to apply scientific methods to experiences of the paranormal. While many of the society's efforts were devoted to unmasking fraud and debunking the claims of popular mediums, some members were genuinely interested in discovering evidence of life after death. These included the society's Secretary Richard Hodgson and psychologists James Hyslop and William James. Each of these individuals became involved in a personal quest to understand the connection between the material and spiritual worlds. All three play starring roles in Brackett's poem.

Hodgson was a poetry loving Australian expat who ended up in London as one of the chief investigators for the Society for Psychical Research. Early on, he traveled to India to explore the claims of the Russian psychic Madame Blavatsky. This cult figure claimed to have a mystical connection to the godlike mahatmas, "great souls" of the Himalayas. Hodgson applied himself like a sleuth, analyzing the handwriting in letters purporting to be from these mahatmas, interviewing witnesses to Blavatsky's séances, finally undermining Blavatsky's claim that every four years letters from the mahatmas dropped from the astral plane into an occult cabinet in a shrine in her home. Hodgson revealed that this supposedly impregnable cabinet contained double-sided drawers that were easily accessible from Blavatsky's boudoir. Back in London, he continued to unmask fraudulent practices until he was invited to come to America to serve as Secretary of the Society's American branch. It was there that he came to investigate the case of the Boston based medium Mrs. Leonora Piper, a case that changed his mind. Through her spirit controls, Mrs. Piper gave Hodgson news of his deceased mother and beloved cousin, as well as the fate of Madame Blavatsky, whose "spirit was in the deepest part of Hell."[261] Mrs. Piper would go on to play an outsized role in the explorations of the American Society for Psychical Research.

James Hyslop was an Ohio farm boy who rejected his family's fundamentalist Christian beliefs, instead earning a philosophy doctorate from John Hopkins University. He became interested in spiritualism following the death of his father, an unforgiving man who never accepted his son's rejection of the family faith. Hyslop became involved with the Society through Hodgson who arranged a session with Mrs. Piper so that Hyslop might attempt to communicate and reconcile with his departed father. Hyslop was so impressed with the results that he devoted much of the rest of his life to studying Mrs. Piper. He would go on to write a four hundred page book titled *Science and a Future Life* (1905) that used the evidence of his sittings with Mrs. Piper to argue for the reality of human survival after death.

William James, like many others, was drawn to spiritualism following tragedy. James' quest was set in motion by the death from pneumonia of his one year old son Herman. While (as we saw in the last chapter) James dismissed the claims of Brackett's favorite medium Mrs. Ross, he was nevertheless anxious to locate a medium whose clairvoyance was authentic. James described his goal as the search for the anomalous "white crow", his metaphor for a medium whose gifts were not subject to natural explanations. Introduced anonymously to Mrs. Piper by his mother-in-law, James was astonished when the medium produced numerous personal details about the James family that she had no way of knowing. His first séance with her culminated in the mention of a dead child named Herman. This was enough to convince James that Mrs. Piper was different from the standard run of mediums he had encountered. Like Hyslop and Hodgson, James came to believe that Mrs. Piper was their "white crow."

Leonora Piper seemed to fit the bill because she was a reluctant psychic and did not seem motivated by personal gain. The wife of a Boston shopkeeper, she had a history of unexplainable clairvoyant experiences. Initially she offered séances to friends and acquaintances free of charge as a service to the bereaved. Like many other mediums, she would throw herself into a trance, after which she was possessed by a rotating cast of ghostly "controls". Mrs. Piper communicated with spirits by handling objects that had belonged to the dead. While James, Hodgson and Hyslop were impressed with her apparent abilities, they tried not to be gullible. They closely examined her séance room. They had her followed to see if she was acquiring information about her sitters from libraries, cemeteries or newspapers. Eventually they sent her to England to be scrutinized by members of the London Society. There she was subjected to numerous inquiries and indignities. To establish that her trances were real, she was pricked with pins and burned with matches. To rule out telepathy, she was given objects whose histories the séance's sitters didn't know. Like the Americans, the British investigators could not detect any obvious fraud.

Upon Mrs. Piper's return to Boston, the American Society's members continued their investigations. They entertained a variety of hypotheses about her gifts. These included the ideas that she was somehow reading the minds of her sitters, that her controls were manifestations of a split personality coming to the fore during her trances and finally, that she perhaps was indeed in communication with the dead. Frustratingly, while they couldn't rule this latter explanation out, they also felt that they couldn't definitively rule it in.

Then they were dealt a blow. Weary of the constant probing and anxious to return to a more normal life, Mrs. Piper announced in an interview with a reporter for the *New York Herald* that she was retiring from mediumship. She came across in the article as a spiritualist skeptic, maintaining that she herself did not know if she was in genuine contact with the dead. She was quoted, "I am inclined to accept the telepathic explanation of all the so-called psychic phenomena, but beyond this I remain a student with the rest of the world." [262]

The interview ignited a firestorm among the spiritualist community and fed tabloid assumptions about the deceptive practices of mediums. Mrs. Piper later clarified to another reporter that she did not intend to debunk the possibility of spiritualism, but to say that she, as a medium, really didn't know what caused her intuitions. Later she recanted her recantation and returned to her activities as a medium.

Mrs. Piper's temporary renunciation served as the inspiration for Brackett's poem. *The Voyagers* borrows its chief motif from Greek mythology, specifically the figure of Charon, the ferryman whose role was to guide souls across the River Styx to the Isle of the Dead. In Brackett's poem the Society's researchers also embark on a voyage to the realm beyond death, though of course they hope to return safely to the land of the living. Their pilot is Mrs. Piper, the "white crow" whom they believe has the expertise to lead them to the other side and back.

The action of the poem centers on Mrs. Piper's explosive interview. In Brackett's telling, Hodgson, referred to simply as the Secretary, is the fraud-busting investigator who hypocritically offers Mrs. Piper's services for sale. (In fact, the Society provided her with a retainer so she would not hire herself out to other clients.) Brackett mocks Hodgson's investigative claims:

"A hundred scalps hung from his belt,
While from his spear aloft he swung
The Russian woman's cloven tongue."

James is the ".professor who claimed to know/ Something about a dear white crow." Hyslop is presented as the author of a mighty book that they hope will save them when all else fails. Together they form a hapless crew whose skepticism undermines their mission. When Mrs. Piper, the Pilot, abandons them, they are stranded on the border of the other world:

"They paddled by night, they paddled by day,
Through ghostly frauds that haunted the way,
Till the pilot refused any longer to guide
Their mystical boat to the other side,
Where those called dead are supposed to reside."

Brackett enjoys describing their efforts to right the boat, and finally to abandon it for Hyslop's tome:

"Then Hodgson said, with hopeful look,
'Almighty friend, hast thou thy book?
If so what care we for this boat?
For come what may we all shall float.'"

But when Hyslop reads from his book, a supernatural force blows them away
to parts unknown. They are never seen again, but their legacy is suggested by
a black crow who steals the mask used by Hyslop to disguise his identity in his
early séances with Mrs. Piper. The crow brings it to her nest, where she produces
five chicks who are white but also blind.

In Brackett's tale the Society fails (as indeed in real life it produced no
definitive proof one way or the other as to the existence of spirit phenomena)
because its members are so focused on fraud and non-supernatural explanations
that they ignore what he sees as incontrovertible evidence of life beyond the
grave. He refuses to criticize Mrs. Piper whom he sees as a victim of sensation-
seeking tabloids. Instead, he places the onus on the narrow-minded researchers.
In an explanatory note that follows the poem, he remarks:

"For more than fifty years I have been a close student of what is known as
spirit phenomena, in all its phases, and I have yet to find any evidence that it is
not what it claims to be. I am not, however, in sympathy with much that passes
under that name, nor am I especially attracted to the work of the American
Branch of the Society for Psychical Research. However honest its members may
be, I regard it as little more than a respectable humbug. They have not sought
to establish the truth of the phenomena, but to prove that it is something else."

Or, as he suggests in the poem, there is a reason the spirits eluded these
researchers:

"Does it pay one, after dying,
To come back and prove the lying?"

Further Thoughts on the Ways of the World

Toward the end of his life, Brackett produced one more extended defense
of his unorthodox ideas. *The World We Live In*, published in 1902,[263] is a set
of essays and literary inventions that present his position on everything from
the relation of democracy to a debased Christianity to speculations about the
origins of the universe. He also reveals an receptiveness to alternative models
of science and religion suggested by the translations of Hindu cosmology just
becoming available in the West.

Many of his observations appear to be a mishmash of prevailing intellectual theories. And again, many of his conclusions are simply wrong. However, the issues Brackett was wrestling with remain urgent. In the text, Brackett decries the despotism of a materialistic age and the corruption of Christianity by politics, comes out against value-free science, explores the limits of the scientific method and the meaning of progress, arguing against materialism's separation of mind from body. His ruminations illuminate a curious layman's unsettled reactions to modern science at a moment when it was professionalizing, splitting from religion, and detaching itself from larger ethical, spiritual and social concerns.

The text is occasionally startlingly prescient: On the subject of women's rights Brackett remarks, "How strange, how sad this debasement, this degradation of woman, who, in the fullness of her nature, in her true individuality, in her noble aspirations, in the glory and splendor of her organization, is the highest embodiment of life! To degrade her, to deprive her of her just inheritance is a crime against humanity and the infinite intelligence that created her."

He debunks the idea of Social Darwinism, arguing that the principle that governs human social evolution is not survival of the fittest, but "survival of the most favored . . . It was opportunity that made Lincoln president when great executive ability was required. It was opportunity that enabled Grant to control the largest army, over the widest extent of territory, ever controlled by one man. The world is full of great men and women kept in the background from lack of opportunity."

And he offers an Emersonian vision of the primacy of Nature: "Whatever may be your station, your surroundings, the closer you adhere to Nature, the more you realize her simplicity and wonderful beauty, the greater will be your progress, both material and spiritual, and the happier you will be."

In *The World We Live In*, Brackett offers a relentlessly optimistic view of human nature and progress. He maintains, "What we call evil is due to appearances, to a deflection of spirit force in its effort to express itself through material and imperfect organisms." And he offers this vision of natural unity: Whether you are conscious or unconscious, sleeping or waking, this pulsation of spirit through matter is always present. You are a part of me and I a part of you, and we are a part of everything that is or has been. The whole world is united through evolution and interchangeable particles of matter."

Such ideas reflect the tenets of what came to be known as New Thought. This philosophy was an outgrowth of spiritualism as it adapted to the widespread discrediting of séances. It was a viewpoint that adopted the language of science to promote an anti-materialist vision of human evolution. New Thought drew on everything from the idealist ideas of Plato and Hegel to Emerson's Transcendentalism and a partially digested Hindu philosophy. It would eventually evolve further into the New Age movement, at which point the progressive social elements it had inherited from spiritualism were overwhelmed by a more individualist, and one might argue, solipsistic view of individual human perfectibility. But in Brackett's hands, New Thought offered a generous, expansive and socially progressive view of mankind's future.

William James, Brackett's sometime antagonist, included a discussion of New Thought in his monumental study of *The Varieties of Religious Experience*. He summed it up as the "religion of healthy mindedness" and saw it as a quintessentially American phenomena, reflecting "the extremely practical turn of character of the American people." His summation of its adherents aptly describes Brackett: ". . . we find 'evolutionism' interpreted thus optimistically and embraced as a substitute for the religion they were born in, by a multitude of our contemporaries who have either been trained scientifically, or been fond of reading popular science, and who had already begun to be inwardly dissatisfied with what seemed to them the harshness and irrationality of the orthodox Christian scheme." Ultimately, however, James finds the optimistic take of New Thought lacking in nuance: ". . . systematic healthy-mindedness, failing as it does to accord to sorrow, pain, and death any positive and active attention whatever, is formally less complete than systems that try at least to include these elements in their scope."[264]

Brackett's faith in the inevitability of humanity's spiritual progress made it impossible for him to accept materialist explanations for the origins of human consciousness. He was convinced that human evolution was being directed by a higher force. Wallace had distinguished between biological evolution driven by the law of natural selection and a spiritual and mental evolution guided by an Overruling Intelligence. Brackett, by contrast, formulated a position that is closer to today's Intelligent Design movement. He stated flatly, "Evolution of species is a theory without any living evidence to sustain it , — an abortive effort to explain the unknowable by methods that do not explain, — to substitute a blind force in the place of divine intelligence."[265]

This conviction was supported by his practical experiences as a farmer and a breeder. He remarks, "If you ask the farmer about his crops, he will tell you that he plows the ground, manures it, plants his corn and carefully keeps down the weeds so that nothing will interfere with its growth. If you tell him that the scientific way is to trust to natural selection and the survival of the fittest, he would tell you that there would be nothing but weeds. If he is at all irritable and lacking in respect for high authority, he may possibly tell you that there is no fool like a scientific fool."[266] For Brackett, the Divine Intelligence was the Great Gardener, lovingly tending its natural creations.

The Practical Science of Conservation

Brackett was not anti science. He acknowledged its success in various fields but he decried its over-reach into matters of the spirit. If Brackett's theoretical musings on science are problematic today, his contributions in the practical field of nature and wildlife conservation remain solid. As Chairman of the Massachusetts Commission on Inland Fisheries, Brackett played an important role in raising the alarm about disappearing species, exhaustion of resources and loss of natural habitat.

The period of the early 1870s when Brackett took up his new position was a turning point for the nascent field of conservation. In England, most natural resources were owned by the Crown, with the result that unauthorized harvesting of fish and game was considered poaching. In the U.S. natural resources were the property of the people. The downside of this democratization of the nation's natural riches was a denuding of wilderness areas of wildlife by overfishing and hunting. This situation was made worse by unregulated tanning, timbering and diversion of water for farm irrigation. Already, by the 1850s, early conservationists were sounding the alarm about drastic declines in fish and wildlife populations. These threatened not only the activities of sportsmen but also the rural and urban communities that depended on these resources for food.

Sometime in the 1860s, Brackett set up a miniature fish hatchery in an old freight car on his property. He was inspired in this effort by his acquaintance with Seth Green, a pioneering pisciculturist who had been experimenting with the artificial propagation of fish since 1837. Brackett's "toy hatchery", as it was described in one account, brought him to the attention of the newly created Massachusetts Commission on Inland Fisheries. Brackett was in the right place at the right time. Government officials at the state and federal level were just waking up to the disastrous state of the nation's waters. In 1869 Brackett was appointed as the third board member of the Massachusetts Commission and in 1873 he became its head. Massachusetts' interest in its waterways coincided with a national conservation drive that resulted in 1871 in the establishment of the U.S. Fish Commission (rechristened in 1940 as the U. S. Fish and Wildlife Service). State and Federal Commissions would work together over the next few decades restore and protect the nation's fish and game resources.

In his official capacity Brackett was in charge of stocking streams and ponds with game fish. Later his purview extended to the propagation of game animals.

He threw himself into these tasks with an energy that he had once devoted to his art career. He expanded his "toy hatchery" in Winchester to become one of the state's official fish hatcheries. Early reports indicate that initially this was an uphill battle. In 1871, at the beginning of his tenure, the Commission's annual report noted the disappointing return from the state hatcheries, remarking that "An evil destiny seemed to preside over this enterprise." The report goes on to point to the small numbers of fish eggs available to be impregnated and laments that many of those which did survive were subsequently lost to unsuitable water in the hatching house and extreme summer heat.[267]

The Report also detailed an expedition led by Brackett to procure salmon eggs for propagation. Again, the process was fraught: "They succeeded in capturing a good number of fine specimens, but lost a part of them owning to the delays of a heavy storm on the lake. . . It was noticed that the females had much less vitality than the males, dying if deprived of proper water. The males, even when placed in a small tank, fought violently and their combativeness could be restrained only by icing the water continually." The report concludes hopefully that this species of fish, if successfully bred, " promises to be a valuable addition to our cultivated species."[268]

Over time the situation improved. In language that echoes Brackett's discussion of the theory of evolution, the report from 1878 maintains: "It is a survival not of the fittest, but of the most favored. Upon our ability to create suitable conditions, to subordinate the lower to the higher forms of life, depends the success of all cultivation." This report also cites much more successful numbers, allowing for the distribution of the fish, free of charge to ponds throughout the state.[269] The Commission reports also find Brackett dealing with petitions for the leasing of ponds for fishing, sorting out rights of public, state and leaseholders, overseeing the distribution of spawn from the Winchester and other fish hatcheries, monitoring the increase or decrease of types of fish and eventually, establishing hunting seasons and limits on catch.

Early on, Brackett's duties embroiled him in a lawsuit that would have far reaching consequences. When he came on board, the commission was already engaged in a battle with the owners of the Holyoke Dam in South Hadley, Massachusetts. In a conflict that presages today's energy wars, the Hadley Falls Company had built a dam on the Connecticut River that prevented shad and salmon from passing up river to their spawning grounds. The company argued that it had paid compensation to owners of fishing rights above the dam and hence had no further obligations. The Commission, then headed by Theodore Lyman III, pointed out that the dam had also destroyed the fishing rights of those below the dam, as fish no longer came to spawn on that section of the river. To rectify the situation, the Commissioners demanded that the company build a fishway that would allow fish to pass over the dam.

When the company refused to accede to its request, the Commission commenced a lawsuit whose full title was *The Holyoke Water Power Company, Plaintiff in error, v. Theodore Lyman and Edward A. Brackett, Commissioners on Inland Fisheries,* (in citations shortened to *Holyoke Company v. Lyman.*) The suit pitted private property rights against public access and use of waterways. The case wound its way to the Massachusetts Supreme Court, where the Commission prevailed and then, following an appeal by the defendants, to the U.S. Supreme Court. The Holyoke Water Power Company claimed that it had fulfilled its contractual requirements while the Commission maintained that the company was sheltering itself behind an erroneous construction of its charter that ignored its public responsibilities. In 1872 the US Supreme Court announced its decision in favor of Lyman and Brackett, ruling that, "Properly construed, neither of the charters [of the Holyoke Company] affords any support whatever to the theory of the respondents, as they do not contain any semblance of a grant to take and subvert the fish rights below the dam".[270]

This was a triumph for the newly established Commission, which could now require the Company to build a fishway. But it had larger repercussions, as it clearly established a public claim to the nation's waterways. As recently as 2018, this court decision provided support to Native American tribes attempting to force Washington State to recognize treaty rights granted them in 1854-55. The tribes maintained they had signed away rights to millions of acres of land in exchange for "the right to take fish" and they argued that the state's system of road culverts had harmed salmon habitats in such a way that threatened their livelihoods. Citing Holyoke Company vs Lyman, this case, Washington v. United States, 584 U.S. ___ (2018) went to the US Supreme Court where the justices let stand a lower court ruling in the tribes' favor.

Throughout the 1870s and 80s, fishways were a popular solution to the problem of moving migratory fish through obstructed waterways. An 1883 exhibition catalog published by the United States Fish Commission extolled the advances of American Fish Culture and mentioned seventeen fishway designs available for use. These included spiral fishways, self adjusting fishways, incline plane return fishways, oblique fishways, deflected current fishways. and chute fishways. Among those listed was a fishway designed by Edward Brackett, who had now adapted his creative skills in the service of his new responsibilities. The report reports on the innovations introduced by the Brackett fishway: "The first section of this fish-way is so arranged that it can be raised, thus entirely shutting off the water at time of freshets or at seasons when the way is not needed."[271]

In his own patent application for his Fishway, Brackett notes another unique feature: his fishway was designed to "retard artificially the rapidity of the current" diverting it "into a circuitous or sinuous course."[272]

Thanks to his position on the Inland Fisheries Commission, the Brackett fishway saw wide use, not only at the Holyoke Dam but throughout the region. It even appeared in an article on fishways published in France in 1904. The 1883 exhibition catalog also mentions the proliferation of hatching boxes to be used for the artificial propagation of fish. Again it includes a design by Brackett for a box that takes advantage of river currents to facilitate the hatching of "semi-bouyant eggs".[273]

Adventures in Animal Husbandry

In 1886, the mandate of the Commission expanded and was rechristened the Commission on Inland Fisheries and Game. Thanks to their success with the fish population of Massachusetts, Brackett (now the Chairman) and his fellow Commissioners were charged with such activities as preserving and expanding the population of game and other birds by restricting hunting seasons, prohibiting the sale of endangered birds and issuing permits for scientific study and collecting. In its annual report, the Commission noted, "The public sentiment in favor of the protection of our song and insectivorous birds is growing, and the moral sentiment of the State is tending strongly in favor of the law for their protection." The Commission also set out to protect various game animals - among them gray squirrels, hares, and rabbits - from such practices as "ferreting, jacklighting, swivel and punt guns."[274] A few years later, the Commissions efforts were bolstered by the passage of the Lacey Act in 1900 which banned the interstate shipment of wild birds and mammals and their products, and greatly limited the species of creatures that could be hunted for sport or food.

As part of this new mandate, Brackett became involved in efforts to ban the use of bird feathers in fashionable women's hats. In the 1880s, the favored feathers came from woodpeckers, terns, grebes, cedar waxwings, robins and blue jays. In the 1890s, high fashion dictated the use of plumes from egrets, herons, birds of paradise, pigeons and sea birds. Not content merely with feathers, women began wearing whole bodies of birds on hats and clothing. A particular favorite was the tiny hummingbird, which species was sacrificed for haute couture in huge numbers during this period. A campaign against these fashions was instituted in 1896 by a pair of socialites—Harriet Lawrence Hemenway and her cousin Minna Hall --who were founders of the Massachusetts Audubon

Society. They were determined to convince their compatriots not to wear feathered hats . Among the tools to gain attention to their cause were tea parties and organized boycotts of feathered products.

As Commissioner, Brackett was happy to get behind this effort by supporting legislation to restrict the feather trade and ceasing to allow permits for private collections of game birds. In an 1900 article in *The Buffalo Commercial* with the headline "The Song Bird Avenged," he suggested a further benefit to the curtailing of feather fashion. Remarking on the onslaught of gypsy moths, an invasive species which can strip a field or forest of foliage in a matter of hours, he argued, "The gypsy moth plague is due to the driving out of the song birds by the milliners and English sparrow." The article goes on to report that "He [Brackett] believed that the sparrows should be exterminated, and that women should cease wearing the wings of song birds and insectivovous birds, and then the gypsy moth would be checked."[275]

As his remarks on the sparrow indicate, Brackett was not opposed to hunting or selective culling. Conservationists of the era realized that sportsmen could be allies if they were persuaded to preserve wildlife habitats and maintain game populations in the service of responsible hunting. In tandem with his efforts to restock the states waterways with endangered fish for the benefit of fishermen, Brackett turned his Winchester property into a breeding ground for a variety of birds and sought-after game animals. These were to be released into the wild for the purposes of sports hunting. Reports from the era mention in particular his work with Mongolian pheasants and Belgian hares. Mongolian pheasants, also known as ring necked pheasants, were prized for their size and meat. Originally from Asia, they began to be imported to the U.S. in the 1880s and arrived in Massachusetts in 1894 under the auspices of a Worcester breeder. Several pairs were turned over to the Fish and Game Commission. Brackett took charge of the propagation and distribution in Massachusetts of what has now become one of the nation's favorite game birds.

Belgian hares, on the other hand, have a somewhat sadder history. Originally developed in Belgium through the cross breeding of domestic and wild rabbits, this large hare arrived in the U.S. in the 1890s. In one of those inexplicable mysteries of speculative demand, the Belgian hare quickly become a highly prized commodity. Much like tulip mania in 17th century Holland, hares began selling for hundreds even thousands of dollars. At one point they reached the price of $5000 for a single rabbit. In a few years over-saturation destroyed the market and prices dropped to under $25 in the early 1900s. Today most breeders have so little interest in the Belgian hare that it has been saved from extinction only through the efforts of a few specialty clubs.

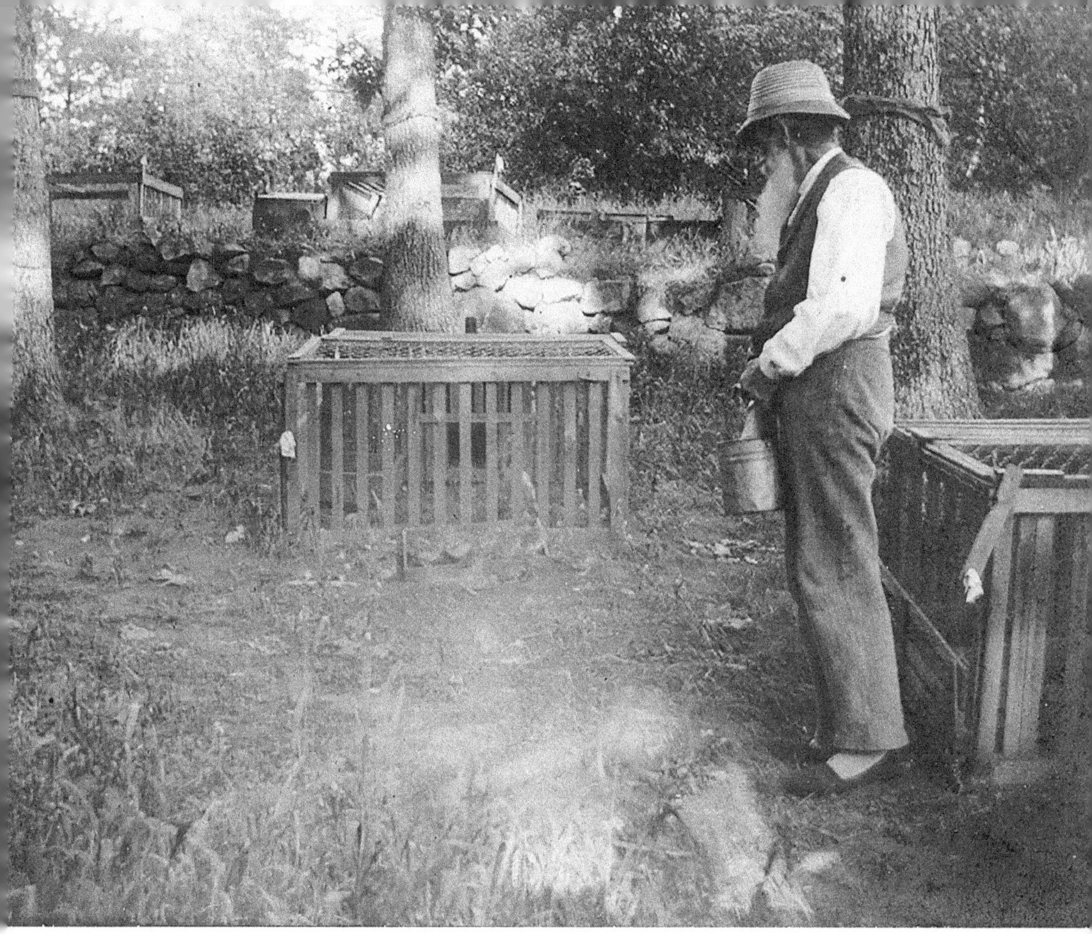

fig. 36 *Edward Augustus Brackett and his animal pens*, undated photograph.
Courtesy of the Winchester Massachusetts Archival Center.

An undated photograph depicts Brackett, his long white beard reaching half way down his chest, grasping a feed bucket as he peruses a cage inhabited by what appear to be part of his collection of Belgian hares.[276] (fig 36) We get an even more vivid sense of his adventures in animal husbandry from an article that appeared in the *Boston Sunday Globe* on April 13, 1902.[277] The unidentified reporter describes his visit to the Brackett property. This tour of the breeding grounds illuminates a more merciless side of Brackett's nature. The article describes the reporter's initial surprise to see the lot encircled by a network of wires. These, it turns out, comprise an electric fence that Brackett installed to protect his brood from predators. The reporter archly notes that the voltage is sufficient "to promptly and neatly dispatch prowling cats and skunks, and sometimes dogs, to the happy hunting grounds." He continues, "Mr. Brackett found it utterly impossible to rear young pheasants and hares because of the marauding felines. Before the adoption of electrocution, Mr. Bracket had recourse to his trusty shotgun, but as he could not sit up nights to watch his tender and valuable brood, the more modern method was put into force with eminent satisfaction and with saving to the state." The reporter adds, "Other thieves than the four-footed kind used to come about and help themselves to the property of the state, but since the deadly wire has encircled the place nimble fingers have had a care of the old adage and refrain from playing with fire."

The article goes on to detail the housing and feeding of Brackett's animals. It becomes clear that proper care is a time consuming process. The reporter describes Brackett's experiments in this regard. For the pheasants he mixes granulated feed and maggots, while the hares are fed oats in the morning and green food in the afternoon, or in the winter chopped hay and clover with moistened bran which has stood for three or four hours before feeding. The reporter remarks that Brackett's success with his hares belies common wisdom about the difficulties of this breed. He notes, "The experience at Winchester shows that the Belgian hares bred by the state are perfectly healthy and more easily raised than their common barnyard fowl. The stock was turned over to the state in the spring of 1900. These were three old and four young does, and from this small stock there have been more than 200 distributed, and there are now some 30 breeders and are sixty young rabbits in various stages of growth. And there has been practically immunity from disease."

A Grand Old Man

The tongue in cheek tone of this article suggests the mix of respect, affection and amusement with which Brackett was regarded in his later years. The once driven young artist had become a grand old man. He was the patriarch of a large and thriving family comprised of sons Frank and Walter, daughters Lena Rose and Bessie, all offspring of his first wife Amanda, and Bertha, his only child with his second wife Elizabeth. He also remained close to his brother Walter, now a painter of some renown who had settled in nearby Boston and to whom he dedicated *The World We Live In*. The dedication reads, "To my brother, WALTER M. Brackett, with whom I have journeyed in this life for more than three - quarters of a century, whose independent thought and action has never marred the affection between us, this little book is dedicated." His last poetry collection contains a bittersweet poem titled *Impromptu* also dedicated to his brother in which he ruminates on the joys of youth, the indignities of aging and the hoped for freedom that will come with death.

As he reached his mid 80s, the *Boston Globe* began to run annual birthday greetings. In 1903, when Brackett had reached the age of 84, an article offered best wishes and described his birthday gathering in Winchester: "During the day and evening a large number of friends called to offer their congratulations, and part of the day was spent by them inspecting the game preserves and fish hatcheries located on his estate."[278] In 1905, the *Winchester Star* has Brackett tooling around town with a friend in an automobile as they survey various town improvements. The article cheerily notes, "Mr. Brackett is enjoying most excellent health at present, except for a little rheumatism, and his mental faculties have suffered no deterioration in the lapse of years." [279] The *Boston Globe*'s 1905 birthday report notes Brackett's recent retirement at age 87 from the State Commission and remarks, "Mr. Brackett is in fine health and daily devotes himself to the care of his extensive fish hatcheries and game preserves. [280]

However, in 1907, when Brackett had attained the age of 89, the *Boston Globe's* birthday greeting notes more sadly, "For some time he has not been in the best of health and this fact made it necessary to forego the usual birthday dinner which he has been accustomed to give to a few intimate friends. A few visitors came today, many letters and telephone calls were received and several friends sent flowers in honor of the occasion." The report concludes, "Mr. Brackett leads an active life, looking after the various matters connected with his work, with the vigor of a much younger man. He has spent much time writing his observations of flowers and fruits as well as fish and game. He is an interesting talker on any subject of nature. His indisposition at this time is only temporary and his friends expect to see him about again soon."[281]

Alas, it was not to be. Brackett passed away on March 15, 1908, six and a half months shy of his 90th birthday. Numerous obituaries in area newspapers recounted his many achievements with varying emphasis on his art career, his service in the Civil War, his poetry and other writings and his work with the Fish and Game Commission. One extensive obituary, published in the Annual Report of Commissioners on Fisheries and Game of Massachusetts, extolled his work in that arena and noted that, "The dominant traits of character were versatility, rugged integrity and perseverance in surmounting obstacles, a sunny optimism and friendliness, — the characteristics of 'a good neighbor' — which made him a notably successful public servant." The Commission resolved that "while bowing reverently to the decree of the Divine will, the undersigned, members of this board, deeply feel the personal loss, the warm friendly greeting and the ripened counsel of our venerated colleague, and extend their profound sympathy to his family and relatives."[282]

But perhaps the best summation of Brackett's life should come from his own pen.

"My House,"[283] the title work in his last published book of poems, captures a sense of an old man surveying a long life with both humor and satisfaction:

"MY HOUSE

This moving house that you call me
Is growing old, and I can see
That it is weak, and here and there
I find some things beyond repair.
You err in thinking it is me,
For I am what you cannot see.
Within, I tread the well - worn floor,
Or stand beside my prison door
That outward swung in days of yore:
'Tis useless now, it swings no more.
Without my house, I see nor hear
Some things that once to me were dear,
And o'er my roof the chilly flow
Of winter piles its drifts of sno.
Yet all within is still aglow
With earnest life, and everything
Wears on its face the joy of spring.

Epilogue
EDWARD BRACKETT AND ME

The origins of this book lie far back in my childhood. They began with what was for many years a vague childhood recollection of a white, life-size sculpture of a woman resting on the stair landing during a rare visit to my great aunt Edna's house in Goffstown, New Hampshire. I was already at this time interested in art and given to sketching anything that came into my field of vision. This interest would evolve later into a career as an art critic. It was no doubt this early fascination with art that lodged the image of the sculpture in my memory, where it lay untroubled for many years. In fact, with time it became so shrouded that I wasn't sure whether I had imagined it. I did know that my great great grandfather was a sculptor named Edward Brackett and I connected this memory to him. Years, later, as an aspiring art writer, I moved to New York City. When I encountered a bust by Brackett of the painter Washington Allston in the American Wing of the Metropolitan Museum of Art, I felt a swell of pride. However, my professional focus at that time was contemporary art. I had little interest in what seemed like the boring academic neo-classicism of 19th century American sculpture.

It took more than three decades for me to turn my attention to my forebear. It was a couple of years before Covid when one day, out of idle curiosity, I googled Brackett to see if there might be any interesting information on him floating around the web. I was astonished to discover several long accounts of the discovery and restoration of Brackett's bust of John Brown by Tufts University Gallery registrar Laura McDonald. The story of Brackett's made-for-TV trip to Brown's jail cell whetted my appetite, and googling further, I discovered reports by Ellen Knight of the Winchester Archival Center detailing Brackett's adventures in spiritualism. I sent the information around to my brothers, who also were pleased to learn something of this fascinating ancestor. And I made a trip to Tufts to meet Laura McDonald. She was delighted to meet a Brackett descendant and provided me with a folder of material she had gathered in her own investigations into the background of the John Brown bust.

However, it took the lockdown and the isolation of Covid to give me the time to dig more deeply into Brackett's story. It was actually a relief during that frightening first year to sink into the 19th century and explore a world with a different set of problems. I was amazed to discover how much material on Brackett was available online. It ranged from facsimiles of his writings to scattered references in memoirs, museum records, government documents and articles on 19th century art and culture. I also reached out to Ellen Knight.

Although the Winchester Archival Center was closed to the public during the pandemic, Ellen was incredibly gracious and helpful, slipping in to the archive to scan and email me newspaper reviews of Brackett's works and other original documents.

I was deep into writing this book when memories of that sculpture from my childhood resurfaced. I had run into several references to a representation of Little Nell still in Brackett's possession at the time of his death. This work was otherwise not accounted for in any list of extant work. I wondered if my mystery sculpture could be Little Nell. At a family reunion I asked my brothers if they remembered seeing a sculpture in Aunt Edna's house. My brother Jim replied that not only did he recall it, but he had a snapshot of it somewhere in an old family album. When he returned home he scanned it and sent it to me. With a bit of digital cleaning, it appeared to conform to contemporary descriptions of Brackett's *Little Nell* in newspaper reviews sent to me by Ellen Knight. (fig 37)

Now I knew the sculpture was not a figment of my imagination. Armed with an actual photograph of it, I enlisted my cousins Heather and David Parker, who are also great grandchildren of Brackett's daughter Bessie. Dave turned out to be an intrepid sleuth, and took on the job of tracing the apparent movements of the sculpture. It must have come to New Hampshire through Bessie, who married Charles Stinson Parker in 1886. It then must have been bequeathed to her son Bill who married Edna Gertrude Fogg in 1918. Bill and Edna had no children and after Bill's death Edna maintained two homes, one in Dunbarton, New Hampshire and the other in Goffstown. This is where I saw the sculpture as a child. (An interesting bit of trivia --great uncle Bill, Brackett's grandson, was an architect who, like his grandfather, built his own house.) Edna died in 1988 and we were able to locate her will. Along with an exhaustive enumeration of every rug, table, item of clothing and houseware in her estate is a listing of a "Large Plaster Statue Known as "Little Nell" Artist Edwin Brackett" (a misspelling of Edward Brackett's name that appears in a few other accounts as well). Its value is given as $750, not a tiny sum in 1989, the date of this inventory.

From here Dave attempted to follow an increasingly tenuous trail. The estate was divided between Edna's nephews Howard and Forrest Fogg. Howard's address at the time of the will signing was listed as Huachuca, Arizona, while Forrest remained in New Hampshire. Forrest got the Dunbarton House and Howard inherited the Goffstown House. Being an out of towner, he sold it and presumably its contents. Dave traced the ownership of both houses, which had turned over several times, up to the present day. I had interesting conversations with several of the current residents, none of whom had any knowledge of the sculpture.

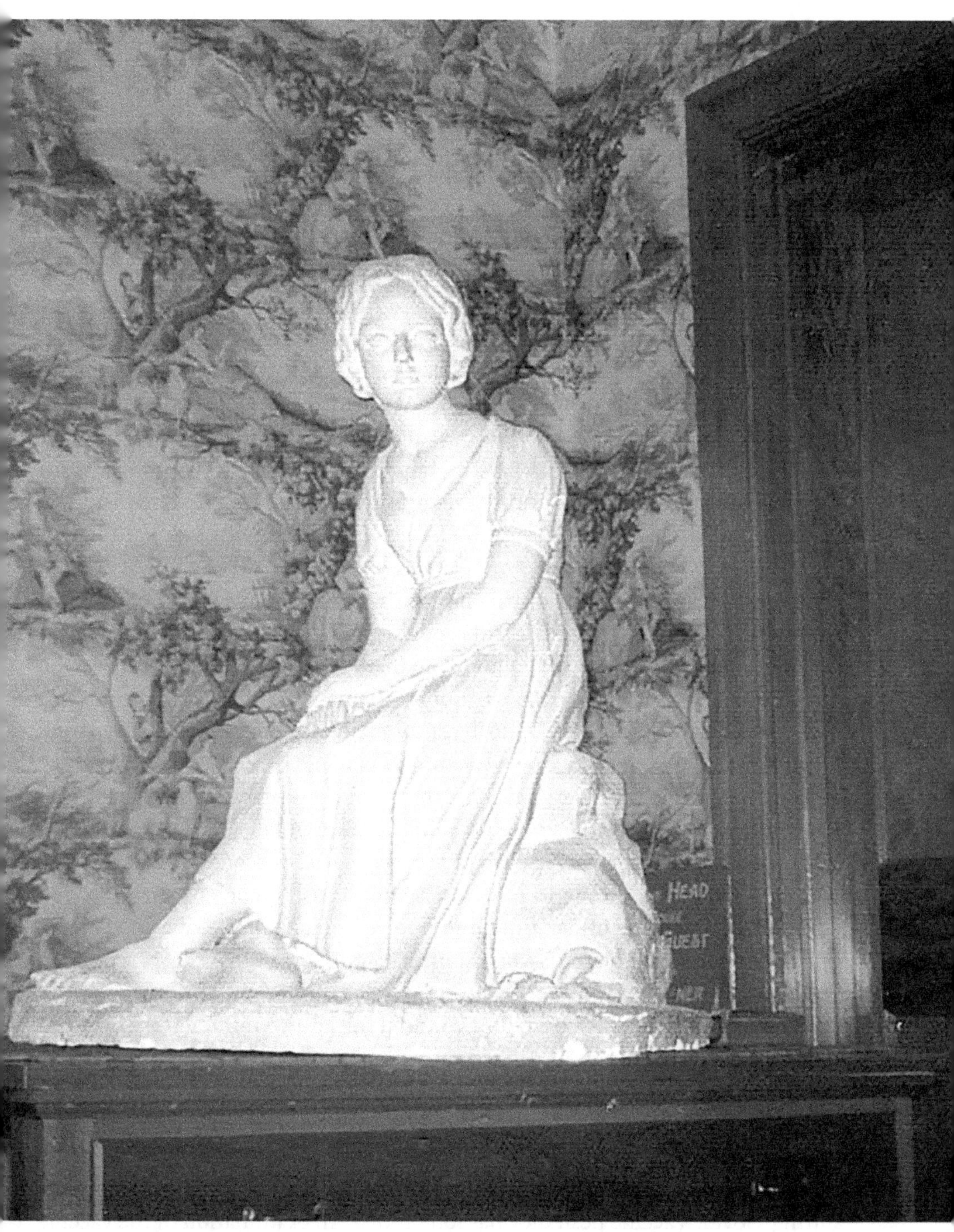

fig. 37 *Little Nell*, by Edward Augustus Brackett, 1842, marble, location unknown, Heartney family snapshot.

There the trail runs cold. But I feel certain that the sculpture is out there, having been seen as recently as 1989. So the search for *Little Nell* continues. Like the *John Brown* bust and *Shipwrecked Mother and Child*, I hope that eventually it will be rescued from oblivion and ensconced in a museum collection.

I have been struck by the unsettling ease with which significant works like *Little Nell,* to say nothing of Brackett's *John Brown* bust and *Shipwrecked Mother,* can disappear. It is often sheer serendipity that brings them back to visibility. This realization underscores the capriciousness of the historical record. When we move beyond the major figures who are firmly etched into our memories and historical narratives, we find a host of others whose inclusion or exclusion appears more or less arbitrary. Why is Darwin hailed as the father of the theory of evolution and why is Wallace largely unknown? How is it that Joseph Holt Ingraham was America's most popular novelist in the 19th century and yet is completely forgotten today? What happens to the legacy of movers and shakers like Nicholas Longworth or Orson Fowler when they slip into historical obscurity? What does it take to bring figures like Edmonia Lewis, or for that matter, Edward Brackett, back into focus?

One of the great rewards of this project has been my discovery of the rich complexity of Brackett's life, art and thought. Another was my introduction to the larger cast of characters who populate this book. Edward Brackett became a portal through which I began to glimpse the passions, tensions, threats and challenges that comprised life in 19th century America. I was continually struck by the foreshadowings of our own dilemmas. Having worked as an art critic for almost forty years, I can very much relate to Brackett's struggles within an art patronage system that prized predictability over originality and set up almost insurmountable barriers to those without proper social or economic connections. Such complaints continue to resonate among artists today. Meanwhile, the stark political divides of our time find a mirror image in the divisions of the antebellum period. The roots causes remain familiar. Conflicts are exacerbated by the legacy of slavery, differing interpretations of the Constitution, frictions between urban and rural communities and unresolved contradictions between the American veneration of rugged individualism and its lip service to more communitarian social ideals. The riots and demonstrations that erupted in the wake of the Black Lives Matter movement are uncannily similar to the racial upheavals that shook communities across the nation in the buildup to the Civil War. Then there is the debate over the efficacy of vaccination that raged during Covid. Vaccine hesitancy has long roots. An examination of the vaccine resistance of figures like Wallace and Brackett suggests that it is not always simply a rejection of science. Even among today's vaccine boosters there is a recognition that different rates of vaccination across the country are related to larger inequities and social problems.

But if such considerations reveal the continuities between Brackett's time and our own, in other ways I became aware of stark differences in our eras. Today it is commonly assumed that religion and science are inevitably in conflict. But in the 19th century they were often seen as mutually supportive. Religious leaders hailed new discoveries as further evidence of God's benevolence. Scientific advances sometimes came about as a result of investigations grounded in questions about the nature of spirit or the possibility of life after death. Scientists and theologians were able to regard each other with interest and respect. They embraced a continuum between the material and spiritual worlds.

Even more stark is the difference in our visions of the future. The end of the Civil War ushered in a period of bracing optimism for many Americans. Reconstruction seemed to point toward a more egalitarian and democratic society. The possibilities opened up by new developments in technology and science promised to unleash human potential in hitherto unimaginable ways. Today, of course, we know how those visions played out over the course of the 20th century. In the 21st century the idea of progress has become problematic. When we look ahead we are more inclined toward trepidation than confidence. To revisit Brackett's world is to become reacquainted with the invigorating emotion of hope.

Working on this book has also led me to ruminate on the nature of inheritance. Retracing the steps of Brackett's life, I came to consider how much I share with a man who entered the world in 1818 and who died forty-six years before I was born. As an art writer my work has often revolved around questions of social justice, environmental restoration and the impact of religion on contemporary artists. I recognize a kindred spirit in my great great grandfather, a man who was deeply immersed in art, politics, nature and spirituality. We both are writers who try to make sense of a confusing time. We both believe deeply that one should leave the world a better place than one found it.

With this book I hope to have brought Edward Augustus Brackett and his times back to life. He believed that our spiritual essence lives on after death. Whether or not that is true, his life is surely evidence that our works and words can carry on and help to shape a future we will never know.

ENDNOTES

1.   Weathersby, II, Robert, *J. H. Ingraham*, (Boston: G. K. Hall& Co., 1980), p. 29.

2.   Poe, Edgar Allan, review of *Lafitte: the Pirate of the Gulf, Southern Literary Messenger* 2 (August 1836), p. 595, quoted in Weathersby, p. 57.

3.   Johannson, Albert, *The House of Adams and Beadle and its Dime and Nickle Novels*, (Norman, OK: University of Oklahoma Press, 1950), digitized by the Northern Illinois University Libraries DeKalb, Illinois, https://web.archive.org/web/20051031095615/http://www.niulib.niu.edu/badndp/ingraham_joseph.html

4.   "The Novelist Divine, *Mississippi Free Trader*, February 18, 1852, p. 1, quoted in Weathersby, p. 40.

5.   Ingraham, J. H., "The Struggles of Early Genius," *Baltimore Phoenix and Budget*, May 1841, reprinted by Google Books: https://books.google.com/books?id=OtURAAAAYAAJ&pg=PA11&lpg=PA11&dq=prof.+ingraham+THE+JUVENILE+GENIUS&source=bl&ots=oTgeC5fEZ1&sig=ACfU3U2OR4hHcQch1jsDWeaSyQTnWoFdA&hl=en&sa=X&ved=2ahUKEwifjdySnYzrAhW3gXIEHUjeCNgQ6AEwBnoECAoQAQ#v=onepage&q=prof.%20ingraham%20THE%20JUVENILE%20GENIUS&f=false and https://books.google.com/books?id=OtURAAAAYAAJ&pg=PA281&lpg=PA281&dq=ingraham+struggles+of+early+genius+baltimore+phoenix&source=bl&ots=oTgeA6lH30&sig=ACfU3U3LCx3qYU9Lp835OWyPpO9J5c7bHw&hl=en&sa=X&ved=2ahUKEwi__OC8YbrAhV4mHIEHY4lBKsQ6AEwDHoECAoQAQ#v=onepage&q=ingraham%20struggles%20of%20early%20genius%20baltimore%20phoenix&f=false

6.   Ingraham, *Baltimore Phoenix and Budget*, April 1841.

7.   Ingraham, *Baltimore Phoenix and Budget*, December 1841, p. 324.

8.   Ingraham, *Baltimore Phoenix and Budget*, December 1841, p. 323.

9.   Ingraham, *Baltimore Phoenix and Budget*, February 1842, p. 402.

10.   Ingraham, *Baltimore Phoenix and Budget*, December 1841, p. 326.

11.   Brackett, Herbert Ierson, *Brackett Genealogy: Descendants of Anthony Brackett of Portsmouth and Captain Richard Brackett of Braintree. With Biographies of the Immigrant Fathers, Their Sons, and Others of Their Posterity*, published by H. I Brackett, Washington D.C. 1907, reprinted in Google Books, https://www.google.com/books/edition/Brackett_Genealogy/qzk3AAAAMAAJ?hl=en

12.   Brackett, Herbert Ierson, p. 53.

13.   ibid, p. 96.

14.   ibid, p. 290.

15.   Ingraham, *Baltimore Phoenix and Budget*, April, 1841.

16.   Wilson, Joshua L. MSS, "Commonplace Book," 1829 (?), *Wilson Papers*, Library of the University of Chicago, quoted in Aaron, Daniel, *Cincinnati Queen City of the West*, (Athens, OH: Ohio University Press, 1992), p. 252.

17.   Wilson, Joshua L, MSS, III, p. 315, quoted in Aaron, p. 179.

18.   Hawthorne, Nathaniel, *The Marble Faun*, Vol 1, (Boston and New York, Houghton Mifflin, 1899) p. 667.

19.   Lee, Hannah Farnham Sawyer, Familiar Sketches of Sculpture and Sculptors, Vol 2, (Boston: Crosby, Nichols and Company, 1854), p. 128.

20.   Ingraham, *Baltimore Phoenix and Budget*, August 1841 p. 166.

21.   Weidman,Jeffrey, *Artists in Ohio, 1787-1900: A Biographical Dictionary*, (Kent, OH: Kent State University Press, 2000) p. 108. https://books.google.com/books?id=ZdICm_W8xKw-C&pg=PA108&lpg=PA108&dq=Edward+brackett+the+poetess&source=bl&ots=s7mHPhN-N9i&sig=ACfU3U1wR6zCNaAtK5ORSiRl_XUkUSRf9w&hl=en&sa=X&ved=2ahUKEwiu8uSdjOvoAhWSUt8KHUUwA34Q6AEwDHoECAsQKQ#v=onepage&q=Edward%20brackett%20the%20poetess&f=false

22.   Thomas, Ebenezer S., *Reminiscences of the last sixty-five years, commencing with the battle of Lexington. Also, sketches of his own life and times*, (Hartford: Case, Tiffany and Burnham, 1840) p. 198.

23.   de Tocqueville, Alexis, *Voyages en Sicile et aux Etats-Unis OC*, V, 1., https://www.city-journal.org/html/alexis-de-tocqueville-urban-critic-12639.html

24.   Trollope, Frances, *Domestic Manners of the Americans*, ed. Donald Smalley (London: Whittaker, Treacher & Co 1832), p. 326.

25.   Jarves, James Jackson, *Art Thoughts: The Experiences and Observations of an American Amateur in Europe*, (New YorK: Hurd and Houghton, 1871) p. 308.

26.   Hawthorne, *The Marble Faun*, vol 1, p. 120.

27.   Harpers Weekly: A Journal of Civilization, Vol VII, No. 323, Saturday, March 7, 1863, *The Late Nicholas Longworth*, p. 1. http://www.sonofthesouth.net/leefoundation/civil-war/1863/nicho-

las-longworth.htm

28. Whittredge, Worthington, *The Autobiography of Worthington Whittredge 1820-1910*, edited by John T.H. Baur, (New York, 1969), p. 17. http://library.cincymuseum.org/topics/l/files/longworth/qch-v46-n1-nic-017.pdf

29. Frankenstein, John P. *American Art: Its Awful Altitude* (Cincinnati, 1864), p. 48.

30. *Harpers Weekly*, p. 2.

31. Ingraham, Seus, Jeff, "Our history: Longworth family influenced arts, politics," *Cincinnati Enquirer*, ˆNov 18, 2018 https://www.cincinnati.com/story/news/2018/11/28/longworth-family-had-impact-arts-politics/2136071002/

32. Ingraham, *Baltimore Phoenix and Budget*, November, 1841, p. 283.

33. Gardner, Albert TenEyck, *Yankee Stonecutters: The First American School of Sculpture 1800-1850*, (NY, published for the Metropolitan Museum of Art by Columbia University Press, 1945), p.21.

34. Gardner, p. 28.

35. Ingraham, *Baltimore Phoenix and Budget*, August 1841, p. 170.

36.   quoted in Thomas, p. 208.

37.   Gardner p. 3.

38. Gardner p. 5.

39. Landor, Walter Savage, quoted in Gardner, p. 4.

40. Jarves, p. 292.

41. Jarves p. 296.

42. Jarves p. 292.

43. Jarves, p. 293.

44. Hawthorne, YS or Marble Faun.

45. Ingraham, *Baltimore Phoenix and Budget*, October 1841, p. 259.

46. Thomas, p. 203.

47. Ingraham, *Baltimore Phoenix and Budget*, November 1841, p. 281.

48. Thomas, p. 207.

49. Ingraham, *Baltimore Phoenix and Budget*, November 1841 p. 282.

50. Ingraham, *Baltimore Phoenix and Budget*, November, 1841, p. 283.

51. Ingraham, *Baltimore Phoenix and Budget*, December 1841, p. 322.

52. Thomas, p. 206.

53. These were provided by Ellen Knight, Reference Archivist of the Winchester Archival Center in Winchester Mass. Most have no author or Newspaper source listed.

54. *Cutty-sark* is a nickname given to Nannie Dee, a fictional witch created by Robert Burns in his poem Tam o' Shanter, after the garment she wore.

55. Lee, Hannah Farnham Sawyer, *Familiar Sketches of Sculpture and Sculptors*, Vol 2, (Boston; Crosby, Nichols and Company, 1854).

56. Weathersby, p. 129

57. Stowe, Charles Edward, The Life of Harriet Beecher Stowe, (Cambridge MA; The Riverside Press, 1889), p. 83.

58. ibid., p. 84.

59. ibid. p. 85.

60. ibid. p. 87.

61. ibid. p. 88.

62. Morse to Mrs. Morse, August 27, 1823, quoted in Harris, Neil, *The Artist in American Society: The Formative Years 1790-1860*, (NY: Simon and Schuster, 1970, p. 112.

63. Henry Kirke Brown to Ezra P. Prentice, March 8, 1844, quoted in Thayer Tolles, "Modeling a Reputation: The American Sculptor and New York City," Thayer Tolles, ed., *Art and the Empire City: New York, 1825-1861* (NY: Metropolitan Museum of Art, 2013) p. 135.

64. Peter Augustus Jay to James Fenimore Cooper, April 1, 1832, quoted in Tolles, p. 141.

65. "Curious Criticism in the Fine Arts," NY *Herald* May 1 1841 p.2 in The Brackett Collection in the Archival Center of Winchester, Massachusetts

66. Katz, Wendy Jean, *Humbug! The Politics of Art Criticism in New York City's Penny Press*, (NY: Fordham University Press, 2020).

67. Katz, p. 1.

68. Katz, p. 66.

69. Katz, p. 252.

70. *New York Mirror: A Weekly Gazette of Literature and the Fine Arts*. Dec 14, 1839, United States: G. P. Morris, p. 199 https://www.google.com/books/edition/New_York_Mirror/J8FCAQAAMAA-J?hl=en

71. Katz, p. 188.

72. Katz, p. 190.

73.	The Indiana Historical Archives lists "Black-and-white lithograph half-length three-quarter portrait of "Major Genl. Wm. Hy. Harrison holding a pen in his right hand and something else in his left, with facsimile signature (drawn and engraved by G. Parker from the bust by E. Brackett)."

74.	Clipping from The Brackett Collection in the Archival Center of Winchester, Massachusetts.

75.	A member of a radical group of New York Democrats organized in 1835 in opposition to the regular party organization.

76.	The Brackett Collection in the Archival Center of Winchester, Massachusetts.

77.	ibid.

78.	see William Freehling, *William Harrison: Campaigns and Elections,* UVA Miller Center, https://millercenter.org/president/harrison/campaigns-and-elections

79.	Cometto, Maria Teresa , *Emma and the Angel of Central Park,* (NY: Bordighera Press, 2023), p. 19-20.

80.	*New York Day Book,* May 6, 1852. http://katzsnewspapers.org/files/original/adb7c86f-442863c353fe46f9876136f7.pdf

81.	"Brackett, the Sculptor," *The Evening Mirror,* Nov 14, 1849

82.	http://katzsnewspapers.org/files/original/a04d3ad2d3157669042d5d43d938df1b.jpg

83.	Letter from E. A. Brackett to G. Forrester Barstow: April 10 1841, Archival Center of Winchester, Massachusetts.

84.	The Brackett Collection in the Archival Center of Winchester, Massachusetts.

85.	"Mr. Brackett, the Sculptor," *New York Mirror,* Saturday December 14, 1839.

86.	Sarna, J. D., *Jacksonian Jew: The two worlds of Mordecai Noah*, (Holmes & Meier 1981) p. 110-111.

87.	Poe, Edgar Allan, "A Chapter on Autography (Part I)," *Graham's Magazine,* November 1841

88.	https://www.mbenjaminkatzfinebooksraremanuscripts.com/product/4027/1848-ORIGINAL-MANUSCRIPT-LETTER-REFERENCING-A-LITERARY-FEUD-HANDWRITTEN-BY-A-BALTIMORE-POET-AND-LONG-TIME-BITTER-RIVAL-OF-EDGAR-ALLAN-POE-RUFUS-DAWES

89.	Harris, p. 306.

90.	Dewey, Orville, *The Old World and the New, or, A journal of reflections and observations made on a tour in Europe* (NY: Harper and Brothers, 1836), p. 162.

91.	Nicholas Longworth to Hiram Powers, April 30, 1840, Hiram Powers and Powers Family Papers, microfilm reel 817, no. frame number, Archives of American Art, Smithsonian Institution, Washington, D.C.

92.	Letter from E. A. Brackett to G. Forrester, op. cit.

93.	"Brackett's Binding of Satan," *Arcturus* vol I, no. VI, (New York: Benjamin Trevett, 1841), p. 373.

94.	"The Binding of Satan," *Boston Post*, July 21, 1841, p. 1.

95.	For a discussion of the cultural ramifications of Greenough's Lucifer see Moll, J. Richmond, "Sculpture and Spectacle: Horatio Greenough's 'Christ' and 'Lucifer,'" *Winterthur Portfolio* 50, no. 4 (Winter 2016): 209-247.

96.	The Brackett Collection in the Archival Center of Winchester, Massachusetts.

97.	ibid.

98.	Stone, William Leete, "Binding of Satan: a clever group in plaster by Brackett, at Chambers," *Commercial Advertiser*, April 1, 1841, p. 2.

99.	Brackett, Edward, "The Group" published in *My House, Chips the Builder Threw Away,* (Boston: The Gotham Press, 1904), p. 19.

100.	ibid. p. 29.

101.	ibid. p. 34.

102.	Brackett, Herbert Ierson, p. 303.

103.	op. cit.

104.	James, Henry, *The Bostonians* (London: Penguin, 1966, 1969), p. 7.

105.	Winthrop, John, "A Model of Christian Charity", sermon delivered March 21, 1630.

106.	quoted in Dowling Adams, Jane Aldrich, "A Study of Art Unions in the United States of America in the Nineteenth Century," 1990, thesis for Virginia Commonwealth University, p. 54, https://core.ac.uk/download/pdf/51292608.pdf

107.	quoted in Harris, p. 113.

108.	Middlesex County, Massachusetts, Registry of Deeds: 555-350.

109.	Newton, James A., "Crows' Nests or Eagles' Aeries? The Octagon Houses of E. A. Brackett and H. P. Wakefield," *Historic New England,* Vol. 67, No. 247 (Winter/Spring, 1977) p. 58.

110.	Bryant to Richard Dana, Mary 21, 1841, Bryant, William Cullen and Voss, Thomas G., The Letters of William Cullen Bryant: Volume II, 1836–1849 (NY: Fordham University Press, 1977,) p. 256.

111. Lester, C. Edwards, *The Artists of America: A Series Of Biographical Sketches Of American Artists; With Portraits And Designs On Steel*, (Baker and Scribner, 1846) p.9.
112. Harris, p. 237.
113. Novak, Barbara, *American Painting of the Nineteenth Century: Realism, Idealism, and the American Experience*, (Wesstport, CT: Praeger Publishers, 1969) p. 45.
114. Gerdts, William H. and Stebbins, Jr., Theodore E., "A Man of Genius": *The Art of Washington Allston (1779-1843)*, exh. cat. (Boston: Museum of Fine Arts, 1979), p. 108
115. Gerdts, p. 108.
116. Lester, p. 24.
117. Gerdts, p. 165.
118. William Cullen Bryant to Richard Dana, Jr. January 16 1844, March 30 1844 and May 17 1844, *The Letters of William Cullen Bryant*, op. cit.
119. Brackett, Edward A., "Lines Suggested on Finishing a Bust of Allston," *Twilight Hours, Or Leisure Moments Of An Artist*, (Freeman and Bolles, 1845) p. 50.
120. Twilight Hours, iv.
121. "The Wreck of the Slave Ship," *Twilight Hours*, p. 74.
122. Reynolds, David S. *Abe: Abraham Lincoln in His Times*, (NY: Penguin Press, 2020).
123. Bode, Carl. *The Anatomy of American Popular Culture, 1840- 1861*, (Berkeley: University of California Press, 1959) p. 188.
124. Justus, James A. "The Fireside Poets: Hearthside Values and the Language of Care" in Lee, A. Robert, *Nineteenth Century American Poetry*, (Cleveland: Vision Press Ltd and Barnes and Noble Books, 1985) p 152.
125. Farnham Sawyer Lee, Hannah, *Familiar Sketches* p. 198.
126. Brackett, Herbert Ierson, p. 303.
127. Brackett's Seedling Grape, *New England Farmer*, Boston, MA, - 07/10/1862. https://www.newspapers.com/clip/19765415/ea-brackett-new-england-farmer/
128. Farnham Sawyer Lee, p. 202.
129. ibid. p. 199.
130. ibid.
131. ibid. p. 200.
132. ibid.
133. Aries, Philippe, *The Hour of Our Death*, (NY: Alfred A. Knopf, 1981) p. 473.
134. Poe, Edgar Allan "The Philosophy of Composition" *Graham's Magazine*, April 1846
135. *The Literary World*, April 10, 1852.
136. Brackett, Edward A., "Sleep and Death," *Twilight Hours*, p. 69.
137. Bode, p. 189.
138. from a clip in the Winchester Archive - *Boston Daily Atlas*, dated March 30, 1842.
139. Greenwood, Grace, "Correspondence of the Era," *The National Era*, January 24, 1850.
140. quoted in Craven, Wayne, Sculpture in America, University of Delaware, 1968 p. 188.
141. Greenwood, op. cit.
142. The Brackett Collection in the Archival Center of Winchester, Massachusetts.
143. ibid.
144. Leland, Charles Godfrey, "Brackett's Wreck," *Sartain's Magazine*, May 1850 p. 370.
145. Edgers, Geoff, "Finding John Brown: How Tufts' art collection registrar Laura McDonald solved the mystery of the lost masterpiece," *Tufts Magazine*, Fall 2016.https://news.tufts.edu/magazine/fall2016/act/finding-john-brown.html
146. Reynolds, David, *John Brown, Abolitionist: The Man Who Killed Slavery, Sparked the Civil War, and Seeded Civil Rights*, (NY: Vintage. 2005).
147. ibid, p. 6.
148. Delbanco, Anthony *The War Before the War: Fugitive Slaves and the Struggle for America's Soul from the Revolution to the Civil War*, (NY: Penguin Books, 2018).
149. *The Middlesex Journal*, Sept. 8, 1855, reprinted in *The Winchester Record*, Vol. III, No. 1 (April 1887), p. 94. Quoted in Knight, Ellen :THE SCULPTOR&THE ABOLITIONIST How Winchester's Edward Brackett Created an Icon for the Abolitionist Movement," posted on https://www.winchester.us/DocumentCenter/View/4401/Sculptor-and-Abolitionist?bidId=
150. Garrison, William Lloyd, "To the Public," *The Liberator*, January 1, 1831.
151. Garrison, William Lloyd to J. May, Rev. Samuel , July 17, 1845, in Merrill, Walter M., ed. *The Letters of William Lloyd Garrison* (1973) 3: 303. *The Liberator*, May 6, 1842.
152. Garrison, William Lloyd , speech at Tremont Temple, December 2, 1859, *The Liberator*, December 16, 1859, https://www.theliberatorfiles.com/garrison-speech/
153. all quotes from *Wendell Phillips, Speeches, Lectures and Letters*, (Boston: James Redpath, Publisher, 1863), pp 7-8. https://www.google.com/books/edition/_/XUUIAAAAQAAJ?gbpv=1

154.	Knight, Ellen, "Abolition and Emancipation", posted on: https://www.winchester.us/Document-Center/View/4304/Abolition-and-Emancipation?bidId=

155.	Speech of Wendell Phillips at Faneuil Hall, May 26, 1854, https://www.loc.gov/resource/llst.019/?sp=7&st=text

156.	Dana, Jr., Richard Henry, "Against the Rendition of Anthony Burns to Slavery," May 31, 1854, *Speeches in Stirring Times*, (Boston and NY; Houghton Mifflin, 1910), p. 215. https://www.google.com/books/edition/Richard_Henry_Dana_Jr_Speeches_in_Stirri/b0IrAQAAIAAJ?hl=en&gbpv=1

157.	Lawrence, Amos quoted in Sutton, Robert K., "The Wealthy Activist Who Helped Turn 'Bleeding Kansas' Free," *Smithsonian Magazine*, Aug. 16, 2017, https://www.smithsonianmag.com/history/wealthy-activist-who-helped-turn-bleeding-kansas-free-180964494/

158.	Sumner, Charles, *The Crime Against Kansas*, Speech on May 19, 1856, (Boston: John P. Jewitt and Company, 1856), p. 5. https://www.google.com/books/edition/The_Crime_Against_Kansas/agwx-Pmo1zYwC?hl=en&gbpv=1&pg=PA1&printsec=frontcover

159.	ibid., p. 9.

160.	"Statement of Hon. George C. Brackett, January 19, 1886", *Proceedings of the Kansas Historical Society*, 1883- 1885 p. 223-225. https://www.kshs.org/publicat/khc/1883_1885_reeder_escape.pdf

161.	Reynolds, John Brown, p. 163.

162.	Bowditch, Vincent Yardley, Extract from his journal,1886, *Life and Correspondence of Henry Ingersoll Bowditch*, (Boston and New York: Houghton, Mifflin and Company, 1902), p. 87. https://archive.org/stream/lifecorresponden02bowdiala/lifecorresponden02bowdiala_djvu.txt

163.	Bowditch, Appendix p. 374.

164.	Child, Lydia Maria, "Brackett's Bust of John Brown," *New York Tribune*, February 11, 1860, reprinted in https://exhibits.tufts.edu/spotlight/john-brown-tufts/catalog/9-600

165.	Sanborn, Franklin, "John Brown and His Friends", *The Atlantic Monthly*, April 1872. reprinted in https://www.theatlantic.com/magazine/archive/1872/07/john-brown-and-his-friends/308739/

166.	ibid.

167.	This would be William Morris Hunt, a Barbizon painter.

168.	Sanborn.

169.	quoted in Reynolds, John Brown, p. 354.

170.	The three accounts spliced together here are found in: *Topeka Daily Capital,* Nov. 14, 1889, quoted in Bowditch, Volume 2, 1902, Mayo, Katherine, "Sculptor's Visit to John Brown," in *The Evening Post*, November 13, 1909 and reports by House, Edward Howard in *New York Daily Tribune*, spread over editions of November 7, 8 and 9, 1859.

171.	In "Edward A. Brackett visits John Brown," a Feb 1, 2013 article for Winchester's *Daily Times Chronicle*, Ellen Knight elaborates on the suspicions that Brackett engendered: "Although Brown was allowed visitors, according to the Anti-Slavery Society Virginians deemed Brackett "if not himself a dangerous man, – to be about a dangerous business.... Anyhow, the Virginian authorities and people appear to have thought so, and Mr. Brackett, after much solicitation, was denied access to Brown. The jailor told him, as we learn from the Tribune's reporter, 'that his mission in town was well known, and that there was an immense opposition to it, some hundreds of people having called on him and insisted, with all the arguments they could bring, that no such thing should be permitted. Under these circumstances, the jailor did not feel willing to open his doors,' for the desired purpose." http://homenewshere.com/daily_times_chronicle/news/winchester/article_43ed70d6-7c40-11e2-8f10-001a4bcf887a.html

172.	Child.

173.	Bowditch, letter from Mrs. George L. Stearns to H. I. Bowditch Oct 28 1889. p. 182.

174.	Ellen Knight of the Winchester Historical Society has discovered references to 15 plaster casts, two marble carvings and one bronze version of the bust. Along with Mary Stearns' marble bust, four other copies have been located. These currently reside at the Boston Atheneaum, Tuskegee University, the Spirit of '76 Museum in Wellington, Ohio and the League of Women for Community Service in Boston.

175.	Bowditch, letter from Mrs. George L Stearns to H. I. Bowditch, May 22 1886, p. 86.

176.	Sanborn.

177.	Jarves, James Jackson, *Art Thoughts,* ibid,, p. 319.

178.	Sanborn. op.cit.

179.	*The Evening Post*, November 13, 1909

180.	Buick, Kirsten Pai, *Child of the Fire: Mary Edmonia Lewis and the Problem of Art History's Black and Indian Subject*, (Durham, NC: Duke University Press. 2010), p. 111.

181.	*Artcurious,* Episode #65: The Coolest Artists You Don't Know: Edmonia Lewis https://www.artcuriouspodcast.com/artcuriouspodcast/65

182.	James, Henry, *William Wetmore Story and his Friends* (Boston, Houghton Mifflin and Co. 1903).

183.	Richardson, Marilyn, "Edmonia Lewis's The Death of Cleopatra," *International Review of African*

American Art, 12, no. 2 (1995): pages 36–52.

184. "Sculptor's Death Date Unearthed: Edmonia Lewis Died in London in 1907," *Artfix Daily.* https://www.artfixdaily.com/blogs/post/51-sculptors-death-unearthed-edmonia-lewis-died-in-london-in-1907

185. "Edmonia Lewis: Interview with the Famous Colored Sculptress," *St. Louis Globe-Democrat* November 20, 1873,

186. ."Medallion of John Brown," *The Liberator* March 4, 1864

187. ibid.

188. Nelson, Charmaine, *The Color of Stone: Sculpting the Black Female Subject in Nineteenth Century America*, (Minneapolis: University of Minnesota Press, 2007), p. 13.

189. "Seeking Equality Abroad," *New York Times*, December 29 1878 https://timesmachine.nytimes.com/timesmachine/1878/12/29/issue.html

190. Buick, p. 12.

191. A MEMORIAL BUST OF JOHN BROWN, RECEPTION TO THE SCULPTRESS, MISS EDMONIA LEWIS—PRESENTATION OF THE BUST TO THE REV. DR. HENRY HIGHLAND GARNET, 1878 reprinted in https://abolitionist-john-brown.blogspot.com/2010/10/memorial-bust-of-john-brown-reception.html

192. Buick, p. 13

193. quoted in "The Vanity of Beast Butler," *Smithsonian Civil War: Inside the National Collection*, Smithsonian Institution, 2013, p. 155.

194. Brackett, Edward A., *Materialized Apparitions: If Not Beings from Another Life, What Are They,* (Boston: The Gorham Press, 1908), p. 34.

195. quoted in "Davis, Andrew Jackson." *The Spirit Book,* (Canton, MI: Visible Ink Press, 2006), https://encyclopedia2.thefreedictionary.com/Davis%2c+Andrew+Jackson

196. Davis, Andrew Jackson, *Principles of Nature*, (New York: S.S. Lyon & Wm. Fishbough,) 1847

197. Davis, Andrew Jackson , *The Spirit Book,* op.cit.

198. Brackett, Edward, A., "Pseudo Science" in *My House, Chips the Builder Threw Away*, (Boston: The Gorham Press, 1904), p. 90.

199. Brackett, Herbert Ierson, *Brackett Genealogy*, op.cit.

200. Brackett, Edward, A., *The World We Live In*, (Boston: Richard G. Badger, The Gorham Press, 1909), p. 11.

201. Brackett, Edward, A.,*ibid.*, p. 42.

202. Brackett, Edward, A., ibid. p. 60.

203. Brackett, Edward, A., *Materialized Apparitions*, op.cit. p. 142.

204. Handbook to Cambridge and Mount Auburn, (Boston: Bricher and Russell, 1864), p. 60.

205. quoted in Kasson, Joy S. *Marble Queens and Captives : Women in Nineteenth-century American Sculpture*, (New Haven: Yale University Press, 1990).

206. Braude, Ann, *Radical Spirits: Spiritualism and Women's Rights in Nineteenth-Century America*, (Bloomington: Indiana University Press, 2020), p. 2.

207. Braude, p. 57.

208. "Swedenborgianism," *New-York Daily Tribune*, June 25, 1845; repr. in *Margaret Fuller, Papers on Literature and Art,* 2(New York: Wiley and Putnam, 1846),160–65.

209. Reynolds, David, *John Brown, Abolitionist*, op.cit.

210. Culkin, Kate, *Harriet Hosmer: A Cultural Biography*, (Amherst: University of Massachusetts Press, 2010), p. 130.

211. "Most Famous of American Women Sculptors," *Boston Globe*, March 1, 1908.

212. Colbert, Charles, *Haunted Visions: Spiritualism and American Art (The Arts and Intellectual Life in Modern America)*, (Philadelphia: University of Pennsylvania Press, 2011).

213. Jarves, Jarves, James Jackson, *Art Thoughts*, op.cit, p. 319.

214. De Tocqueville, Alexis, *Democracy In America, Book Two*, (London: Saunders and Otley,1935), p. 489.

215. Walters, Charles Thomas, "Sculpture and the Expressive Mechanism in Pseudo Science and Society in 19th Century America" in Wrobel, Arthur, *Pseudo Science and Society in 19th Century America*, (Lexington: University Press of Kentucky, 2021).

216. Fowler, Orson *A Home for All, or a New, Cheap, Convenient and Superior Mode of Building*, (NY: Fowlers and Wells, 1848).

217. Adamian, John, "Dr. Octagon," *Believer Magazine*, May 1, 2009, https://believermag.com/dr-octagon/

218. Fowler, *A Home for All*, p. 17.

219. Colbert, Charles, *A Measure of Perfection: Phrenology and the Fine Arts in America (Cultural Studies of the United States)*, (Chapel Hill: University of North Carolina Press, 2009), p. 243.

220. Fowler, p. 12.

221. Brackett, *Materialized Apparitions*, p. 12.

222. Brackett, *The World We Live In*, p. xvii.

223. Brackett, *My House*, p. 50.

224. William James, "Society for Psychical Research Presidential Address", *Science*. 19 Jun 1896. Vol 3, Issue 77.

225. Brackett, *Materialized Apparitions*, p. 11.

226. ibid., p. 18.

227. ibid., p. 11.

228. ibid. p. 47.

229. ibid.

230. ibid, p. 68.

231. ibid. p. 85.

232. ibid. p. 90.

233. ibid. p. 25.

234. ibid. p. 101.

235. letter from Alfred Russel Wallace to William James, 1 June, 1886 accessed from   https://people.wku.edu/charles.smith/wallace/S712AC.htm

236. *Banner of Light*, 60,, January 8, 1887, p. 4, referenced in https://www.google.com/books/edition/Essays_in_Psychical_Research/eWgvirLiO9sC?hl=en&gbpv=1&dq=Mr.+Brackett%E2%80%99s+niece+Bertha,+came%3B+she+was+quite+strong&pg=PA402&printsec=frontcover

237. Wallace, Alfred Russel, *My Life: A Record of Events and Opinions, vol. 2*, (London: Chapman and Hill, 1905), p. 356.

238. ibid.

239. James,William, "Letter on Mrs. Ross, the Medium," 1887, reprinted in James, *Essays in Psychical Research*, (Cambridge: Harvard University Press, 1986), p. 31. https://www.google.com/books/edition/Essays_in_Psychical_Research/eWgvirLiO9sC?hl=en&gbpv=1&bsq=mrs.%20ross

240. ibid.

241. "A Spiritualist Exposed. How a Boston Audience Captured the Spirits," *New York Times*, February 4, 1887, p. 1. https://people.wku.edu/charles.smith/wallace/ztAnon1887NYTimes.pdf

242. James, "Letter on Mrs. Ross"

243. Letter from Alfred Russel Wallace to *Banner of Light*, published March 5, 1887. p. 4 retrieved from https://people.wku.edu/charles.smith/wallace/S396.htm

244. Letter from Edward Brackett to *Banner of Light*, published February 26, 1887, p.5, quoted in https://www.google.com/books/edition/Essays_in_Psychical_Research/eWgvirLiO9sC?hl=en&gbpv=1&bsq=Ross

245. Newton, E. A. "Test Séance with Mrs. H. V. Ross," *Facts*, Vol. 6, pp. 111-115.

246. ibid.

247. "Confessions of a 'Spirit", reprinted in *Some Account of the Vampires of Onset, Past and Present*, (Boston: Press of S Woodberry & Co, 1892). http://iapsop.com/ssoc/1892__beard___vampires_of_onset.pdf

248. Conan Doyle, Arthur, *The History of Spiritualism*, vol. II, 1922 reprinted by Project Gutenberg, posted 2003, p. 44.

249. "N. Riley Haegerty and Circle of Light Research," *The Phenomena of Spirit Materialization*, (Morrisville, N: Lulu Press, 2021).

250. Brackett, Edward A., *Materialized Apparitions*, p. 100.

251. "43rd to 46th Annual Report of Commissioners on Fisheries and Game of Massachusetts (1908-1911)" https://archive.org/stream/43rdto46thannual00mass/43rdto46thannual00mass_djvu.txt

252. Brackett, Edward A. "Pseudo Science", in *My House, Chips the Builder Threw Away*, (Boston: The Gotham Press, 1904), p. 105. This and all subsequent quotations from "Pseudo Science" pp 103-122.

253. Wallace, Alfred Russel, "Sir Charles Lyell on Geological Climates and the Origin of Species," *Quarterly Review* 126 (April 1869): 359-94. https://people.wku.edu/charles.smith/wallace/S146.htm

254. letter from Charles Robert Darwin to Alfred Russel Wallace, 14 April 1869, "WCP1920," in Beccaloni, G. W. (ed.), *psilon: The Alfred Russel Wallace Collection*, https://epsilon.ac.uk/view/wallace/letters/WCP1920

255. Wallace, Alfred Russel *Social Environment and Moral Progress*, (London: Cassell & Company, 1913), p. 43.

256. "Fish and Game Commissioner Fears the Pasteur Treatment," *Boston Herald*, Feb 17, 1907, reprinted in *Our Dumb Animals*, a publication in the early animal advocacy movement and found in p. 160 of a contemporary facsimile: https://books.google.com/books?id=VWVFAQAAMAAJ&pg=PA160&lpg=PA160&dq=edward+brackett+pasteur&source=bl&ots=wcVhv1suN_&sig=ACfU3U3iSwASTu9tjl7jZYxyV2EPHA8VqQ&hl=en&sa=X&ved=2ahUKEwjk7Nvlp_LoAhUJd-

98KHd19AD8Q6AEwCnoECAwQLA#v=onepage&q=edward%20brackett%20pasteur&f=false

257. quoted in *Sir James Marchant. Alfred Russel Wallace: Letters and Reminiscences,* Vol. 2. (London: Cassell and Company, 1916), p. 241.

258. Tresch, John, *The Reason for the Darkness of the Night: Edgar Allan Poe and the Forging of American Science,* (NY:Farrar, Straus and Giroux, 2021).

259. ibid, p. 302.

260. ibid, p. 341.

261. Brackett, Edward A., "The Voyagers," in *My House, Chips the Builder Threw Away,* All quotes from this poem from pp 123-144.

262. Lavoie, Jeffrey D. *The Theosophical Society: The History of a Spiritualist Movement.* (Irvine, CA: BrownWalker Press, 2012).

263. quoted in Blum, Deborah, *Ghost Hunters: William James and the Search for Scientific Proof of Life After Death,* (NY: Penguin Books, 2006) (kindle location 4935)

264. Brackett, Edward A. *The World We Live In,* op.cit.

265. James,William, "Lectures IV and V: The Religion of Healthy Mindedness" in *The Varieties of Religious Experience,* (NY: Longmans Green & Co., 1902).

266. Brackett, *The World We Live In,* p.24

267. ibid. p. 25

268. "Fifth Annual Report of the Commissioners on Inland Fisheries," *Commonwealth of Massachusetts,* January, 1871, p.14, https://archives.lib.state.ma.us/bitstream/handle/2452/781585/ocm01521340-1870.pdf?sequence=1&isAllowed=y

269. ibid. p. 15

270. "Thirteenth Annual Report of the Commissioners on Inland Fisheries," *Commonwealth of Massachusetts* for the year ending September 30, 1878, p. 28. https://archives.lib.state.ma.us/bitstream/handle/2452/781593/ocm01521340-1878.pdf?sequence=1&isAllowed=y

271. The "Board of Commissioners" Years 1866-1919, Summary, p. 26 https://www.mass.gov/files/documents/2017/09/15/board-of-comm-yrs-1866-1869-pages-20-58.pdf

272. Earll, R. Edward, "Great International Fisheries Exhibition, "London 1883, United States of America, *Catalogue of the Fish Cultural Exhibit of the United States Fish Commission,* p. 50. https://repository.si.edu/bitstream/handle/10088/30377/1884_Goode_1155-1249.pdf?sequence=1&isAllowed=y

273. PATENT EDWARD A. BRAGKETT, OF WINCHESTER, MASSACHUSETTS. IMPROVEMENT IN FISH-WAYS. https://patents.google.com/patent/US132349

274. Earll, p. 57

275. The "Board of Commissioners" Years, p. 32.

276. "The Song Bird Avenged," *The Buffalo Commercial,* Buffalo New York, March 1, 1900 p. 8. https://ma-winchester.civicplus.com/517/Agriculture

277. "Tales of the Innocent", *The Boston Globe,* Sunday Apr 13, 1902, Page 50.

278. "Congratulations in Order," *The Boston Globe* Friday, Oct 2, 1903, Page 7

279. "Newsy Paragraphs," *The Winchester Star,* October 20, 1905.

280. "Edward A. Brackett is 87," *The Boston Globe,* Monday Oct 2, 1905, Page 2.

281. "Edward A. Brackett, 89," *The Boston Globe,* Tuesday, Oct 1,1907, Page 3.

282. "43rd to 46th Annual Report of Commissioners on Fisheries and Game of Massachusetts." (1908-1911)

283. Brackett, *My House, the Chips the Builder Threw Away,* op.cit.

FURTHER READING

HISTORICAL SOURCES:

Brackett, Edward A., *Materialized Apparitions: If Not Beings from Another Life, What Are They,* (Boston: The Gorham Press, 1908)

Brackett, Edward, A., *My House, Chips the Builder Threw Away,* (Boston: The Gorham Press, 1904)

Brackett, Edward, A., *The World We Live In,* (Boston: The Gorham Press, 1909)

Brackett, George C., "Statement of Hon. George C. Brackett, January 19, 1886", *Proceedings of the Kansas Historical Society,* 1883- 1885 p. 223-225.

Brackett, Herbert Ierson, *Brackett Genealogy: Descendants of Anthony Brackett of Portsmouth and Captain Richard Brackett of Braintree. With Biographies of the Immigrant Fathers, Their Sons, and Others of Their Posterity,* published by H. I Brackett, Washington D.C. 1907

Braude, Ann, *Radical Spirits: Spiritualism and Women's Rights in Nineteenth-Century America,* (Bloomington: Indiana University Press, 2020),

Child, Lydia Maria, "Brackett's Bust of John Brown," *Tribune,* February 11, 1860,

Conan Doyle, Arthur, *The History of Spiritualism,* vol. II, 1922 reprinted by Project Gutenberg, posted 2003

Fowler, Orson *A Home for All, or a New, Cheap, Convenient and Superior Mode of Building,* (NY: Fowlers and Wells, 1848)

Ingraham, J. H., "The Struggles of Early Genius," *Baltimore Phoenix and Budget,* April 1841-March 1842. ames, Henry, *William Wetmore Story and his Friends* (Boston, Houghton Mifflin and Co. 1903)

James,William, "Lectures IV and V: The Religion of Healthy Mindedness" in *The Varieties of Religious Experience,* (NY: Longmans Green & Co., 1902).

Jarves, James Jackson, *Art Thoughts: The Experiences and Observations of an American Amateur in Europe,* (: Hurd and Houghton, 1871)

Lee, Hannah Farnham Sawyer, Familiar Sketches of Sculpture and Sculptors, Vol 2, (Boston: Crosby, Nichols and Company, 1854)

Sanborn, Franklin, "John Brown and His Friends", *The Atlantic Monthly,* April 1872.

Some Account of the Vampires of Onset, Past and Present, (Boston: Press of S Woodberry & Co, 1892)

Thomas, Ebenezer S., *Reminiscences of the last sixty-five years, commencing with the battle of Lexington. Also, sketches of his own life and times,* (Hartford: Case, Tiffany and Burnham, 1840)

Wallace, Alfred Russel *Social Environment and Moral Progress,* (London: Cassell & Company, 1913) Wallace, Alfred Russel, "Sir Charles Lyell on Geological Climates and the Origin of Species," *Quarterly Review* 126 (April 1869): 359-94.

Wallace, Alfred Russel, *My Life: A Record of Events and Opinions, vol. 2,* (London: Chapman and Hill, 1905)Wallace, Alfred Russel, *Vaccination: Proved Useless & Dangerous,* (London: E.W.Allen, 1889)

CONTEMPORARY SOURCES:

Blum, Deborah, *Ghost Hunters: William James and the Search for Scientific Proof of Life After Death,* (NY: Penguin Books, 2006)

Bode, Carl. *The Anatomy of American Popular Culture, 1840- 1861,* (Berkeley: University of California Press, 1959)

Buick, Kirsten Pai, *Child of the Fire: Mary Edmonia Lewis and the Problem of Art History's Black and Indian Subject,* (Durham, NC: Duke University Press. 2010)

Colbert, Charles, *A Measure of Perfection: Phrenology and the Fine Arts in America (Cultural Studies of the United States)*, (Chapel Hill: University of North Carolina Press, 2009)

Colbert, Charles, *Haunted Visions: Spiritualism and American Art (The Arts and Intellectual Life in Modern America)*, (Philadelphia: University of Pennsylvania Press, 2011)

Cometto, Maria Teresa , *Emma and the Angel of Central Park*, (NY: Bordighera Press, 2023)

Culkin, Kate, *Harriet Hosmer: A Cultural Biography*, (Amherst: University of Massachusetts Press, 2010)

Delbanco, Anthony *The War Before the War: Fugitive Slaves and the Struggle for America's Soul from the Revolution to the Civil War,* (NY: Penguin Books, 2018)

Edgers, Geoff, "Finding John Brown: How Tufts' art collection registrar Laura McDonald solved the mystery of the lost masterpiece," *Tufts Magazine*, Fall 2016

Gardner, Albert TenEyck, *Yankee Stonecutters: The First American School of Sculpture 1800-1850*, (NY, published for the Metropolitan Museum of Art by Columbia University Press, 1945)

Katz, Wendy Jean, *Humbug! The Politics of Art Criticism in City's Penny Press,* (NY: Fordham University Press, 2020).

Knight, Ellen, Brackett secretly aids N.Y. Tribune, *Daily Times Chronicle*, Woburn, MA, Feb 22, 2013 https://homenewshere.com/daily_times_chronicle/news/winchester/article_9b098b2c-7d0b-11e2-a1d5-0019bb2963f4.html

Knight, Ellen, Edward A. Brackett visits John Brown, *Daily Times Chronicle*, Woburn, MA, Feb 21, 2013 https://homenewshere.com/daily_times_chronicle/news/winchester/article_43ed70d6-7c40-11e2-8f10-001a4bcf887a.html

Knight, Ellen, THE SCULPTOR & THE ABOLITIONIST. Posted at www.winchester.us/480/Winchester-History-Online

Knight, Ellen, Winchester's Brackett creates icon for Abolitionists, *Daily Times Chronicle*, Woburn, MA Feb 20, 2013, https://homenewshere.com/daily_times_chronicle/news/winchester/article_5e72c7c0-7b7e-11e2-baa3-001a4bcf887a.html

Knight, Ellen,A SÉANCE AT THE OCTAGON HOUSE, Posted at www.winchester.us/480/Winchester-History-Online

Nelson, Charmaine, *The Color of Stone: Sculpting the Black Female Subject in Nineteenth Century America*, (Minneapolis: University of Minnesota Press, 2007)

Newton, James A., "Crows' Nests or Eagles' Aeries? The Octagon Houses of E. A. Brackett and H. P. Wakefield," *Historic New England*, Vol. 67, No. 247 (Winter/Spring, 1977) p. 58

Reynolds, David S. *Abe: Abraham Lincoln in His Times,* (NY: Penguin Press, 2020)

Reynolds, David, *John Brown, Abolitionist: The Man Who Killed Slavery, Sparked the Civil War, and Seeded Civil Rights,* (NY: Vintage. 2005)

Slotten, Ross A., *The Heretic in Darwin's Court*, (NY: Columbia University Press, 2004)

resch, John, *The Reason for the Darkness of the Night: Edgar Allan Poe and the Forging of American Science,* (NY:Farrar, Straus and Giroux, 2021)

Tufts Online Exhibits, https://exhibits.tufts.edu/spotlight/john-brown-tufts, "The Magnet and the Iron: John Brown and George L. Stearns: The Stories Behind the Busts."

Walters, Charles Thomas, "Sculpture and the Expressive Mechanism in Pseudo Science and Society in 19th Century America" in Wrobel, Arthur, *Pseudo Science and Society in 19th Century America*, (Lexington: University Press of Kentucky, 2021)

Weathersby, II, Robert, *J. H. Ingraham*, (Boston: G. K. Hall& Co., 1980)

Weidman,Jeffrey, *Artists in Ohio, 1787-1900: A Biographical Dictionary*, (Kent, OH: Kent State University Press, 2000)

INDEX

ACKNOWLEDGEMENTS

Bringing a historical figure to life is quite a different prospect from the kind of contemporary art writing that is my usual stock in trade. This project involved a great deal of research on the internet, in family archives and sifting through historical documents and publications. I could not have completed this book without a great deal of help from others. I would like in particular to thank Laura McDonald, the Tufts University registrar who set me on this quest with her discovery and copious documentation of Edward Brackett's John Brown Bust. Equally indispensable was Ellen Knight, historian and Reference Archivist for the Winchester Archival Center who made the Brackett files available to me, even going so far as to let herself into the archives during the Covid lockdown in order to scan and send me vital research materials. Her updates and comments on the manuscript were invaluable. Paula Artal-Isbrand at the Worcester Art Museum did a remarkable job restoring Brackett's *Shipwrecked Mother and Child* and provided me access to the sculpture and to information about the conservation process. I also owe a debt to my cousins Heather and David Parker who assisted me in sleuthing out the possible whereabouts of Brackett's as yet elusive sculpture of *Little Nell* and to my brother Jim who located a photograph of this lost work in a family album.

I was also fortunate to have a number of perceptive readers to whom I sent chapters of the manuscript draft. Their comments and suggestions helped steer me forward and helped me avoid various pitfalls. Thanks for this goes to my feminist comrades Helaine Posner, Nancy Princenthal and Sue Scott and to Betsy Baker, Lanny DeVuono, Sara Lynn Henry and Sylvia Bullett. I am also most grateful to the lenders who provided me with images, in most cases at little or no cost.

The book itself has been made a reality with the help of Aldo Sampieri, whose sensitive design has made this volume a thing of beauty. And finally of course, I must thank my partner Larry Litt who has shared this journey with me and provided unflagging support to my at times obsessive desire to pull the remarkable life of Edward August Brackett back into the light.

ABOUT THE AUTHOR

Eleanor Heartney has been writing about contemporary art for leading art magazines since 1981. She is also the author of numerous books, monographs and catalogues about contemporary art and artists. Among her books are important studies of art and religion, art and politics, and art and feminism. This biography of her great-great-grandfather has allowed her to extend these interests back into the 19th century, where the roots of so many current crises and conflicts can be found. Heartney is a longtime contributing writer and editor to *Art in America, Artpress*, and *The Brooklyn Rail*. She also has contributed to such other publications as *Artnews, Artnet, Art and Auction, the Washington Post and the Times.* Her books include *Critical Condition: American Culture at the Crossroads (*Cambridge University Press), *Postmodernism* (Tate Gallery Publishers and Cambridge University Press) *Postmodern Heretics: The Catholic Imagination in Contemporary Art* (Midmarch Arts Press with a reissue by Silver Hollow Press) *Defending Complexity*, (Hard Press Editions), *Art and Today,* (Phaidon) and *Doomsday Dreams: the Apocalyptic Imagination in Contemporary Art* (Silver Hollow Press). She is also a co-author of three books examining feminism's impact on contemporary art: *After the Revolution: Women who Transformed Contemporary Art* and *The Reckoning: Women Artists in the New Millennium* (both from Prestel,) and *Mothers of Invention: the Feminist Roots of Contemporary Art,* (Lund Humphries.) Heartney was the 1992 recipient of the College Art Association's Frank Jewett Mather Award for distinction in art criticism was honored by the French government in 2008 as a Chevalier dans l'Ordre des Arts et des Lettres. She is also past President of AICA-USA, the American section of the International Art Critics Association.

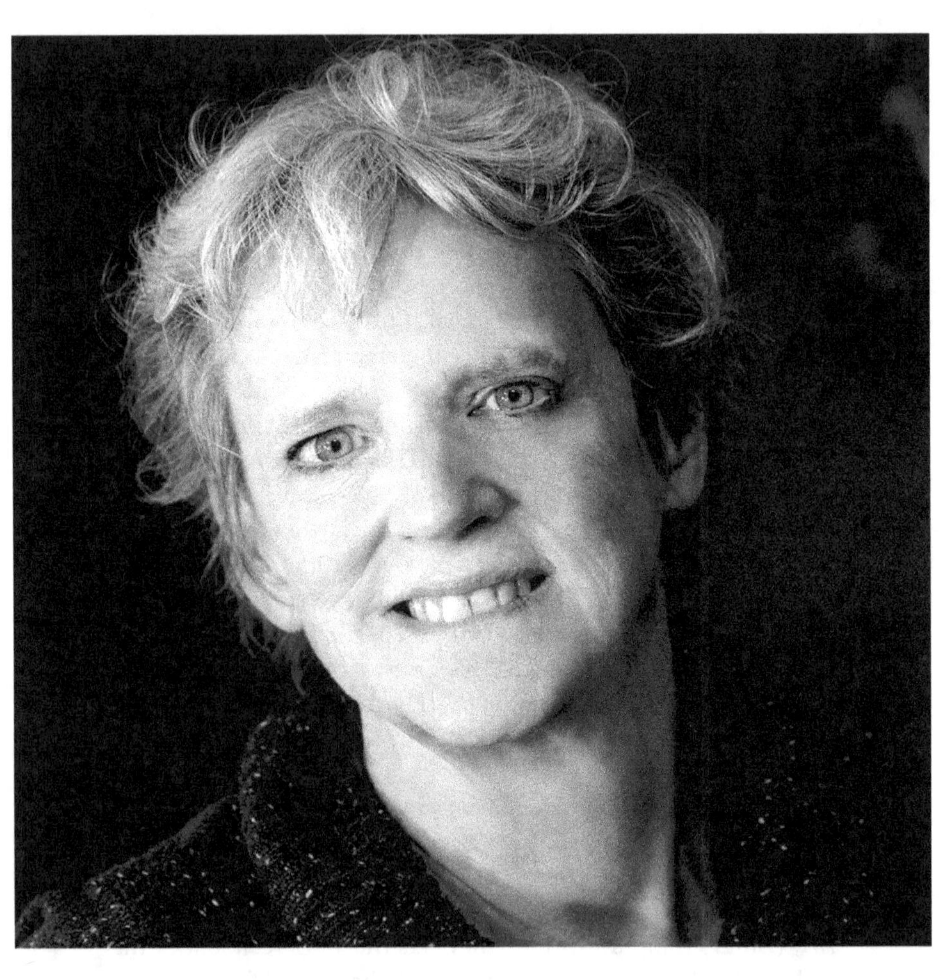

Eleanor Heartney
Photographed by Grace Roselli, Pandora's BoxX Project

www.ingramcontent.com/pod-product-compliance
Lightning Source LLC
Chambersburg PA
CBHW051515030726
47592CB00006B/2281